Enjoy Looking!

Chris

LEARN FROM
LOOKING

LEARN FROM
LOOKING
How Observation Inspires Innovation

Written and Illustrated by

CHARLIE SZORADI

LEARN FROM LOOKING
HOW OBSERVATION INSPIRES INNOVATION

iUniverse books may be ordered through booksellers or by contacting:

iUniverse
1663 Liberty Drive
Bloomington, IN 47403
www.iuniverse.com
1-800-Authors (1-800-288-4677)

ISBN: 978-1-5320-2517-4 (hc)

Library of Congress Control Number: 2016916772

Printed in the USA

iUniverse rev. date: 08/02/2017

For my son, Calvin, and daughter, Carter,
whose creativity inspires
and energizes me

CONTENTS

PREFACE

This book is about seeing the world in new ways, challenging preconceptions, and presenting opportunities for positive change. At a time of increasing digital overload, we can still choose to pause and look harder at relevant aspects of the physical world with attention to detail and context.

The Writing Process for This Book

Over two decades, I have traveled the planet, drawn what I have seen, and learned from the act of looking. Out in the field and immediately following the travels, I have taken notes and then over many years written the insights included in this book. The content centers on innovation, critical thinking, and sustainable design. I have also included some personal experiences as well as professional insights to accompany the travel drawings and observations. The act of looking and documenting has been constructive for me on many levels, so I am pleased to present this work for your consideration.

The Structure of This Book

Printed books are bound and linear by nature, with sequentially numbered pages. The binding structure is well suited for narrative content and storytelling in fiction and nonfiction. However, this book is more of a resource with nonlinear interconnected content, some of which spans multiple continents over multiple years. Plus, some of the content may appeal to certain readers over others. The table of contents and the comprehensive index are intended to help you get the most out of this book for the highest and best use of your time.

Learn from Looking is organized into five parts, with multiple chapters within each. The parts include the following:

Part 1: The Foundation
Part 2: Travel Drawing and Insights
Part 3: Commercial Impact
Part 4: Conclusions
Part 5: Support Information

The Multiple Audiences for This Book

General Market: Anyone who is intellectually curious and open-minded.

Tip for the readers: Start at the beginning, and see where this book takes you. Note that you may find information about topics that you never expected, ranging from high-speed bullet trains in Japan to making pickles on sunny windowsills in Hungarian villages. Some of the text includes technical details, specifically for readers such as design and energy professionals, so I hope that you just advance through those paragraphs or pages and continue onward through the book.

General Market—Subset Travelers: Anyone who has already traveled or plans to travel in the United States or overseas.

Tip for the readers: Start with part 2 in the table of contents to identify your geographic area of interest from North America to Asia. Then drill into the relevant chapter to gain perspective on what you have seen or what you may want to see in advance of your trip. The index also includes a deeper dive into the places, from New York to Tokyo, so that you can search more specifically and then navigate accordingly through the book. Safe travels!

Design Professionals: Architects, city planners, industrial designers, interior designers, and all others who help shape our world.

Tip for the readers: Start by reviewing part 2 with the extensive drawings, or use the index to find topics as broad as renewable energy or as granular as Pennsylvania bank barns that have passive geothermal advantages. As a Leadership in Energy and Environmental Design accredited professional (LEED AP), I welcome feedback from other architects, US Green Building Council members, and design professionals.

Real Estate Professionals: Building owners and managers, real estate investors, developers, and contractors from general to the specialty subcontractors.

Tip for the readers: Similar as for design professionals, start with part 2.

Energy and Sustainability Professionals: Sustainability directors, energy auditors, clean technology manufacturers and service providers in categories such as solar, wind, water, HVAC, lighting, and others.

Tip for the readers: Similar as for design and real estate professionals, but definitely look into parts 3 and 4 as well as part 2.

Students and Educators: Undergraduate and graduate architecture and other design, environmental studies, city planning, public policy, and sustainability, plus high school students interested in science, technology, engineering, and math (STEM).

Tip for the readers: Read the whole book.

Parents of School-Age Children: Parents of any age, plus grandparents and other family members.

Tip for the readers: Start with the part 1 chapters "Powers of Observation" and "Critical Thinking" as well as the part 5 appendix sections "Fostering Critical Thinking at the Earliest Ages" and "Creativity for Children."

Public Sector Officials: Leaders and their policy advisers who want to create more jobs—mayors, state legislators, US senators and representatives, governors, the president, and anyone who works for the government in a position of authority.

Tip for the readers: Start with part 1, chapter "Sustainability and Clean Tech for America," part 3 "Key to US Economic Revival," and part 4 "Local First." You are most likely as busy as any of us, but if you take a few minutes to pause and read these few chapter sections en route to a meeting or vote, you will learn about cost-effective paths to create jobs and support sustainable economic revival.

Sharing Information

The mantra for sustainability in the 1970s centered on the three Rs: reduce, reuse, recycle. "Reuse" is key when it comes to sharing. If you like what you read and see in this book, please pass it along for reuse by a family member, friend, or colleague. The intent of publishing this book was to share the information and inspire positive change. You can become a change agent just by passing it along.

Beyond the Book

Given that innovation never sleeps, I welcome feedback and insights from all types of readers with all types of experiences and mind-sets. I will share relevant content by posting it online at www.LearnFromLooking.com. The website will hopefully grow with some of the content from this book as the springboard. Together, we can collectively advance innovation, critical thinking, and sustainable design.

Dig In

Enjoy looking at this book, following the path through the chapters or skipping ahead in your journey. I hope that you will take away a sense of value in pausing and appreciate how looking closer inspires innovation.

INTRODUCTION

Thank you for purchasing this book. If you received it as a gift from a friend, colleague, or family member, then I appreciate that he or she saw the value in sharing it with you. You may have also picked it up from someone's coffee table or bookshelf. In that case, I hope you enjoy browsing through a few of the drawings and reading the accompanying observations.

The drawings and insights in *Learn from Looking* are intended to provide actionable intelligence to improve our lives and strengthen America. The content will hopefully encourage you to look at the world around you in new ways with fresh perspective relative to our homes, buildings, transportation, food, energy, job creation, education, ecosystem, and more.

Active observation can fuel critical thinking, which is often a key driver of innovation. In turn, innovation can support sustainable design that is cost-effective and practical. Collectively, we can build a triple bottom line[1] that supports people, the planet, and profit. This multiwin approach is at the core of sustainable design and this book.

By focusing on a range of US and international examples, *Learn from Looking* includes many in-field drawings that lead to insights. Instead of following the leader, this strategy is more about following the clues. The premise is to look *well* and *thoroughly*—to first observe and then apply the learning to innovate and rethink paths forward. Details count throughout this book, along with supporting research data to provide the context. The idiom "Look before you leap" is a concise way of capturing the idea of taking a pause to gain perspective before taking action.

This book is a *perspectiventure*. It provides fresh perspective and ventures down paths of potential extraordinary opportunity that are inspired by many ordinary elements across the global landscape.

Perspectiventure is an unusual word for an unusual book. I created the meldword by simply combining two underlying themes in my career and in this book: perspective and venture. I have used perspective-drawing techniques for the sketches in this book, completed over two decades and across many countries. As an entrepreneur, I undertook the business venture in 2010 of bringing our manufacturing from China to the United States for our energy-saving light-emitting diode (LED) technology. This book connects perspective and venture by illustrating examples and shedding light on new mutually beneficial journeys for people, business, and the public sector.

Perspective has two relevant definitions. The first definition is a specific drawing term that is about representing our three-dimensional world on a two-dimensional surface, and the second more general definition is about a distinct point of view. This book includes hundreds of drawings that are in perspective and add perspective. The point of view comes through the notes that I have written on new ways to think about sustainable design and the ways that we live, work, and play.

Venture also has two relevant definitions. The noun is a risky or daring journey or undertaking. The verb is about daring to do something or going somewhere that may be dangerous or unpleasant. This book includes many insights that are outside of mainstream approaches. The views are not risky at the life safety level, but many of the recommendations are challenges to the status quo. Benjamin Franklin said, "Nothing ventured, nothing gained!" As an inventor, author, and founding father of our country, Franklin sits high on my list of critical thinkers. He is also particularly appealing to me, because he appreciated efficiency at its core, and many efficiency paths are interwoven throughout this book. Franklin said, "Waste neither time nor money, but make the best use of both. Without industry and frugality, nothing will do, and with them everything." Franklin may embody the sprit of perspectiventure, especially in an example such as his exploration into electricity where the kite and key became the springboard for his lightning rod invention.

Here are my two definitions of the new word:
> perspectiventure
> per·spec·ti·ven·ture
> *Noun*
> 1. A journey that starts by looking at something from a curiosity perspective, without the goal of justifying a preconception or finding something, and leads to learning that can have a positive impact. Perspectiventure is the act of learning from looking rather than looking for something. "The architecture graduate student embarked on a perspectiventure around the world." Synonyms: path to accidental discovery and surprise observation journey.
>
> 2. A business venture that is inspired by studying something unrelated to the final products or services offered by the business. "The high-tech lighting entrepreneur built a perspectiventure inspired from low-tech solutions." Synonyms: nontraditional business, disruptive business, and unexpected source enterprise.

Your Perspectiventure into This Book

Take the journey to turn the pages in this book with curiosity. You may find something that you were not looking for or expecting to find. You may end up relooking at your own world with fresh perspective.

1 THE FOUNDATION

1 GETTING STARTED

Sustainable Observations: *Twenty Years of Looking*

From a very early age in grade school, I started drawing and documenting the world around me. Since then, international work and travel have provided very fortunate opportunities and access. This book is a means of sharing some of what I have seen and learned along the way.

To date, many authors have shared their ideas about sustainability, energy consumption, and the impact on our climate. Their works have been instrumental in bringing information to the forefront. This book is not about looking for a way to support a belief or strategy. This book is about the learning that has come from the looking. This book is also intended as a catalyst that may inspire others to document what they see and share their insights.

The excerpts from my travel sketches in part 2 of this book capture a long journey to different places around the world. There was not a scheduled or linear path that led to some of the commercial impact results in part 3, such as a sustainable smart home and an energy-intelligent lighting company. There was, however, always an underlying curiosity to look closer at how things work with an eye on how we might be able to use the findings as a springboard to shape a more sustainable modern world.

Many years after I started drawing these sketches in the field, I learned about Charles Darwin's discovery process.[2] The process made sense to me at a core level. He apparently followed a guiding force to "Start looking, and learn from the looking, rather than looking for something." In my research for this book, I could not attribute this quote to Darwin. I sought out the feedback from Darwin scholar and Harvard University professor Janet Browne. Professor Browne let me know that she doubted if this quote was from Charles Darwin, since she had never come across it before, and it did not sound like nineteenth-century prose. Regardless of the source or the exact language, the act of observation and recording enables one to see things that would not have otherwise been noticed. The written support text, which I have added to my drawings in this book, dates back in some cases twenty years to the time of the earliest drawings. Hopefully, the combination of images and words will help shed additional light on what I have seen across my travels.

START LOOKING,
and learn from the looking,
rather than looking for something.

The Origin of the Drawings in This Book

As an architect, inventor, and entrepreneur in the energy-saving marketplace, I am one of many foot soldiers in the trenches of a global sustainability and energy revolution. This collection is about taking the time to draw some details in the field and make some observations. The drawings are made in ink on paper with accordion-style foldout sketchbooks. The books are ideal for on-site illustrations, because the foldout structure allows me to continue drawings across multiple pages and also easily carry the books in my back pocket or backpack.

In the 1980s and early 1990s, I was trained as an architect right at the bridge of analog and digital design. Hand drawing was still the key foundation of expression. I was one of the very last groups of architects to take the comprehensive multiday registration examination on a drafting board versus a screen. Drawing was not an option but simply a requirement.

In the middle of the second decade of the twenty-first century, digital photography on our smartphones provides an unprecedented ease of documentation. However, the act of capturing information from our eyes through our brain to hand illustration encourages what I have started calling "observational pause." The change in tempo lets us look closer at certain things that we may otherwise have taken for granted. In my case, I have also found that the act of drawing inspires thinking about what we can learn and apply to our lives today. I love the ease of taking photos and videos with my phone and sharing them with friends and family, so this observational pause is certainly in addition to using technology and not by any means a nostalgic attempt to revert to a simpler time.

Technology is outstanding when used in balance. With grade-school children, my wife and I have had to find ways to manage their love of screens that range in size from TVs, desktops, laptops, and touchpads, to smartphones. My brother and I were limited as kids to a certain amount of TV time each week, but now for our kids we need to limit the ubiquitous screens and balance "screen time" with "sneaker time." So we encourage outdoor activities as much as possible, from playing with the neighborhood kids to hiking and biking.

At so many age and socioeconomic levels, we love to watch versus look. The number of cable channels and online videos is overwhelming to say the least. Watching is largely passive, while looking is more active. The physical act of engagement in an interactive three-dimensional world rather than a two-dimensional screen world will most likely create a stronger body and brain, as well as create a few moments of observational pause along the way. What is old is often new again, and some of the documentation in this book covers design and innovation dating back hundreds of years. Hopefully this work inspires some critical thinking to rethink and provide perspective on how we can thrive in the twenty-first century with the technology that has shaped our communications.

The foldout *Stretch-A-Sketch* books, as I call them, in this collection are the result of a simple multicultural phenomenon. As a graduate architecture student at the University of Pennsylvania in the early 1990s, one of my professors, Kinya Maruyama,[3] inspired me to look at the world with fresh perspective. Kinya is a Japanese architect who has dedicated his career to innovation and sustainable design. He expanded on what I had learned from my parents about how to look more closely at details and natural structure and study the habitat and process of how people live, work, and play together.

One of the first assignments that Kinya gave us was to crack open a walnut shell and look closely at the inside to envision what it would be like to inhabit the space. He wanted us to explore the possibilities of turning traditional architecture inside out and taking clues from natural structure to advance design. He taught me to learn from looking and how looking closer inspires innovation.

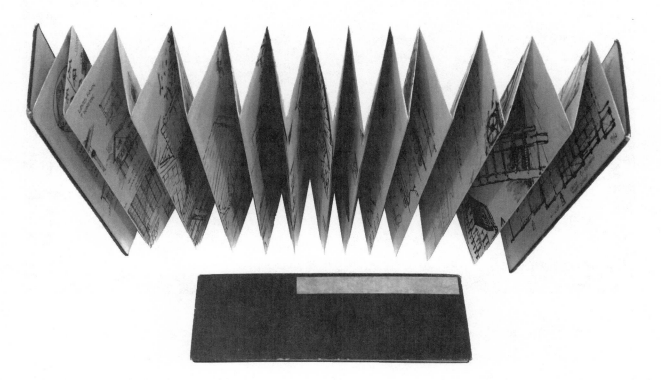

Kinya was a visiting professor at the University of Pennsylvania, and he gave me, and each of my fellow classmates, very unique Japanese books of blank paper that he had brought over from Tokyo. The books measured 11 1/2" tall by about 3 3/4" wide. The special aspect of these books was that the paper was not bound on a single edge but linked through a zigzag accordion form that unfolded to almost eight feet long. Historically, the Japanese used these books to write vertically and tell stories that would unfold across the length of more than two-dozen panels.

Kinya also gave us each a unique writing tool. The brush pen had ink in the handle and a brush tip so that you could squeeze the handle to release the ink and actually paint the surface with varying degrees of pinpoint and sweeping strokes.

Kinya encouraged us to sketch in the books. Without any training to write vertically in Japanese, sketching became the obvious highest and best use of our architectural skills at that time. More than two decades later with travel around the world, I have filled a massive collection of books and used hundreds of brush pens.

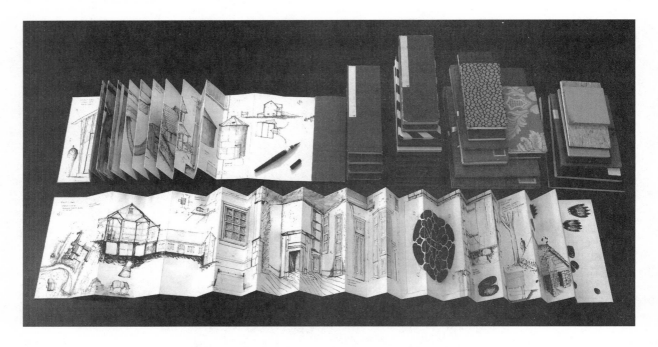

I needed so many books that I found a Philadelphia book bindery to make custom-sized folded paper and the book cover structure for me, rather than buying the books from Japan. This was my earliest foray into American manufacturing in the middle of the 1990s, and it gave me some foundational experience when we moved our light-emitting diode (LED) manufacturing from China to Pennsylvania about fifteen years later in 2010.

My travel opportunities have included destinations where I have been able to live and sometimes work directly with people in remote countries that many Americans do not have the chance to see firsthand. Each sketchbook depicts a leg of an ongoing journey, from a three-month adventure working in Japan to equally as much time in Eastern Europe; from a six-month study of Amish culture to explorations into island cultures like Virgin Gorda and Hawaii; from the Mayan ruins of the Yucatan Peninsula to the hilltops of Los Angeles. Each image is also a reflection of what I see standing on site at the very place and the very time that I make the drawings. As I see new things that appeal to me, I include them along the sequence of what is now a set of multiple books comprising about a thousand panels. There is no predetermined "mural" or draft sketch since all of the work is done in ink. The sense of discovery literally unfolds, as one observation leads to another over the different days and weeks and months in the field.

Given that the average sketchbook is over seven feet long, this publication includes an outline of a human figure for each book to show the scale.

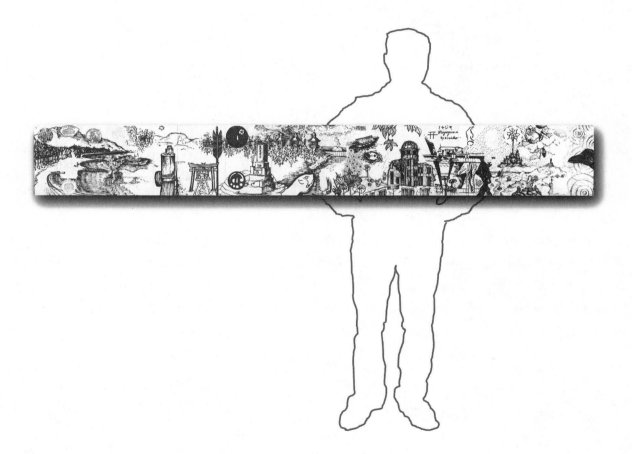

The documentation includes detail images as well. Within this collection, each sketchbook includes at least one detail or section enlargement on the page following the whole layout of the book, as well as notes and observations.

Sample Detail Enlargement

Students and enthusiasts of architecture may also notice 360-degree illustrations of cityscapes, such as in Budapest, and town squares, such as the one at the center of Prague. The foldout aspect of the sketchbooks gives me the ability to make murals dynamic explorations. In many cases, the cityscapes took the better part of an afternoon to complete, while other books took multiple weeks to complete as I traveled to different places.

The foldout books also provide an opportunity to draw full-size items such as the wooden slats of a corncrib on an Amish farm in Lancaster County, Pennsylvania, or a curved metal brace to hold open a shutter.

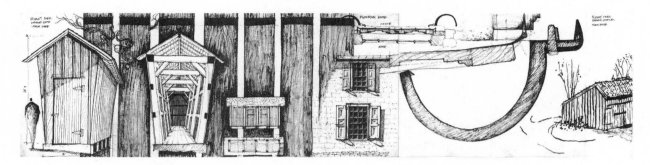

The ink drawings in the field are from a combination of brush pens plus some felt-tip pens for detail work. This *en plein air* "in the open air" approach and stream of consciousness style has its challenges with weather and scheduling. However, if it starts to rain, I have often found an overhang or taken a break with a few locals who sometimes provided their words of wisdom and encouragement. This process of embedded documentation has embossed invaluable memories for me through the sequence of transmitting information to paper. In a fast-paced and high-tech digital world, this slow-paced and low-tech methodology creates the moments to reflect and look closer at details that are often overlooked. The images that I chose to capture resonate with me, in part because they have some combination of beauty, function, sustainability, and relevance to our current culture.

Influence comes in many forms, and my parents sparked my early interest in looking closer at the world and drawing. My father was an architect who escaped through the Soviet Union's Iron Curtain and came over to America in the 1950s from Hungary. My mother, who was raised in Pennsylvania, is a retired teacher and champion marathon runner. Their creativity, energy, and spirit of exploration have served as my foundation.

Sketching naturally takes some practice at a functional level, and my brother and I were encouraged to draw at a very early age. Beyond the execution of the drawings, some friends have expressed curiosity over what I have chosen to draw at any given time in any given country along my travel journeys. I have told them that in many cases the subject matter is about a solution that demonstrates some form of critical thinking on behalf of the builder, designer, or local creator. In some cases, the solutions involve an elegant reduction of energy consumption, while others may have an appealing aesthetic.

Overall, I have been interested in how people live within the built environment at a sustainable level, and this exploration with drawings is about relooking at the world to gain new perspective through firsthand observation.

The next chapter is about the power of observation, and it focuses on some ways to cultivate looking skills, starting at a young age.

② POWER OF OBSERVATION

Active observation is about training the brain and honing skills. By contrast, passive observation can lead to missing out on a broad range of facets of life that may go unnoticed. Just as an athlete practices to build muscle memory, the act of looking intently requires some work to build expertise. I have identified four main areas of focus that are interconnected sections within this chapter on the power of observation:

1: Active Selection
2: Look Closer
3: Find It
4: Invention

1: Active Selection

Training young eyes is similar to giving children exposure to multiple languages and multiple sports at an early age. An early start simply increases the potential adoption of the skills as the brain and body develop. My parents would take my younger brother, Stephen, and me to the Smithsonian Institute and specifically the National Gallery on weekends. We grew up in Washington, DC, and the free price of admissions to the museums was certainly the right ticket. Shows ranging from King Tut to Degas would come to Washington, and we learned the history of art from a very young age in a similar way that a child might learn a second language without effort through bilingual parents or exposure.

Specifically at the National Gallery, we had to pick out our top three paintings, sculptures, or works of art and then explain to my parents why we picked them as our favorites. I remember that my brother and I resisted on many occasions, but the net impact was "active" observation versus a more "passive" walk-through of a gallery show. This early encouragement to look closely, shape an opinion, and then verbalize the rationale may have been more formative than any of us imagined. We were invested in our choices, and we often learned that two or more of us in the family shared a top pick among our three favorites.

We also had to read the biographical highlights of the different artists that were often displayed at the entrance to each show along with a super-sized photograph or illustrations of their face. Over a decade, from age four to about fourteen, we covered hundreds of artists, and we learned about historical trends through the lens of artistic representation. In high school, I remember taking the advanced placement (AP) exam in art history, and I was able to breeze through essays much more easily than completing the AP physics and AP calculus problems. The AP exams for American history and European history were loaded with the expected data points, but knowledge of the history of art at least helped put a face on players and events. Preparation for the AP English literature exam required all of the classes and readings that one would imagine, but we had an excellent comparative literature class at Saint Alban's School for Boys that gave us tremendous perspective. I remember that Professor Paul Barrett would show us paintings ranging from the Enlightenment to midcentury modern, and we could start to see how authors were in sync with artists in how they reflected something as simple as human connection to nature. One of the other positive by-products of the early art observation and communication was a comfort in sharing information and public speaking.

This early exposure to art history and comparative literature became foundational to my later focus on critical thinking and sustainable design. Artists and authors have their own points of view and express them in many different ways. I learned that the same thing can be seen and represented in dramatically differently ways without a binary right-versus-wrong outcome. Solutions may come from a middle ground through combinations and interconnections that are not immediately apparent from inception.

2: Look Closer

The natural world is an excellent landscape for honing active observation skills. In the spring and fall, our parents would pack my brother and me into the car to go hiking down on the canal in Washington, DC, across the river in nearby Virginia, or over in Maryland. I remember specifically being tested on leaves. In the woods, my father would pick up a leaf or point to a tree and ask my brother and me if it was a white oak or red oak tree. He would explain that the white oak has curved "fingers" on the points of the leaf and the inside edges, while the red oak has sharply pointed tips and inside edges. When you glance at the trees among others with the leaves high in the air, the difference is not obvious until you look closer. We also learned to look closer at how an oak tree's branches asymmetrically bend like the curled fingers of an old man or woman, while the branches on an elm tree more gracefully and more symmetrically rise up and away from the trunk. We were also tested on identifying oak tree bark versus sycamore tree bark, which peals away like it is "sick" of staying on the tree. Further, we would look at evergreens in addition to deciduous trees to identify the difference in needle length and thickness from white pines to other conifers. By hiking at different times of the year, we saw the shading capacity of deciduous trees and learned about the advantage of having them on the south side of a house for shading in the summer. Since my father had explored passive solar architecture in the 1970s, he also shared with us how deciduous trees could add value in the winter by allowing the sunlight to help heat a house after the trees had lost their leaves in the fall.

Looking back, these exercises shaped my design interest as an architect to incorporate nature at a fundamental level. When I designed our solar house in Wayne, Pennsylvania, outside of Philadelphia, I made sure to plant a fast-growing deciduous river birch tree on the south side of the bedroom wing for shading, and evergreens like the blue atlas on the north side for wind shear reduction. These help reduce the air-conditioning and heating load cost on the home, which was featured in the Cisco documentary series "One Million Acts of Green" as one of the most ecofriendly residences in the United States. The right type and placement of trees was one of over a hundred sustainability measures that my wife and I deployed. The breadth of the energy intelligence work became the foundation for the return on investment (ROI) analysis for the online resource that I created: www.GREENandSAVE.com.

Circling back to the childhood experiences with my brother, I remember other explorations into the natural world. As we grew a little bit older in grade school, we would climb Old Rag Mountain each year. Old Rag is about three thousand feet high and located in the Blue Ridge Mountains of the Shenandoah National Park in Madison County, Virginia. I remember that we had to look for the trail blazes on the trees and also identify which direction was north at various rest points. We learned that moss often grows on the shady north side of trees and that lichen grow on the north side of rocks. Years later, I climbed the significantly higher twelve-thousand-foot Mount Fuji while working in Japan and thought back to those early years on Old Rag Mountain. My brother, Stephen, has taken climbing to an extreme. After working in the Swiss Alps, he then moved to Aspen, Colorado, where he currently runs Aspen Alpine Guides. He is the family hero, because he literally saves lives through his work with Mountain Rescue Aspen (MRA). I get a terrific thrill and source of family pride when he sends me photos that include jumping out of high-altitude helicopters over the Rockies on search-and-rescue missions.

When hiking or traveling by car, my father would also give us topographical maps that had the contours of the terrain without the road names, numbers, and layers of information that are now on our vehicle navigation systems and smartphones. He explained that we could see where we were by learning how to read the topo lines, and he had used similar maps to get through the woods of Eastern Europe on his escape from the communists to come to America.

The parallel to the topo map lessons came with the exposure to nautical charts. Over summer weekends, we grew up sailing in Ocean City and Annapolis, Maryland. My parents bought a small piece of land on an inlet development, with the hopes of building a vacation house. The lot was covered with poison ivy and pine trees, and we kept our sloop on the end of a small dock. My brother and I would sleep up in the bow with the spinnaker bag and anchor lines. We learned how to sail on Sunfish, Lasers, 420s, and Hobie Cats. I remember learning how to spot the ripples on the water from a wind shift, and it paid off to get a jump on a tack over the other skippers and win regattas.

Only years later, I started to piece together that observing the leaves and the bark, the topo maps and the charts, along with the wind on the water—it was all a foundation for looking closer at the nuanced details that surround us every day. In the part 3 "Commercial Impact" section of this book, the "Sustainable Smart House" and other chapters address some of the fruits of the early labor.

3. Find It

Cities are excellent landscapes for honing active observation skills. Hunting and gathering are not just about survival in the wild. For my brother and me, the regular Smithsonian visits, hiking, and sailing were part of a broader set of weekend activities. Stickball in the street and cops and robbers with our bikes in the neighborhood were par for the course. In the 1970s, there was nothing remotely close to the level of travel sports for kids, let alone the sophistication and appeal of video games that exist now. We were often left to our own unscheduled devices. As part of the Atari "Pong" generation, we were amazed when *Space Invaders* came out. Since there were only a few TV channels in a pre-cable universe and very few of us on the block had video games, we were outside in the small backyard or in the back alley behind our row house much more than in front of any screen.

We became highly skilled urban hunters and gathers. We were trained to see opportunity and then pounce. I remember one weekend in grade school playing with friends in the back alley when a neighbor threw out a vacuum cleaner. The trash pickup on our street was behind the houses in the alley that ran as a spine between the two rows of town houses on either street. This was a protected zone with very little car traffic, and it was largely out of sight of any of our parents. The prize was the vacuum motor. We took to the busted old vacuum cleaner like hyenas take to the carcass of a slain gazelle on the African Maasai Mara in Kenya. More than a decade later at age twenty-one, I would get to see in person the cycle of life on the African savannah. Back in the alley, the heart of the vacuum cleaner was the coveted engine, and we had screwdrivers and wrenches on hand, taken from our parents' toolboxes. Over multiple years of weekend alley hunting and gathering, Stephen and I amassed a sizeable collection of motors and mechanical parts, and the act of taking things apart instilled in us a love of discovery and invention. This expanded into a love of building. We both studied architecture, and decades later we purchased and renovated multiple properties in different cities. Stephen's work focused on residential properties ranging from Chicago to Zurich and most recently Aspen. My real estate development focus included a narrower geographical range from Washington, DC, to Philadelphia but a broader property mix that included transforming homes, warehouses, churches, and even a squirt gun factory into mixed-use properties.

For both of us, the real estate transformations incorporated found objects, local materials, and an underlying sense of energy-efficiency and sustainability that was not yet as defined in the mainstream as it is today. I wrote my 1993 architecture master's thesis on energy intelligence, titled "Eco-Humanism," and it set the stage for a career centered on advancing American energy independence.

The sustainability and the hunter-gatherer instinct came from our parents. We would have field trips and collect railroad spikes along abandoned track lines or go to marinas and find old chipped propellers. My grandparents on my mom's side lived in Lancaster, Pennsylvania, and they bought a beach house on the New Jersey Shore in the 1960s. Our family summerhouse is in Stone Harbor, and just south of the town on the end of the seven-mile island is the nature reserve at the point. Growing up, we called it the "Wild Beach." I remember that on one summer weekend, we walked down to the end of the Wild Beach and found a skate, which looks like a manta ray, washed up on the sand. In addition to sea life and shells, we would also collect debris that had washed up on the beach. We called the man-made finds "trash treasures," and they ranged from deep blue beach glass to bright orange strings and floats from commercial fishing nets.

On the home front, my mother was particularly dexterous as well as creative. I remember Christmas wreathes that were made from the pinecones either collected from the wooded lot near our sailboat in Ocean City or from one of many hikes. She made baskets out of wooden slats but took it up to a high art with woven pine needle baskets. This simple idea of using resources at hand has carried over to me. She would go to nearby farms in Virginia to have wool sheared from the sheep, card it, dye it in huge boiling caldrons in our kitchen, dry it, spin it on two different sized colonial spinning wheels, and weave it on a loom wider than a dining table into "groovy" 1960s and '70s wall hangings.

She would take some of our drawings as kids and turn the designs into these wall hangings with terrific vibrant colors. I was only flattered years later when I saw the crayon drawings manifested in artwork up on our wall. Her work became popular enough to sell as fine art, but we were happy to have a good portion of it in our home gallery. In the spirit of finding and applying materials, my mom also dug into the art of quilting. My three favorite works of hers are a quilt made from my brother's old flannel shirts, a coverlet from my grandfather's old neckties, and a bedspread made from the indigo dye and other fabric scraps that I specifically found in Japan for her to use back at home.

Both of our parents instilled in my brother and me a curiosity in finding and making things from the objects other people discard. The remnants of a disposable society can become assets in a new form. My brother's early sculpture included found objects, and his photography focused as well on industrial castoffs. One of my favorite photographic series from Stephen's work was entitled "Blue Collar Cathedral" and it focused on documenting steel mines. The epic scale of the structures with the long and high framework shares the feeling of a nave of a church, and we have many of his images at our home, some printed as large as five feet across with key objects or human figures for scale.

4. Invention

Active observation skills can lead to invention. When we look at something intently and question why or why not something else, we have planted the seed of invention. This compilation of sketchbooks and insights is loaded with global "inventions" that in many cases are improvements and practices handed down over multiple generations. Parents inspired children and their children to follow.

The year 2013 marked the celebration of one hundred years of innovation across four generations of my family. Since 1913, the spirit of invention and "made in America" manufacturing has driven innovation and job creation through patents, production, and improvements in the ways that we both live and work within the built environment. This century-old commitment has inspired me to continue innovating. The US Patent and Trade Mark Office (USPTO) granted my first patent in 1993 on a modular building construction system, and a year after the hundredth anniversary of my great-grandfather's thirteen patents on indoor plumbing, my patent for light-emitting diode (LED) technology was granted as a step toward the next hundred years. In the LED market, the patent is part of an ongoing focus on energy-saving technology for Independence LED Lighting, which I founded and where I currently serve as the chairman and CEO.

The innovative and strong men and women in my family have profoundly influenced my work. The "One Hundred Years of Family Innovation" section in the appendix of this book includes biographical highlights on multiple generations of influential family members.

Summary of the Power of Observation

The power of observation is about empowering all of us with active observation skills to look more intently at the world around us versus defaulting to a less engaged passive approach. Good things happen with active observation. The good things could be as small as improvement to soil in a personal backyard garden or as large as a paradigm shift in global food production. Imagine seeing a neighbor grow bigger tomatoes, then applying the new compost technique, and then scaling the results to create efficiencies in large-scale vegetable farming.

Situational awareness is a key requirement and advantage to active observations. Innovation and invention often spring from critical thinking, which in turn springs from active observation. The power of observation starts the chain of positive events.

The next chapter addresses some examples of critical thinking, which often involves the ability to question why certain things are done a certain way and not taking anything for granted.

3 CRITICAL THINKING

Definition of Critical Thinking

Critical thinking[4] is the intellectually disciplined process of actively and skillfully conceptualizing, applying, analyzing, synthesizing, and/or evaluating information gathered from, or generated by, observation, experience, reflection, reasoning, or communication, as a guide to belief and action.

Overall, I like the definition and the idea of thinking how knowledge makes sense in a world that has plenty of knowledge but often less time to pause and think. We put a man on the moon without smartphones and text messages, so I sometimes feel like we are working harder but not smarter. The words from the critical thinking definition that appeal to me most are "observation" and "action."

Too often we think that we know something, and then we don't necessarily act in the best interests for ourselves or for our larger economy or community. This was true for several decades when it came to lighting in our homes and offices. Certainly our founding fathers looked around, and their observations led them to take action. The twenty-first-century energy revolution now follows the late twentieth-century information technology revolution, the nineteenth-century Industrial Revolution, and the eighteenth-century democracy revolution. Hopefully, this book inspires you to pause, observe, think critically, and then ask key questions that lead to constructive actions in multiple areas of your life.

Diverse Geographic Perspective

Perspective provides power. From East Africa to Eastern Europe and from Asia to Central America, I have had the great fortune of conducting research and traveling in countries around the world. Greater Philadelphia is the home that I have loved for the past two decades and expect to continue loving for many more, regardless of the success or failure of our sports teams.

Philadelphia is also naturally the home of American independence and the birthplace of our Declaration of Independence, which may serve as the ultimate example of critical thinking. Our founding fathers embodied the spirit of innovation and courage to challenge preconceptions and ignite the fire of democracy. Now, American energy independence is within reach, and we have an opportunity to think critically about how to seize the moment.

In my research on different continents, I have studied how people live with and without energy. I also drove across the United States between college and graduate school and experienced the power of the heartland at an impressionable age. Self-reliance is such a fundamental part of the American frontier spirit, and I always enjoy returning to Idaho, Colorado, Oklahoma, and Texas. Before settling in Greater Philadelphia, I lived in American cities ranging from the political machine of Washington, DC, to the financial machine of New York. By contrast to city living, along my travels, I have tracked silverback gorillas in East Africa, climbed Mount Fuji, and seen firsthand the failures of communism from inside the Soviet Iron Curtain, before the wall came down. These global multicultural and diverse socioeconomic experiences have provided me with some fresh perspective on power consumption and sustainable design in cities, towns, suburbs, farms, and the wilderness.

Over the past few years of my career, I have spent over ten thousand hours, met with over one thousand companies, and personally trained over five hundred people to look up and make a case to switch the lights to LEDs for energy-savings and overall sustainable design. Light-emitting diode (LED) technology is still disruptive relative to traditional incumbent lighting, so we have had to think critically to engineer cost-effective products and also think critically to communicate cost-effective solutions over commodity purchases.

Definition Conclusion: The definition of critical thinking centers around analyzing and synthesizing information gathered from absorbing outside information. In short, critical thinking is about opening your senses without bias to make connections that others may not have made. Travel and personal and work experiences become spokes in a critical-thinking wheel that continues to grow larger and turn more smoothly. As the spokes increase, they start to overlap and inform each other. The following examples are at the intersection of critical thinking and sustainable design.

Examples of Critical Thinking for Sustainable Design

In my exploration of renewable energy, efficiency strategies, and technology related to my "green" architecture practice, I found hundreds of examples of critical thinking. Here are just a few examples of critical thinking relative to how we interact with energy and sustainable design in the built world. The following pages highlight the critical thinking for each.

- □ window shutters
- □ shoji screens

- ☐ showerheads
- ☐ light-emitting diodes (LEDs)
- ☐ pens and pencils
- ☐ moving mountains

Window Shutters: In a village outside of Budapest, Hungary, I saw a set of shutters that had a set of double hinges. The primary hinges were on the sides so that the shutters could open out, similar to what you would expect to see with operational American shutters on homes from the last two centuries. However, these village shutters included an insert panel on each side with the hinge at the top. The idea was pretty simple. If it was raining and the residents wanted to have the shutters open for natural ventilation in their homes (most of which did not have air-conditioning), they could lift up and out the insert panel and use the surface to protect the opening from the rain. The same move worked well for shading the opening of the window on bright sunny days. This low-tech solution piqued my interest into how cultures without an abundance of electricity were able to improve their interior climate control.

Shoji Screens: The sliding translucent rice paper and wooden panels that are so prevalent in Japanese culture intrigued me. When I worked in Japan for one of my graduate school architecture professors from the University of Pennsylvania, I saw how they were able to divide and transform spaces as well as share light between the spaces. The shoji screens were walls and doors as well as windows. Some critical thinker ages ago challenged the very preconception that a wall needed to be static and opaque versus active and translucent. Professor Koyama, who teaches at Tokyo University, said, "Why does the window open and not the wall?" The shoji panels piqued my interest in mobility and illumination. Our home back in Philadelphia now includes interior doors with translucent glass that share light between spaces, sun tunnels, skylights, and transoms. As I looked into even more ways to use natural light, I started to explore the implications on commercial architecture. The challenges were steep. Since the deployment of fluorescent lighting in the 1950s and air-conditioning systems, commercial buildings no longer needed to use as much natural light or natural ventilation. I could not help but look up at the ceiling to the sea of tubes.

Showerheads: I saw in my travels that water was a much more precious commodity than here in the United States. We sometimes forget that millions of people around the world have to carry water to their homes each day. We take for granted running water, and some research shows that we may run out of fresh drinking water on the planet before we run out of fossil fuels. I looked into low-flow showerheads that reduce the typical 2.5 gallons per minute down to 1.5 gallons. The problem was twofold. First, the name low-flow is terrible for marketing. I started referring to the ones I tested as "high-performance" showerheads, because "high" is better than "low," especially when it comes to water pressure. The second problem was that many of the low-flow showerheads did not create a shower experience that was as pleasant as the high-flow heads. After testing showerheads on site in hotels and homes in different countries where I have stayed around the world, I continued the testing with showerheads from different manufacturers back at our home.

Finally, I found one that used less water but felt like the same pressure via an aeration technology. When I ran the calculations on the savings, the return on investment (ROI) was solid. A gallon of domestic water costs about a penny out of the sink or shower (far less than bottled water), and by saving a gallon a minute on a ten-minute shower, the ten cents saved each day adds up to about $36.50 per year. With a forty-dollar showerhead, the ROI was over 90 percent, and the payback was just over a single year. The surprise came when our monthly gas and electricity bill was lower over the first month, which I discounted for seasonality. After several months of savings, I put on my detective hat. Our bill was very low to start with, given that I designed our home outside of Philadelphia with both solar photovoltaic panels for electricity production and solar water panels for hot water heating. Plus, I installed one of the first on-demand water heating systems as well to back up the solar system. With dual net metering, I monitored the daily utility cost of operations.

The learning was profound. By reducing ten gallons a day, for both me and my wife, Cynthia, we were not using as much natural gas to heat the water. The savings on the natural gas was higher than the savings on the water. The takeaway is counterintuitive: a $40 high-performance showerhead saves over $80 each year, which is more energy than the energy produced by a $400 solar panel. We have tens of thousands of dollars of solar panels on our roof, and this discovery aligns with the 1970s mantra of the green movement, "reduce, reuse, and recycle." The first word is "reduce," and by reducing the water, the savings is dramatic on both water and energy consumption.

Light-Emitting Diodes (LEDs):[5] I repeatedly saw that fluorescent tube lighting was the dominant form of commercial illumination at a global level. I asked, why? The answer lies with inertia over innovation. Fluorescent tube technology was more efficient when launched over fifty years ago than incandescent bulbs. So the commercial market readily adopted the change. Since then, the form factor has stayed largely the same, with the typical four-foot (120 cm) tubes. I saw a path to double the efficiency and reduce the 32-watt tubes to 15 watts with LEDs back in 2009, and in so doing also eliminate the toxic mercury vapor in each fluorescent tube and reduce the air-conditioning load. I expected the world to respond. However, disruptive technology takes time. The next year in 2010, we developed a robust thermal management system to keep the LEDs cooler, and we moved our manufacturing from China to southeastern Pennsylvania to increase quality assurance. The superior engineering and made-in-America reliability triggered the sales to major corporations and the US government.

According to the US Department of Energy (DOE) there are over 2.3 billion fluorescent tubes in American ceilings.[6] As an architect with a master's thesis on energy intelligence, I take that data as an awesome challenge to switch the lights and save 50 percent or more on energy, create American jobs, and reduce CO_2 emissions along the way. A link to critical thinking lies in the fact that lighting accounts for about a third of commercial electricity but it is *not* sub-metered on the electricity bills. Simply, business owners can't see the breakout expense on lighting. It is a costly cancer that grows in each utility bill. For about fifty years, no one really asked the question, "How much do my lights cost to operate?" Taking anything for granted is the opposite of critical thinking, and since 2009, my team has been beating the drum of energy efficiency through lighting. We have had to assess and count many lights in many locations to calculate the annual kilowatt-hour consumption. The calculations let us show property owners their burden of electricity for existing illumination, and the savings potential with LEDs. We have proudly retrofitted some "firsts" in property categories like commercial high-rises, retail, health care, education, hospitality, automotive, industrial, and the military. Each spring, I think that the mainstream tipping point will come, and we'll see if it happens soon.

Critical thinking is often about connecting the dots that are not immediately apparent. The act of digging deeper with something as common as a showerhead, that saves water and energy relative to heating the water, sets the stage for explorations into how LED technology could reduce electricity for lighting and also reduce air-conditioning costs since LEDs run cooler than other less efficient types of lights.

Pens and Pencils: During the 1960s space race between the United States and Soviet Union, a story unfolded that NASA was spending millions of dollars to develop a pen that would work in a gravity-free environment, while the Soviets just used pencils. The story turns out to be an urban myth, because both programs used a form of pencil. Our American astronauts initially used mechanical pencils with high-strength outer casings while the Soviet cosmonauts used wax pencils. Both writing implements had their downsides, because the unintended material waste could damage sensitive electronic equipment in the space capsules. Plus, the broken graphite from the mechanical pencils or the peel-back paper from the wax pencils could float around and get into someone's eye. Both programs eventually ended up using the Fisher Space Pen.[7]

The innovation by Paul C. Fisher used nitrogen under pressure to force the flow of ink. This resulted in a pen that would write in zero gravity, upside down, in a vacuum, and also underwater.

A floating barrier separated the nitrogen from the special high-viscosity ink, and a tungsten carbide roller ball helped prevent the ink from leaking out into the space capsule.

I share this story, because I like the message of the myth more than the reality of the historical facts. Solutions that use readily available materials versus high-tech alternatives have a certain simplicity and elegance.

See the appendix for more on situational awareness for writing implements.

Moving a Mountain: In 2014, when my son, Calvin, was eight years old, I asked him one of the questions that I have asked high school seniors that are at the very top of their class, during interviews that I help conduct for my alma matter, the University of Virginia, for the Jefferson Scholarships. I ask, "How would you move Mount Fuji?"

Many of the high-performing students respond with answers that are literally about moving Mount Fuji through earth-moving equipment, which is similar to what is expected of employees in interviews for companies like Microsoft, McKinsey, or Booz Allen Hamilton. In his book *How Would You Move Mount Fuji,*[8] William Poundstone provides details into the earth-moving calculations and many other thought-provoking questions and answers.

The idea of the "big" questions is to see how people respond to breaking down the steps necessary to tackle seemingly insurmountable challenges like moving a mountain or walking on the moon. As a second-grade student, my son, Calvin, answered the Mount Fuji question with a question, "Dad, isn't the real question how to stop it from moving?" As he asked, he spun his finger around and then widened the circle radius to mimic the earth rotating and revolving around the sun. The next day, he asked me, "In what time do I have to move that mountain?" I asked if he meant how much time did he have to move it, and he said, "No, when do I have to move it, because if it is now, it would be easier than with old technology, but if it is in the future, it would be easier because I could use future technology like lasers and hovercrafts." In both of his first two responses, I loved that he skipped over trying to wrestle with the earth-moving calculations and questioned the question.

The next day on our morning drive to school, he asked me to ask him the same question again. I looked in the rearview mirror and said, "Calvin, how would you move Mount Fuji?" He looked back at me through the mirror and with a calm and almost unaffected demeanor said, "What am I?" I asked what he meant, and he said, "Well, you said how would 'I' move Mount Fuji. What if 'I' am magma and can move it by erupting tomorrow?" Since then, I have proudly shared his set of rotation, time, and existential responses with friends.

In the twenty-first century, we have some potential mountains to move. Given that human population has doubled since the 1970s, and we face energy, natural resource, and climate challenges, we will need to rethink prior solutions. We may need to also question the questions in order to open opportunities for productive paths forward.

See the appendix for more on fostering critical thinking at the earliest ages and creativity for children.

Summary on Critical Thinking

Overall, critical thinking starts with observation and the act of asking questions versus having preconceived answers. I now have many more questions than answers. By embedding in communities around the world at urban, suburban, and rural levels, my preconceptions were challenged daily. In many cases, drawing something like a town square involved multiple hours of documentation. The time-consuming act of drawing enabled me to absorb local social interactions. In different countries, I have seen a surprising range of commuter "shift changes" in bustling cities and interaction between merchants and customers in towns and villages. The social observations and personal interactions have certainly shaped some of my critical thinking about the people side of the triple bottom line: people, planet, and profit.

Drawing on observations from prior experiences or from other countries and synthesizing those observations is what elevates critical thinking from just … thinking. The most effective synthesizing is often when a number of apparently disparate things are combined into a coherent whole. The whole may become an insight, tactic, or strategy. The next chapter focuses on how critical thinking can inform sustainability and a new clean technology approach for America.

4 SUSTAINABILITY AND CLEAN TECH FOR AMERICA

Sustainable Design Approach

Sustainable design is a child of sustainability and a sibling of sustainable innovation. So understanding the family is important for clarity.

Sustainability is about endurance through interdependence at the social (people), environmental (planet), and financial (profit) levels. This triple bottom line relies on complex connections, and that complexity of interconnectivity is what makes it so difficult to achieve.

Sustainable innovation is a process that aspires to reach the triple bottom line while cultivating new ideas within a company from inception through to sales. All of the complexity of engineering, research, and refinement along the way make sustainable innovation difficult to achieve as well.

Sustainable design is an approach to design and build structures, develop and manufacture products, and provide services that adhere to the principles of social, economic, and ecological sustainability.

Synonyms include environmental design, environmentally sustainable design, and environmentally conscious design.[9]

Execution of Sustainable Design

The founding three Rs of sustainability—reduce, reuse, and recycle—form a compelling triangle of interconnectivity. I have added "rethink" as the fourth to create cornerstones that provide a solid foundation for sustainable design.

Reduce

Reduce negative impacts on the environment:

- reduce nonrenewable energy consumption;
- reduce water consumption and contamination;
- reduce packaging waste, especially in single-use packaging;
- reduce transportation, especially through local options;

- reduce toxins in products and building materials;
- reduce energy waste by adopting high-efficiency technology (from lighting to air-conditioning, and many more systems). Note: lighting and indoor climate control each account for over a quarter of building energy consumption.

Reuse
- reuse resources and goods when possible, especially over single-use packaging;
- repair versus replace when possible with equipment, finished goods, and buildings.

Recycle
Recycle whatever cannot be reused or repaired. Remember, recycling uses energy and transportation, so it comes after reduce, reuse, and repair.

Rethink
- health and comfort for people;
- delivering function and style with sustainability;
- productive living and working environments;
- alternative and renewable power production;
- optimization of operational and maintenance practices;
- optimization of site potential for building locations;
- life-cycle impact on the environment of products, services, and buildings;
- prioritization of social and economic impact—local products and jobs placed first.

Clean Tech for America

Clean Tech for America is an example of a strategy to promote sustainability across many different socioeconomic sectors. The debate over energy resources and weather impact may continue for decades. In the ramp up to the 2012 presidential election, the debate over the science of climate change started heating up. I thought that conservatives and liberals could focus more on solutions for natural resource allocation and sustainable ROI than the weather. So I developed the concept "Clean Tech for America" to focus on creating new jobs and business opportunities along with building a stronger and more sustainable country in the new global energy economy. Since we had moved the manufacturing for our LED lighting business from China to southeastern Pennsylvania in 2010, I had started to see firsthand the sales traction and benefits of energy-smart job creation through American manufacturing. My thought was that America needed more jobs, and we had rallied to fight for independence 235 years ago, and now we could rally for energy independence.

The Concept

Create a tipping point that makes America stronger as a change agent for positive economic growth and environmental sustainability. In his book *The Tipping Point,*[10] Malcolm Gladwell writes, "The Theory of Tipping Points requires, however, that we reframe the way we think about the world." In this case, I felt that we needed to reframe the perception that economic growth was counter to environmental sustainability. Mr. Gladwell also writes, "In the end, Tipping Points are a reaffirmation of the potential for change and the power of intelligent action." This Clean Tech for America concept includes examples of intelligent action and mission with ten pillars for positive change.

To succeed in executing this concept, I looked at relevant examples of cultural change to learn from their strategies and tactics. The conservative Tea Party had ignited tens of millions of Americans to take action and hold rallies, which over the course of the 2010 midterm election impacted the nation and sparked dialogue. The Republican Party gained sixty-three seats in the US House of Representatives, recapturing the majority and making it the largest seat change since 1948.[11] Clean Tech for America is about the American ideal of self-reliance, technology leadership, and smart government. While Tea Party supporters often spoke about our need to stop wasting money, my idea for Clean Tech for America was to attract both liberals and conservatives by focusing on our need to stop wasting energy. The concept was to attract Americans from college age to the baby boomers and focus on "smart" government, not just small or large government. Smart government would create incentives as the carrot versus penalties as the stick to work with rather than against private sector interests.

A Clean Tech Definition

Clean tech is a term used to describe knowledge-based products or services that improve operational performance, productivity, or efficiency while reducing costs, inputs, energy consumption, waste, or pollution. This definition is intended to be universally appealing because it is not the stereotypical "green" language. Instead, it speaks to efficiency and cost reduction in the same breath as reducing pollution.

Declaration of Independence

The preamble has two phrases that are relevant to sustainability and Clean Tech for America (italicized):

> When in the Course of human events, it becomes necessary for one people to dissolve the political bands which have connected them with another, and to assume among the *powers of the earth*, the separate and equal station to which the

Laws of Nature and of Nature's God entitle them, a decent respect to the opinions of mankind requires that they should declare the causes which impel them to the separation.

We hold these truths to be self-evident, that all men are created equal, that they are endowed by their Creator with certain unalienable Rights, that among these are Life, Liberty and the pursuit of Happiness.

Ten Pillars of the Clean Tech for America Mission (From Original Draft in 2011)

#1: American Self-Reliance: We believe that our unalienable rights come with the responsibility to leverage the "powers of the earth," referenced in the Declaration of Independence, to their highest and best use so that America reduces its reliance on overseas oil and thrives in the new global energy economy.

#2: American Jobs: We believe that that the breadth and scope of clean technology will become the foundation of a new energy revolution in the twenty-first century just as mechanical automation became the foundation for the Industrial Revolution that shaped the twentieth century. With this change comes an opportunity for Americans to intelligently train and rethink manufacturing and services to participate as creators as well as buyers of a whole new generation of consumer, business, and industrial products.

#3: American Health: We believe that clean tech is also about the process of making products with fewer toxins that we touch and digest. This form of preventive medicine in advance of a business or consumer sale may serve as a highly cost-effective solution over the life cycle of products to reduce unforeseeable diseases and sick-building syndrome for our children and ourselves.

#4: American Property Value: We believe that measurement is the key to management and American real estate offers an immediate platform to create efficiencies. According to the US Department of Energy (DOE), buildings account for over 40 percent of all US energy consumption. It takes energy to make a new property, but it saves energy to retrofit an existing one. We believe in energy auditing and scoring properties on operating cost per square foot to determine the most cost-effective paths forward.

#5: American Transportation: We believe that America can create better fuel economy through electric cars, given improved battery technology with longer life and lower costs, in addition to advancements in clean diesel. These technologies are bridges to the ongoing development of hydrogen vehicles, and fleet and public transportation can lead the way with natural gas as another bridge option to hydrogen. We also believe in a more robust development of car share and ride share carpool programs as well as mass transit and high-speed rail where reasonably possible within return-on-investment targets.

#6: American Five-Star Rs: We believe in the three founding Rs of the early environmental movement: reduce, reuse, and recycle, plus a fourth one for "renewable energy" and a fifth one for "rethink." Reduce waste, reuse materials, recycle trash … and renewable energy through renewables such as solar, wind, hydro, geothermal, tidal, and other sources. Rethink—all of the ways that we have done things in the past to find new opportunities for efficiency, growth, and prosperity.

#7: American National Security: We believe that we need to focus on manufacturing and product development and intellectual property, because we are increasingly vulnerable to other countries.

#8: American Energy Mix: We believe in a balance with multiple renewable energy spokes, in concert with nuclear and traditional power supply, and efforts to diminish the percentage of dependency from coal, offshore oil, and natural gas. According to the US Department of Energy (DOE), we use 25 percent of the world's power and we only have 5 percent of the world's population, so we have to reduce wasted energy. We will also need to transition off of existing power supplies.

#9: American Political Candidates and Legislation: We believe in supporting candidates who look beyond party ideology to find local, state, and national solutions with an eye on American job creation and long-term sustainability. Beyond any candidate or public servant, we believe in supporting legislation that encourages American job creation and rewards clean tech and energy-smart performance, without handicapping corporations from growth.

#10: American Stewardship: We believe in respecting the "Laws of Nature" referenced in the Declaration of Independence as they relate to human interaction with plants and animal life so that we strive to lead the world by example and coexist as better stewards of the environment for ourselves and future generations.

Conservative Perspective

About four years after writing the ten pillars for Clean Tech for America, I saw an interview with conservative thought leader William J. Bennett. Over the early fall of 2015, he was promoting his new book, *America the Strong: Conservative Ideas to Spark the Next Generation*.[12] Mr. Bennett is the former secretary of education under President Ronald Reagan and director of the Office of National Drug Control Policy under George H. W. Bush. He cofounded K12, a publicly traded online education company in 2000, and as of 2016, he hosts the syndicated radio program "Morning in America." Mr. Bennett is a highly respected conservative and the author of twenty-four books, including the number-one *New York Times* best sellers *The Book of Virtues* and *The Death of Outrage*.

Mr. Bennett and his coauthor, Mr. John T. E. Cribb, write in *America the Strong* about the need to balance incentives for economic prosperity with environmental and energy consumption considerations. They describe that conservatives do not want to live on a polluted planet and that *conservation* and *conservatism* are offspring of the Latin root *conservare*, which is about preservation and ensuring safety. They also acknowledge that environmentalism has had positive impacts and certain laws are required to reduce negative environmental impact.

Mr. Bennett and Mr. Cribb are spot-on that certain laws are key to success. Unsensible laws have surprising negative impacts. Some examples of negative impacts were highly informative. In 2014, coauthors Steven D. Levitt and Stephen J. Dubner released their book *Think Like a Freak*,[13] and it became another one of their *New York Times* best sellers. Mr. Levitt is the professor of economics at the University of Chicago, and Mr. Dubner is an award-winning author, journalist, and radio and TV personality. Their prior best-selling books, *Freakonomics*[14] and *SuperFreakonomics*,[15] have earned them popular and critical acclaim, and have inspired this author. Among the many data points and thought-provoking stories in *Think Like a Freak*, the book includes examples of environmental laws that backfired. In Mexico City, single-passenger car drivers had to leave their vehicles at home one day a week to help reduce pollution. Mr. Levitt and Mr. Dubner describe how the law did not work as intended to increase public transportation, because many people dodged the license-plate tracking process by purchasing a second car. The second cars were often lower-cost used cars with even worse emissions than their primary vehicles.

In the drawings and insights on sustainable design in this book, I address urban traffic at several points. The overall theme is about providing better pedestrian access and public transit as a "carrot" incentive versus a regulatory "stick" penalty.

When it comes to human impact, in *America the Strong*, Mr. Bennett and Mr. Cribb describe that many conservatives think that human behavior is not necessarily creating a negative impact on the earth. Here is an example that may provide some perspective. If we put rising sea level and storm surge debates aside, we have reduced the world's marine vertebrate fish population by an alarming 49 percent since the 1970s. This report from the World Wildlife Fund was analyzed by the Zoological Society of London.[16] The local and commercial fish populations have been nearly cut in half due to habitat depletion and the increased global population, which has doubled since 1970.

Human activity is outpacing and impacting natural wildlife reproduction. It is not statistically strange that twice the number of people would eat twice as many fish, create pollutants that increase ocean acidity levels, or deposit 250,000 metric tons of plastic in the ocean. I share this example because the planet is unemotional, and what we do as humans is more likely "bad" for us than it is "bad for the planet." I like to eat fish as well as just about every other type of food. Fewer fish will increase food costs through the time-tested laws of supply and demand. In the part 3 "Commercial Impact" section of this book, I preview a recent innovation to produce fish intelligently through advanced aquaponics, lighting, and renewable energy technology. We can start solving big problems if we first accept that the problems exist. Big problems are often complicated, so we can start by identifying and solving the subset smaller problems first.

In the *Freak* books, Mr. Levitt and Mr. Dubner challenge preconceptions, and *Think Like a Freak* includes key insights into why we should "Think Small."[17] They write about how many interrelated small challenges often make up the larger problems. Given the complexity of large-scale problems, they recommend focusing on solving the smaller ones first. As I have drafted and illustrated this book on sustainable design, I have focused on numerous small problems and small solutions while also taking a critical look at how those micro-moves can influence larger solutions.

Conclusion: Embracing clean technology can solve economic and environmental challenges. Conservatives and liberals may have more in common than appears on the political stage. Tackling small problems is a cost-effective strategy to solve for larger issues. We just need to shed some of the "green" bias to roll up our sleeves and find which programs and policies will have the most cost-effective impact.

Sustainable ROI: *Seven Insights and Actions*

The percentage increase in global population since the first Earth Day in 1970 is surprising. A few friends and colleagues thought that the increase was between 10 and 25 percent. The perception is far from the reality. Global population has doubled with an increase of almost 100 percent in just forty-five years. American home and business owners can take steps with cost-effective return on investments (ROI) for lifestyle improvements and profit benefits while also reducing our impact on the environment. We can individually lead by example to build American energy independence, energy security, and sustainability while the governments of the world try to do their part. Here are seven points that I have identified through research to add perspective and inspire action.

Insight #1: Population[18]

Global population has increased from 3.6 billion to over seven billion in 2015. This is an unprecedented lift, given that up until the midnineteenth century, the global population was under one billion.

Action #1: Imagine what would happen to your house if visiting family members stayed indefinitely after Thanksgiving or an Independence Day party. Ask your spouse or a friend what little things might get damaged or depleted by doubling the residents of your home. Damage may start with spilled glasses of wine or running out of paper towels and then extend to jammed garbage disposals or running out of hot water for morning showers. You may accept that we would statistically break and deplete some things within our homes. The same realization applies to our ecosystem by the sheer stress from an increasingly crowded "house party." Stop debating the climate science and start focusing on the small actions that you can take to yield a cost-effective and positive impact.

Insight #2: Water[19]

Water is integral to life, and fresh water is only 2.5 percent of the water on earth. Within the 2.5 percent, 68.7 percent of it is in glaciers, 30.1 percent is groundwater, and only 1.2 percent is actually on the surface. With population increases projected to nine billion by 2050, we may run out of drinking and irrigation water before we run out of fossil fuels. The massive High Plains Ogallala aquifer covers 174,000 square miles across eight states, holds over 978 trillion gallons of water, and supplies 30 percent of US irrigation. We pump the Jurassic reservoirs faster than fresh water can replenish it. Over the past century, the average hundred-foot reservoir depth has dropped by ten to fifty feet. A cheeseburger requires between 660 and 1,300 gallons of water to produce depending on its size versus vegetables that yield six times more protein for the same water. Beans, lentils, peas, and so on, win with only five gallons of water per gram of protein, followed by chicken at nine gallons/gram, while beef requires about thirty gallons/gram of protein. We eat about 171 pounds of meat a year, which is three times the international average and twice the recommendation for good health.

Action #2: Make or order a salad for lunch, go for "meatless Mondays," buy a high-performance showerhead, and for business owners, use faucet timers in bathrooms, dual-flush toilets, waterless urinals, draught-tolerant landscaping versus sprinkler-intensive planting. Whenever possible, buy locally grown food or grow vegetables in your backyard or on the roof of your office. When we transport food across the country in massive truckloads every day, the water within the food goes with it. This disrupts the water cycle. In regards to water quality in local communities, we need to conserve forests near any body of water. These areas are natural biofilters called *riparian zones*, and they help reduce polluted surface runoff. We often take small streams and wetlands for granted, but they are key spokes on the total wheel of fresh water. Imagine the potential water pollution from the construction of an office park or the daily runoff from a large parking lot at a shopping mall.

Insight #3: Paper[20]

America uses 25 percent of the world's paper and we only have 5 percent of the world's population. The digital revolution has not reduced paper at expected levels, and 95 percent of business documents are still stored on paper. New York's largest export out of the Port of NY is waste paper. We use over 700 pounds of paper each year per capita, and we currently only recycle about 45 percent. The average American attorney uses one ton (2,000 pounds) of paper every year. Recycling one ton of paper saves 682.5 gallons of oil, 7,000 gallons of water, and 3.3 cubic yards of landfill space.

Action #3: Buy a microfiber cloth to use at home for big spills versus paper towels, and at work, set up paper recycling programs, print less, and print on double sides. If offices increased two-sided photocopying from 20 percent to 60 percent, we could save the equivalent of about fifteen million trees.

Insight #4: Transportation[21]

America uses 25 percent of the world's energy and we only have 5 percent of the world's population. Transportation is 28 percent, and personal vehicles account for 60 percent. America is home to one-third of the world's automobiles. Transportation is a hidden energy cost of products and single-passenger commuting is a key place to explore cost-effective savings.

Action #4: Buy local and American-made products to reduce the transportation energy and also create more American jobs. Consider public transportation or ride sharing for one or more weekdays. The ROI is excellent, given fuel savings and reduced wear. Business owners can also offer incentives for staff and use sustainability to attract employees and customers.

Insight #5: Energy[22]

Our homes and buildings use over 40 percent of US energy. Cost-effective energy savings are right overhead.

Action #5: Add extra insulation in your attic to save energy at a terrific ROI. Look up and change the lights at home and at work. Energy-efficient lighting, such as LED technology, is the low-hanging fruit of energy cost reduction with ROI over 33 percent in many cases and multiple-decade longevity. Energy reduction is typically more cost-effective than renewable energy production. Saving energy and money is easier than making more power from alternative sources.

Solar panels may have a ten-year payback, while lighting, insulation, or upgrades to heating and air-conditioning may have a payback in less than half the time. Plus, new zero-dollar upfront cost financing yields cash-flow positive results from the start. Technology and financing have improved so dramatically since the first Earth Day that home and business owners are empowered with "energy intelligence" at entirely new levels.

Insight #6: Agriculture[23]

With population increases, farm-ready arable soil is depleting around the globe at such high rates that experts believe by 2050 we will need to produce 70 percent more food than 2015 levels. Natural methods of agriculture actually have the best crop yields and guarantee healthy soil for years to come. Healthy soil takes about a thousand years to develop. When farmers use methods such as herbicides, synthetic fertilizers, and tilling, and they grow only one crop each year, they eventually destroy arable soil.

Action #6: For soil preservation, personal solutions include food composting, backyard and rooftop gardens, and buying locally grown food. At the corporate business level, developers and real estate investors may not realize that building on arable land has long-term negative impacts on our food supply. Individuals that invest in real estate investment trust (REIT) companies, or mutual funds focused on real estate, most likely do not think that their investment may negatively impact soil for about a thousand years. Farmers can use more natural methods such as crop rotations, natural pest eliminators (e.g., birds and bats), managed grazing, multicrop systems, as well as new innovations in urban farming, hydroponics, and aquaponics. The "hydro" and "aqua" systems have the added benefit of water conservation and fish protein production. The final chapter of this book highlights an innovation in aquaponics that also ties in urban farming through LED light technology.

Insight #7: Suburbanization[24]

Suburban sprawl, which has resulted from global population increases, has a negative impact on water, transportation, energy, and fertile soil. Major loss to biodiversity (animal and plant life) and arable farmland will negatively affect the environment and human health while also stressing infrastructures.

Action #7: Instead of building on undeveloped land, we can rethink the city and more proactively refurbish abandoned buildings and houses.

Sustainable Re-view: *What Is Old Is New Again*

As the earliest members of humankind faced the challenges of their environment, sustainability was not an option but a survival requirement. Over 100,000 years ago, early Homo sapiens focused on reducing wasted human energy and reusing resources as a default. The early cave-dwelling men and women only had so much energy in a given day to hunt and care for their families. So they sourced local food or moved to find better sustenance and shelter. Today, buying local products is one of the strategic directions of twenty-first-century sustainability. Only since the Industrial Revolution and the advent of transportation and food preservatives have we as a species eaten food that was not primarily sourced locally. Everything used to be organic, because there were no processed foods. American students typically learn about how Native Americans used every part of a resource such as a bison or deer. We would benefit from remembering what we were taught at a young age. The animals were not just a source of protein, but the parts were used for tepee covers, bedding, belts, footwear, glues, thread, bows, and more. They used and reused the resources at hand, without creating toxins or waste for landfills.

Overall, our ancestors at different stages have lived relatively lightly on the land. As recently as the middle of the last century, the "milkman" was a reflection of the spirit of reuse. The milkman would take the empty bottles back for cleaning and refilling rather than undertaking the much more energy-intensive meltdown and recycling process. The same was true for the longneck beer bottles, which were designed so that regional facilities could clean and refill the glass bottles. Plastics changed the game. While adoption of recycling is increasing, billions of plastic bottles and packaging materials end up in the landfills each year. While one-time-use plastic bottles cost less than multiple-use glass bottles, the lifetime total cost of ownership (TCO) is less in certain cases for glass.

Perspective is the key to finding balance in a modern world with global trade and advancing technology. We do not want to go nostalgically backward, but we should also be careful not to steam ahead without learning how to apply relevant lessons from the past. Here is a small example of a sustainability move with a high ROI. When my wife, Cynthia, and I were renovating our home outside of Philadelphia, we priced out the new driveway and back patio. The gravel for underneath the driveway asphalt and the patio flagstone was going to come from a local quarry, and it was more expensive than I had expected. Having lived in the heart of Philadelphia for my master's of architecture at the University of Pennsylvania, I remembered occasionally seeing row homes and other dilapidated buildings demolished for new construction. In many cases, dump trucks full of crushed bricks and concrete blocks would roar out of the city in a cloud of dust.

I found out that the vast majority of the debris was just going to landfills. The American Institute of Architects estimates that anywhere from 25 to 40 percent of the national solid waste stream is building-related waste, and only 20 percent of construction waste or demolition debris is actually recycled.[25] After a few calls, I was able to find a demolition company that would sync up the "drop" of the crushed and sorted masonry debris at my home on the day that I had the excavation team on-site with the backhoe and front-end loader. The results: I paid less than buying newly quarried gravel, yielding a high ROI on the brief time it took to source and coordinate the demolition stone delivery. The overlay asphalt and flagstone look great, and no one will ever see what is beneath. The demolition company did not have to pay to dump the debris, and the landfill has less waste. This approach to cost-effective sustainable ROI was a key driver for over a hundred different decisions in the construction of our eco-smart solar home that we transformed from an old 1950s house. Many of the lessons learned over the two decades of travel that are documented in this book influenced the sustainability choices for our home and my career as an architect and US manufacturer of energy-saving LED lights.

Dating back to the origins of humankind, we have had sustainability in our DNA. Now we can look harder at what we have and what we need. We can then analyze the true cost to determine the mix of conserving resources, managing consumption, and investing in new technology. We are fortunate in America to have such a breadth of natural resources and energy options. Intelligent strategies with cost-conscious tactical deployment plans and incentives will enable us to thrive for generations to come.

Summary of Sustainable Design

We have the tools and the strength in numbers to make a cost-effective and positive impact. Debate over climate science has stalled mainstream adoption of clean technology initiatives, and we should focus on high-performance ROI tactics. Terminologies such as "global warming" and "climate change" have been divisive in that they focus on weather without capturing the larger systemic challenges to the system.

All of us should accept that massive increases in population with billions more people will result in human activity that has some impact on the system. If we accept interrelationships, then we can work more productively together to find solutions that help the triple bottom line of people, planet, and profit. Sustainability and environmental advocates should maintain their passion while also speaking in the language of business to propose and rank solutions based on ROI, such as the number of kilowatt-hours saved per dollar invested and the number of pounds of CO_2 saved per dollar invested. We can also change the terminology to broaden the dialogue beyond weather.

Consider themes such as ecosystem change, eco-disruption, and eco-overload. Top eco-ROI tactics will reduce energy waste to improve business net operating income (NOI), build American energy security, increase quality of life, and foster environmental stewardship for future generations.

The next section, part 2 of this book, includes the travel sketches and observations relative to sustainable design.

2 TRAVEL DRAWINGS AND OBSERVATIONS

The following chapters include drawings from over two decades of field observation and documentation. The pens used for the field drawings ranged from different sized brush pens with ink cartridges to felt-tip pens for detail work.

Extensive travel across America has provided me with incredible inspiration into the strength and innovation of our great country. Some of my earliest travel drawing experiences in Asia and Europe set the stage for my focus on sustainable design.

The international travel served as a springboard in part because so many other countries do not have the combination of low fuel costs and natural resources as the United States. They have had to make do with less, and efficiency solutions have come over centuries of innovation.

5 ASIA

JAPAN

Japan seems to be a country of juxtaposition and contradiction. A profound love of nature coexists with an equally deep love of technology. Both loves are rooted in a microcosm of quality over quantity. "Nature" for the Japanese is anything from the detailed engineering and markings on an insect to a walk through an immaculately manicured and controlled garden. "Technology" is anything from fast-food sushi to miniaturized electronics. Steeped in tradition that has evolved over two thousand years, this nation struggles with maintaining its culture while rushing into the twenty-first century with the enthusiasm of nineteenth-century American prospectors.

I had the good fortune of traveling extensively throughout Japan and also working for Kinya Maruyama, one of my master's of architecture professors, from the University of Pennsylvania. Kinya is a pioneer in environmentally sustainable architecture and a celebrated architect who teaches as a guest professor at Penn. Kinya's office is in Tokyo, where I worked in his studio, Atelier Mobile, in 1992. He not only gave me the work experience and a place to live in a small apartment, but he set in motion the thinking process that has shaped my work ever since. The observations from Japan resonate today, as America strives to build sustainable practices and energy independence.

Japan 1

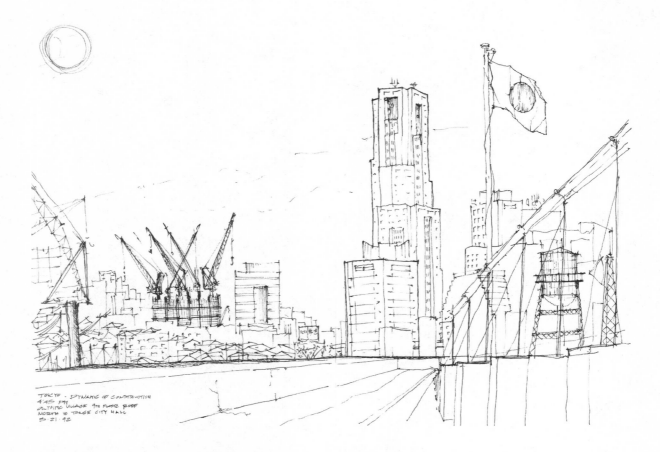

TOKYO - DYNAMIC OF CONSTRUCTION
4:45 PM
OLYMPIC VILLAGE 9TH FLOOR ROOF
NORTH TO TOKEE CITY HALL
5-21-92

Japan 1: Highlights Relevant to Sustainable Design:

We can look to more proactively build *up* in cities versus *out* in suburbs to reduce the burden on sprawl and automobile transportation.

From the roof of the Olympic Village hostel where I initially stayed in Tokyo, I drew the first image of my Japanese odyssey in 1992. The skyline was more dynamic than any I had seen in other cities. Imagine dozens of cranes swinging, churning, moving, and grinding as they rushed to expand the capital city. Over the past two hundred years, Tokyo has been destroyed at least four times by either fires or earthquakes. Remarkably, the city officials consistently return plots and streets to their original layout. The result is that often ten-story buildings sit on twelve-foot-wide parcels that most likely used to be someone's house. As well, the streets wind and dogleg with the organic-ization of limbs on an old oak tree, making navigation less than simple for the unfamiliar.

Tokyo for all intents and purposes is the largest village on earth. The sense of urgency and crowding, which we share to a slightly lesser degree in large American cities, is perhaps palatable to the Japanese people in part because of the oasis parks and the natural experiences they find outside of the cities.

Japan 1: (a) Interior spreads 2 and 3

Japan 1: (a) Interior spread 4

 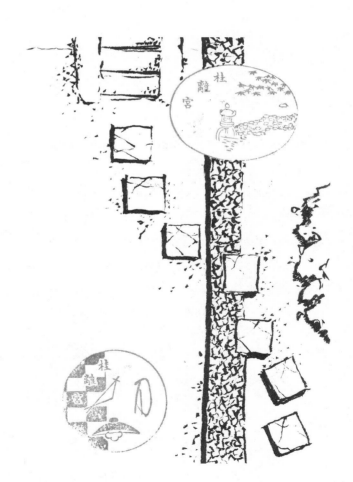

Japan 2

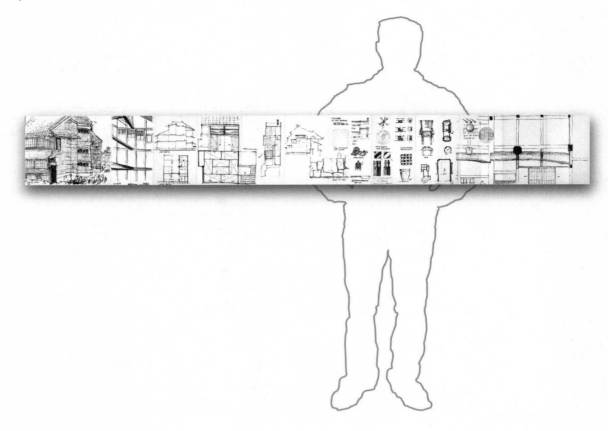

Japan 2: Highlights Relevant to Sustainable Design:

Preserve technique over material.

Traditional Japanese houses have steadily made way for the innovations of modern construction. To preserve a few exemplary physical structures and maintain a thread of cultural memory, the Japanese government has funded parks that include regional architecture and craft museums. The history of "craft" is something that struck me as a telltale difference between our current American process of making things and even thinking about making things. I was fortunate to work with both a master carpenter and a master Shikkui mason. Shikkui is a special Japanese lime plaster that includes seaweed extract additives for stability, soybean oil for improved workability and water repellency, natural plant fibers for reduced cracking, and other natural aggregates such as eggshells. Both master craftsmen had trained for years to hone their skills, repeating and copying traditional methods.

Only after decades of looking and learning did they try to improve the process and the product. Our American reputation is based on a force to invent and reinvent the mousetrap of America and products. Often we do so without first understanding the mouse. This sketchbook also includes large wood beams, modular tatami mats, shoji screens, and light fixtures.

Japan 2: Left Side

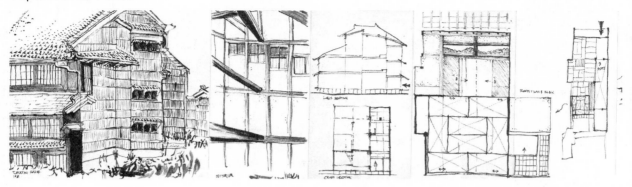

Japan 2: Right Side

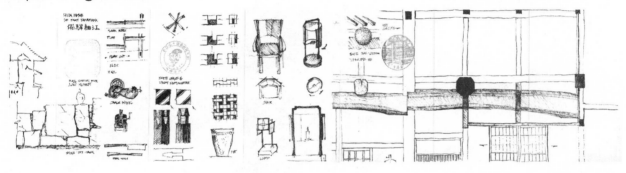

Japan 2: Detail (a)

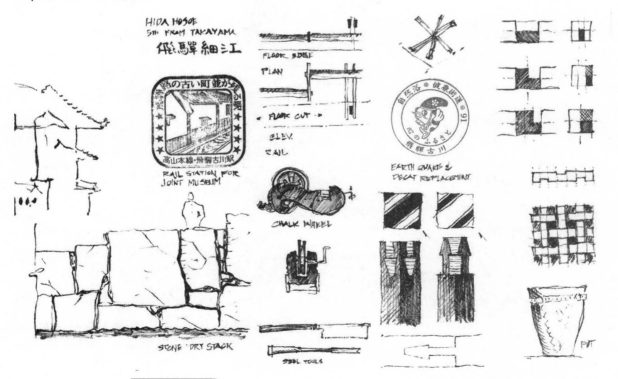

Japan 2: Detail (a) Highlights Relevant to Sustainable Design:

Local material use reduces transportation costs and pollution from fossil fuels.

    The stone wall illustrated here is comprised of multiple-sized stones. Notice that the stones are skillfully pieced together like a puzzle. The largest stone in the center fits especially well with the smaller one to its right. When the stones do not line up exactly, the masons use smaller stones to fill the gaps. These walls last for hundreds of years, and one of the hallmarks of sustainability is longevity. These walls take longer to build than mass-produced concrete block or retaining paver walls, but they last longer and leverage the local materials despite the irregularity of the stone shapes and sizes.

Japan 2: Detail (b)

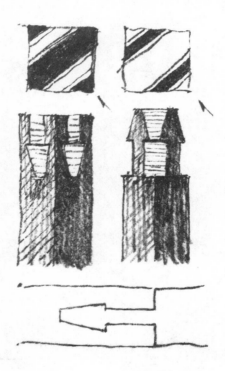

Japan 2: Detail (b) Highlights Relevant to Sustainable Design:

Look for component modularity and longevity.

    This sketch illustrates a diagonal carpentry detail used to connect the lower part of the post to the one above. This detail is used so that about twenty years after construction, when the lower post rots and decays from weather, the bottom two-foot piece can be removed and replaced. In modern construction, we typically choose to save time by not cutting such a joint for the future and instead use pressure-treated lumber to combat the problem. Of course, we have had to regulate and invent a way to keep the chemical by-products of the pressure-treated process from killing river fish and contaminating groundwater.

The component modularity and long twenty-year cycle of replacement reminds me of the long twenty-year life of the LED lights. The initial LED investment is higher than a fluorescent tube or compact fluorescent lights (CFL), and the equivalent of pressure-treated chemicals in the wood is the toxic mercury in the fluorescent tubes and CFLs. Just as we have to manage the toxins in the wood, we have to manage under controlled disposal the hazardous mercury in the fluorescents. By contrast, the modularity of LEDs, with an external driver, allows us to replace only the part that is damaged over time and not the whole product.

Life-cycle cost and environmental-impact analysis often shed light on the winners that are not always the least expensive to start but the lowest total cost of ownership over time. This is the difference between return on investment (ROI) as a sprint and lowest total cost of ownership (TCO) as a marathon.

Japan 2: Detail (c)

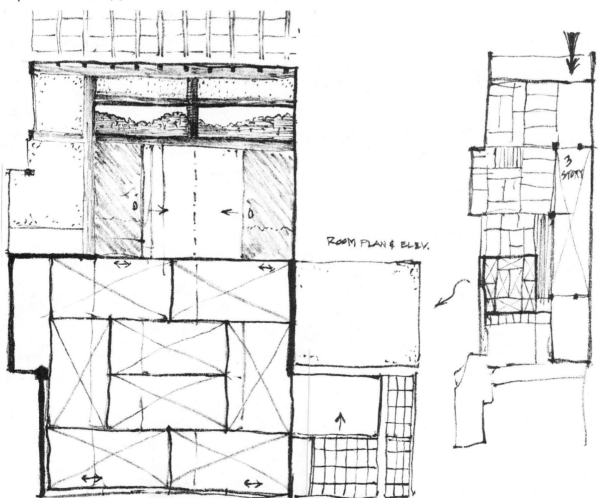

Japan 2: Detail (c) Highlights Relevant to Sustainable Design:

Modular flooring streamlines design and maintenance.

   We sometimes take for granted systems in commercial flooring like carpet tiles or the modular ceiling grids overhead in facilities, from offices and schools to hospitals and retail stores. The ubiquitous commercial ceiling grid that holds fluorescent tube fixtures is typically 24" x 48" with a length that is exactly twice its width. The modular tatami mats that have been used in traditional Japanese structures for hundreds of years are a distant ancestor with the same geometric proportion that is also twice as long as its width.

   Tatami mats are 35 1/2" x 71" or about three feet wide by six feet long. The surface is typically made from rush grass with cotton borders, a rice straw core, and protective backing. The long rush grass is dyed with natural clay to produce a golden-yellow color, and it is tightly woven and stitched in precise tension to prevent warping. The core made of rice straw is naturally treated, kiln-dried, and set in layers that are compressed to two inches before yarn is used to stitch them together for a durable and level flooring system. With care, the tatami floors will last up to twenty years. The modularity is key in that if a mat is damaged, the whole floor does not need to be replaced. Unlike roll-out carpet and matting, the tatami mat can be repaired or replaced. In America, between 25 and 40 percent of our solid waste stream is building-related debris[26] of which some portion every day is discarded carpets. On the longevity front, carpets are often priced according to five-, ten-, fifteen-, and twenty-year lives, and the longevity of the tatami mats puts them at the upper tier.

Japan 3

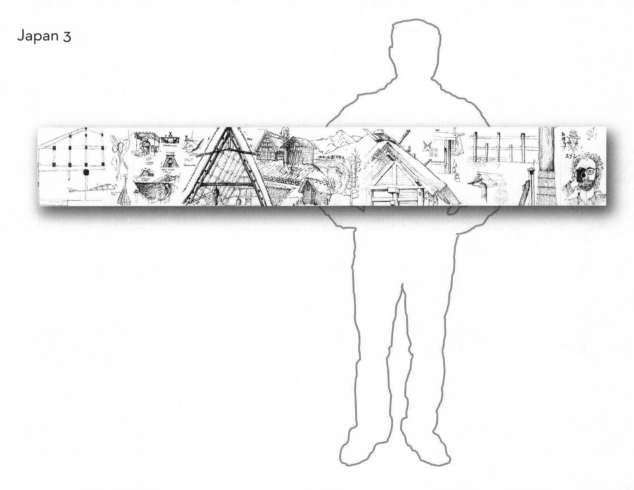

Japan 3: Extended—Metaphysical Speed Bump between Sketchbooks

We cannot bridge differences on major issues like climate change and create meaningful solutions unless we first accept that there are no exact right answers to many questions.

My professor and mentor, Kinya Maruyama, wore rectangular glasses. He could sleep practically standing up, and when awake, he would draw in his sketchbook illustrations of meals that he found particularly interesting. Mariko was an architect from Kinya's studio who traveled with us. She was a trusted member of Kinya's architectural practice, where I later worked in Tokyo. She always wore a hat and taught me something about color, shape, and life. One day, I asked Mariko one of the questions that Walter Gropius would ask students at the Bauhaus School, which he founded. Gropius lived from 1883 to 1969, and he is considered one of the pioneers of modern architecture, along with other modern design leaders such as Ludwig Mies van der Rohe, Le Corbusier, and Frank Lloyd Wright.

The question is seemingly very straightforward but layered with complexity: "How would you assign the primary colors to a circle, an equilateral triangle, and a square?" Like many architects, I had always thought of yellow as a light source well suited for the circle, like the sun, blue as a calm, steady color belonging in the square, and red the most active and fiery color, occupying the more dynamic triangle. Architecture is about how one thinks about the environment and materials. The example of primary colors in geometric shapes challenged me to find balance, an important part of sustainable design, so I thought it would be important to see what others thought about this topic. Many of my architecture student colleagues provided the same color-to-shape match as me, but Kinya's fellow architect, Mariko, said, without knowledge of our decision and reasoning, the following, "Blue is calm, so it should be offset by going in the most active of shapes, the triangle. Red, the opposite, needs to relax in the square, leaving yellow to shine on both from the circle." Her reasoning is nothing short of a balance of yin and yang tranquility, previously elusive to me. Miles was also with us, and he had traveled extensively in Japan prior to my trip. He enjoyed seeing the country through the lens of his new toy.

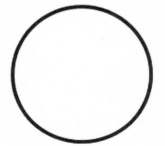 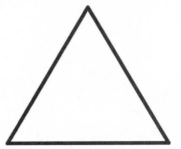 

Matchmaking: Primary Colors in Basic Geometric Shapes

For the comparisons:

Y = yellow

R = red

B = blue

Which color would you put in each shape?

Circle = yellow, red, or blue   Why?

Triangle = yellow, red, or blue   Why?

Square = yellow, red, or blue   Why?

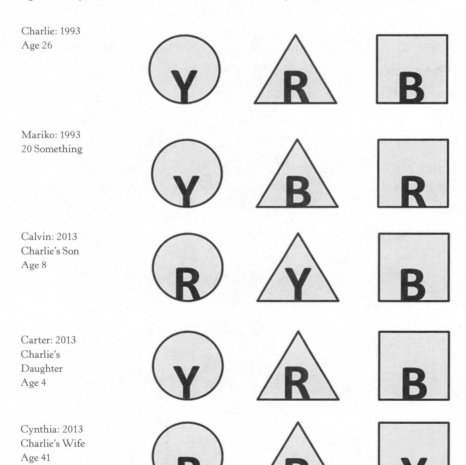

Charlie: 1993
Age 26

"Yellow as a light source belongs in a circle, like the sun, blue as a calm steady color belongs in the square, and red the most active and fiery color belongs in the triangle."

Mariko: 1993
20 Something

"Blue is calm so it should be offset by going in the most active of shapes, the triangle. Red, the opposite, needs to relax in the square, leaving yellow to shine on both from the circle."

Calvin: 2013
Charlie's Son
Age 8

"I put my favorite colors in the shapes I like most. My favorite color is black, then green, then blue, then red, followed by yellow. I like squares best because you get to see them a lot."

Carter: 2013
Charlie's
Daughter
Age 4

"My favorite color is purple. I like yellow in the circle because it rolls. I like red in the triangle, because it looks like a pizza slice. A book looks like a square."

Cynthia: 2013
Charlie's Wife
Age 41

"Blue is in the circle because it reminds me of the earth. Red in the triangle reminds me of a hazard sign. Yellow in the square is the leftover."

Japan 3: Detail (a)

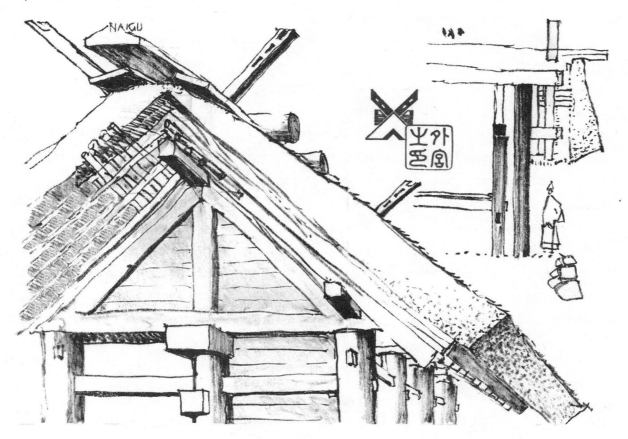

Japan 3: Detail (a) Highlights Relevant to Sustainable Design:

We can look at preservation with new perspective and rethink the "tear down" culture as it relates to job creation and the preservation of construction trade skills.

The Ise Grand Shrine is one of the most sacred of Shinto shrines, and it is a building that may always look like it did over a thousand years ago. I initially had trouble understanding why the Ise Shrine was being torn down in front of me. Simultaneously, behind protective screen walls, an identical shrine was being constructed right near the first one. Well, it turns out that the first one was not first at all but merely one of the many in a continuous cycle of reconstruction every twenty years. I hope my children and grandchildren have a chance to see the reconstruction process. I was there in 1992 to see the beginning of the reconstruction, and the current buildings, from 2013, are the sixty-second version since the original (20 years x 62 cycles = 1,240 years ago). The next rebuilding is scheduled for 2033. I am not aware of any corollary at this scale in the United States.

The reasoning behind the tradition as far as I can determine is threefold:

Reason one: weather breaks down the unprotected, natural materials like thatch roofs and stucco walls over two decades.

Reason two: the apprentices and sons of the master craftsmen who built the previous one can work on the current one and learn the trades.

Reason three: the ritual is a way to mark time at a different scale than by year or decade, and the shrine is forever young.

The seeming redundancy of Ise is sublime in the context of American preservation efforts. Currently, we go to a large effort to preserve the way "original" building construction materials look. The science of keeping materials like wood beams at Monticello or Nantucket's oldest house intact may involve using hidden reinforcing steel or perhaps even fiberglass rods. Recent history proves that we are very good at preserving materials but not as good at preserving technique. The elevated costs of high-quality craftsmanship are a result of supply and demand and a philosophy of material over technique.

The Ise Grand Shrine is in the city of Ise in Mie prefecture, Japan. Please do not confuse it with the Yasukuni Shrine that is another Shinto shrine, located in Chiyoda, Tokyo, Japan. The Yasukuni Shrine is controversial relative to war criminals, since it was founded by Emperor Meiji and commemorates anyone who had died in service of the empire of Japan during the wars from 1867 to 1951.

Japan 3: Detail (b)

Japan 3: Detail (b) Highlights Relevant to Sustainable Design:

We can look harder at local manufacturing for job creation and also reduce transportation cost and pollution.

This is an example of the interior cross section of a silkworm farm, with the exterior in the background. Local manufacturing has historically been micro versus macro before the factories of the Industrial Revolution and the mega industrial complexes such as the Detroit auto hub. In this case, silk production for fabric was small and local instead of at large textile mills that exist around the world. Local jobs simply support the local economy. With the advent of the information age, small may come back into favor over large because small business owners can connect to resources and supply chains via the Internet cloud.

Japan 4

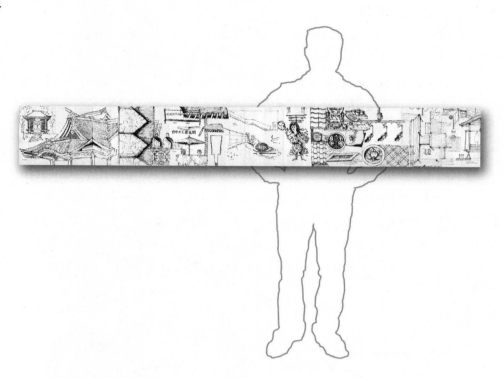

Japan 4: Detail (a)

Japan 4: Detail (a) Highlights Relevant to Sustainable Design:

Rethink walls.

This familiar roofline of the Buddhist Bible store is typical of traditional Japanese roof shapes but unique in that the wall construction is made up of diagonally, wedge-cut logs. One of the intentions of the thick wall log design is to allow more expansion over humid summers to deter moisture from damaging the Bibles.

In America, two-by-four vertical studs and two-by-six studs are still the most popular form of construction for residential construction. Plywood sheathing is often fastened to the outside of the studs with weatherproofing membrane stapled to the surface prior to siding or stucco. Using thicker two-by-six studs allows for more insulation than the thinner studs.

These thick construction members in Japan inspired me during the design of our solar house years later in America. I ended up using vertical studs, but I was able to create ten-inch thick walls by combining two-by-six studs for structure with a two-by-four interior wall. This combined approach not only allowed me to pack the studs with ten inches of insulation for energy savings in both heating and cooling seasons, but I staggered the placement of the studs to reduce the thermal bridge that typically transfers the exterior temperature into a structure. The by-product was also a quieter home, since exterior sound waves do not have a direct path through the staggered studs.

Japan 4: Detail (b)

Japan 4: Detail (b) Highlights Relevant to Sustainable Design:

Rethink the simple tools that have shaped our world.

The saws in this sketchbook, with teeth directed toward the handle, are typical of Japanese hand tools. The direction allows the user to pull the cut rather than push the cut. Western saws are the opposite in that the cutting takes place on the push action. One saw in particular has two different sized and shaped teeth flanking the tool. The difference is that the tight or smaller teeth are for the crosscut versus the larger ones that are used for the rip-cut running parallel to the wood grain. The saw design seems a small reflection of the Japanese attention to detail and respect for not only materials like wood but also for the process involved with the art of its manipulation.

Since Japan is an island, and islands by their nature have finite resources, this respect for the wood is also about maximizing available resources with the least possible waste. Reduced waste is at the heart of sustainable design. Rethinking a tool such as a saw is a springboard for rethinking the much larger outcome of the tools that we often take for granted.

Japan 4: Detail (c)

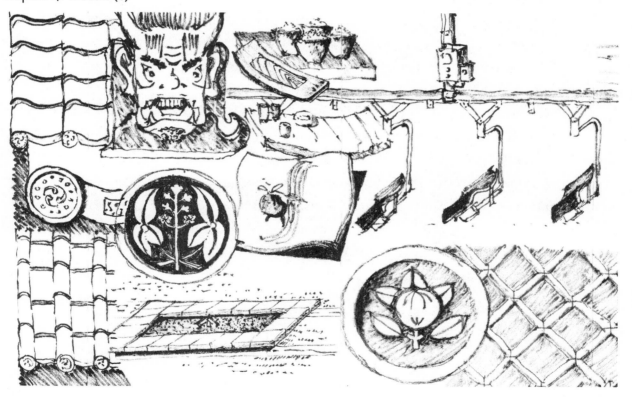

Japan 4: Detail (c) Highlights Relevant to Sustainable Design:

Rethink the lifetime total cost of ownership of building envelopes starting with the roof.

Asphalt roof shingles are commonplace across the roofs of American homes. Many countries have used ceramic tiles for hundreds of years. In my travels to Italy, at the end of the 1980s, I saw firsthand the ubiquitous orange terra-cotta tiles that covered the roofs of residential and commercial buildings in Florence. Years later in Japan, I saw the use of equally ubiquitous roof tiles. The orange Italian tiles are curved symmetrically like a shallow tunnel, while the gray Japanese tiles are curved more like a shallow wave. The upper left of the sketch below illustrates the wave curve. To learn more about the tiles, I visited a tile factory in Japan, and this sketch also shows, on the right side, an illustration of how hanging armatures carry the tiles in and out of the glazing booth.

The Japanese tiles often include significantly more ornamentation via round end caps than the Italian counterparts. The three different circular configurations are examples of regional ornamentation on the ends of roof tiles. The glazed ceramic tile may last hundreds of years, assuming they are spared from exceptionally violent earthquakes. When there are violent earthquakes, the light wood structures will rock from side to side, and in many cases, they collapse under the heavy weight of the roof tiles. All that remains is a pile of sticks covered with tile. Contemporary construction includes more reinforcement to prevent the earthquake damage. The S curve of the tiles is distinctive as is the cool blue-gray tint of the traditional glaze.

We have an abundance of clay in America, as evidenced by the extent of our brick buildings dating back to the eighteenth century, so I could not help but wonder why we did not adopt clay tiles. They typically last over fifty years, more than twice the average life of wood shakes or asphalt. I think that American settlers found it easier to cut wood and split logs into shingle "shakes" rather than build kilns for clay tiles. Slate was also prevalent as a resource and became a popular upscale solution. We should now perhaps reconsider clay tiles over asphalt, because they do not rely on petrol products. Clay tiles also reduce the waste in landfills and reduce the energy used in manufacturing and transportation, because they last so much longer than asphalt shingles. This approach speaks to the overriding theme of "Do it right from the beginning, and save money and energy down the road."

Japan 4: Detail (d)

Note: the low square entrance of a teahouse at the top of this sketch is described at the end of this chapter.

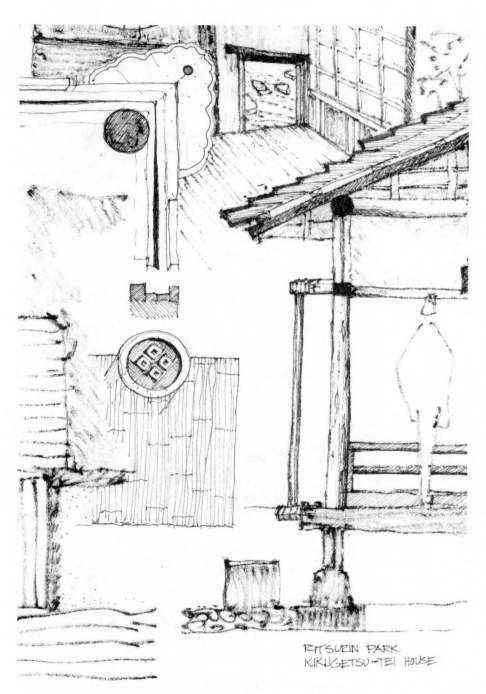

RITSURIN PARK
KIKUGETSU-TEI HOUSE

Japan 5

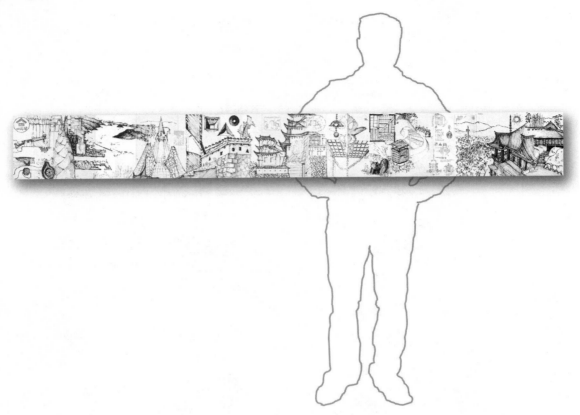

Japan 5: Detail (a)

Japan 5: Detail (a) Highlights Relevant to Sustainable Design:

We can learn to leverage more out of raw materials.

I worked with bamboo on different projects, and its potential impressed me at multiple levels. Bamboo grows from the ground straight up at the same thickness that it leaves the earth. It is a grass that has incredible tensile strength and has multiple applications for the Japanese people. The drawing on the left side is what a bamboo plant looks like when it leaves the ground. In this case, the diameter is 3 3/4". The size of any given bamboo shoot within a "system" mirrors the size of the other family members. When you see a bamboo grove, it is not a cluster of individual plants but a single macro-organism. Some of the Japanese "giant" bamboo may grow at a rate of a foot or more in a day. We cut down some that was over fifty feet tall. The material is still used today for anything from scaffolding in building construction to basket making. More than two decades after my work in Japan, my wife and I incorporated bamboo for the floor in one of the rooms that we were renovating for our solar home outside of Philadelphia.

I have also seen the versatility that bamboo offers for fabric and even replacements for the disposable paper towels that we too often churn through. Bamboo is an excellent fast-growing renewable resource with many more potential applications. We have an opportunity in America to align botanists with material scientists and explore more ways to leverage cost-effective applications of renewable resources with building needs.

Japan 5: Detail (b)

Japan 5: Detail (c)

Japan 6

Japan 6: Detail (a)

Japan 6: Detail (a) Highlights Relevant to Sustainable Design:

We can build cultural memory into our architecture and personalize objects in our world.

The gateway at this temple includes little stones that visitors place on top as a means of signifying their visit. Years later when I was in Idaho, I saw a gate that reminded me of this simple but meaningful way to mark an entrance. See sketchbook USA 2: Detail (a).

The circles on the right are the metal hilts for swords. They include openings that are ornamental to personalize the weapons for the warriors. Local craftsmanship and manufacturing has the potential to reemerge in the twenty-first century. Local equals less transit costs of fuel and less emissions. Part 5, "Conclusions," of this book speaks more to the sustainability advantages of local production in the chapter "Local Future."

Japan 6: Detail (b)

Japan 6: Detail (b) Highlights Relevant to Sustainable Design:

Some solutions have elegance in their simplicity.

In the center, there is a Japanese rock garden with a pair of rectangular stepping-stones. They are set parallel to each other but offset. This simple design lets you know that you can go in either direction. I loved seeing the elegance of this solution. Going from indoors out, the transition from the tatami mats to the exterior includes a wooden perimeter and then a bed of stones before the raked pebble rock garden. The bed of stones holds the majority of the large stepping-stones and also catches the rain from the roof eave overhead. This transition is common in traditional Japanese architecture and creates a dynamic interconnection of interior and exterior space that is not binary. In sketchbook Islands 8: John's Island Club—Vero Beach, Florida, I share more insight into this appealing shared relationship with nature. The appeal is based on the connectivity between indoor and outdoor spaces that links us as inhabitants to the natural environment rather than creating a wall between inside and outside space.

Japan 6: Detail (c)

Japan 6: Detail (c) Highlights Relevant to the Sustainable Design:

History should not repeat itself for human sustainability on earth.

The sobering memorial for the Hiroshima atom bombing includes one of the only buildings that was left standing. Near the drawing of the building, I sketched the outline of a bottle that was twisted from the massive heat of the atomic impact. Nuclear power may earn an ongoing place in the greater mix of our American energy portfolio, but hopefully we do not need to resort to using it as a weapon again.

We should remember to split atoms for utility power versus political power. Pressure will continue to mount to meet growing energy needs in America, and natural gas may start to replace coal-fired power plants. While natural gas power has fewer emissions than coal, the CO_2 output is still high. The "not in my backyard" syndrome may prevent the construction of new nuclear power plants, especially after the devastating meltdown at the Fukushima Daiichi nuclear power plant in 2011. So this leaves more expensive solar and wind options. As the efficiency of the technology increases and the costs come down, renewables become more economically viable. In conjunction with energy efficiency in buildings and transportation, the blended mix of solutions is promising.

Japan 6: Detail (d)

Japan 6: Detail (d) Highlights Relevant to Sustainable Design:

We can remember how life is precious.

This is a cemetery for babies and small children who died well before they had a chance to live a full life. I visited the site in the rain, and there was a surreal quality about it with a few small pinwheels spinning as the raindrops hit the fins at each turn. A raven flew into the cemetery when I was there, and its flight along with its periodic caws added an even more strange and sad quality to the experience. As so many of us race full speed ahead in the digital world, moments like this can cause us to pause and add perspective on the fleeting nature of life. If you are reading this, then you are as fortunate as I am to have lived long enough to learn how to read. I cannot imagine the devastation and heartbreak of losing a child. We can hopefully give our children and grandchildren a bright future.

Japan 7

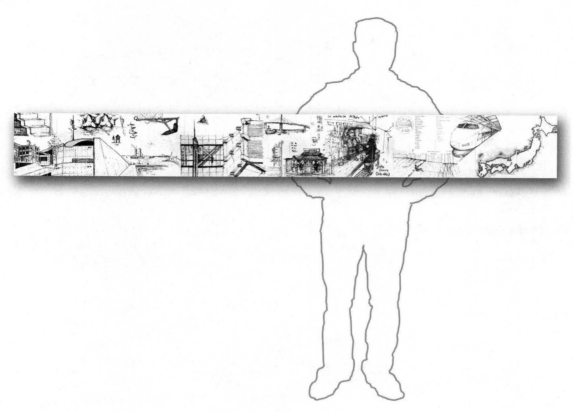

Japan 7: Detail (a)

Japan 7: Detail (b)

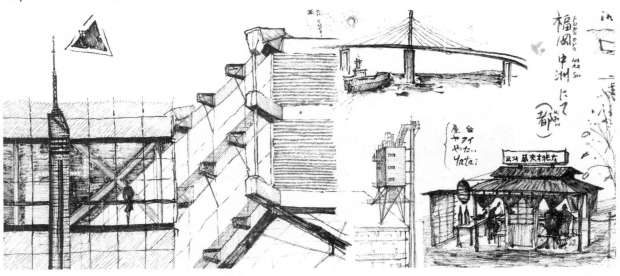

Japan 7: Detail (c)

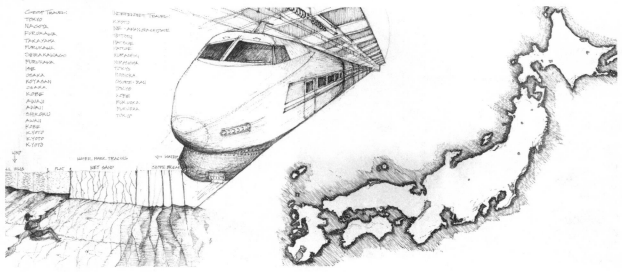

Japan 7: Detail (c) Highlights Relevant to Sustainable Design:

Energy-smart transportation could start with rethinking rail in America.

One early morning, as I waited on the platform of the Shinkansen, Japan's ultra-high-speed bullet train, I thought about how great it would be to have a magnetic levitation (maglev) train in the United States running from Miami to Boston, with stops at each major city. The engineering would most likely require an elevated track to ease the curves of the existing Amtrak line. So this might require a massive elevated platform running between the northbound and southbound lanes of I-95. We put a man on the moon, so almost anything is possible. The advanced Shinkansen technology in the early 1990s delivered tremendous speed and comfort, because the train floated given the polarization of the magnetic "levitation." Reduced friction lets the maglev train fly down the tracks.

That morning, I was the first one on the platform. Within a few minutes, I discovered something that I have remembered ever since. I heard a faint *swishing* sound from around the corner of the ticket booth, and I looked to find a tiny woman under five feet tall hunched over with a bamboo broom. The broom was made with thin bamboo shoots, bound like the stereotypical broom that witches use at Halloween. At first, I thought that it was so ironic that such a low-tech tool was used to sweep the platform of such a high-tech means of transportation.

In America or other countries, the respective Department of Transportation might be tempted to put out a request for proposal (RFP) or design challenge to make a high-tech broom out of molded plastic or some advanced sweeping machine to match the aesthetics of the state-of-the-art trains. The Japanese culture is so old that they have an ability to comfortably have the "old" right up against the "new." This juxtaposition makes sense when you look at the broom's utility and socioeconomics. The bamboo broom simply works well, the technique to make it has been refined over countless generations, and the raw materials are readily available. Plus, the little old lady has a job, and Japan has found all kinds of ways to put people to work as part of their overall employment strategy.

Beyond sustaining jobs, high-speed trains can reduce auto transportation emissions at massive levels. The level of commuter congestion in major US cities and rings of suburbs will hopefully create pressure to include high-speed rail in the budgets for public works over the next decade. Comprehensive total cost of ownership (TCO) analysis may highlight the fact that we are already collectively spending more than we may think on road construction, road repair, auto purchase, auto fuel, auto repair, and lost time waiting in traffic. We can rethink what is perceived as "expensive" for new technology in the context of a holistic review of what we now spend to move millions of people to work and back every day, week, month, and year.

Japan 8

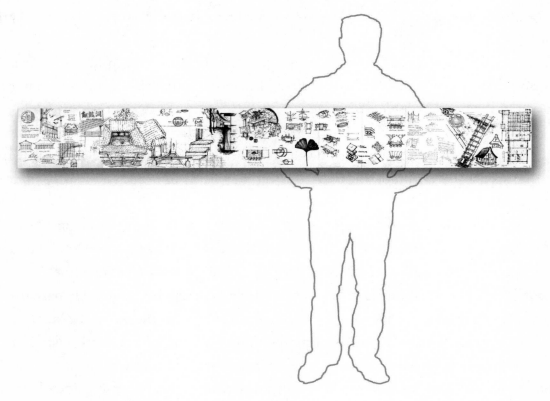

Japan 8: Highlights Relevant to Sustainable Design:

We can rethink natural light over artificial light.

Professor Koyama teaches at the University of Tokyo, and he is a friend of Kinya. When we met, one of the points he raised was about windows as holes in the wall. He simply asked, "Why does the window open and not the wall?" He then proce\eded to show us his design for a house that has windows with fixed glass and walls that have hinged portions that open up and out. This level of thinking is appealing in dealing with a range of historical observations. Rather than just repeating or copying what is old, why not take the idea and put it through a metamorphosis? Too often here in America, we become enamored with how something looks rather than how it works. We love an Italian villa, so we build a slightly smaller scale one in Palm Beach. We don't try to figure out what it is that makes the villa look and work the way it does.

The natural light, the air circulation, the texture, sound, and even smell are all so special. These factors too often play a secondary role to the visual style. Japan 9: Detail (a) shows an atrium roof design that effectively and elegantly allows light to enter four different interior walls, provoking the question of why the Japanese are now enamored with American-style suburban box houses. This system also shows an overlapping system of shoji screens, which takes on a cubist transparency. Often in Skia style, strict geometry is juxtaposed with something that is natural.

In the midst of an exacting grid of wooden slats, one column is taken directly from the tree, with its full curve, bark, and imperfections included. This is one more example of design juxtaposition and contradiction. Sustainability is about embracing our connection to the natural world, and the organic form is a subtle but powerful reminder.

Japan 8: Detail (a)

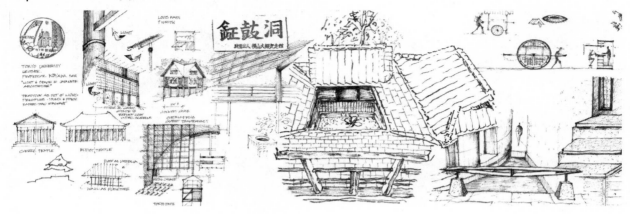

Japan 8: Detail (b)

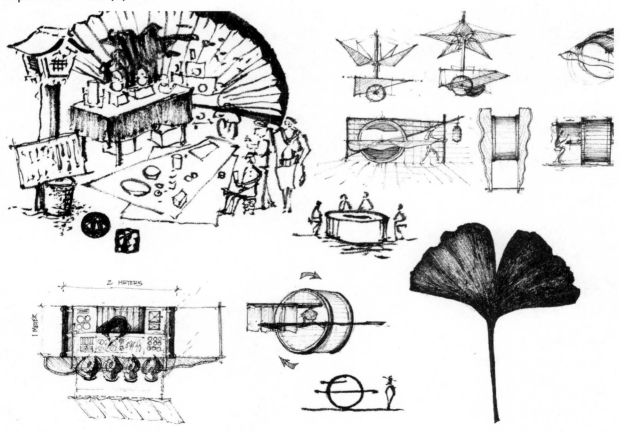

Japan 8: Detail (c)

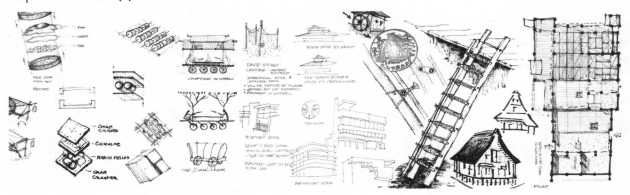

Japan 9

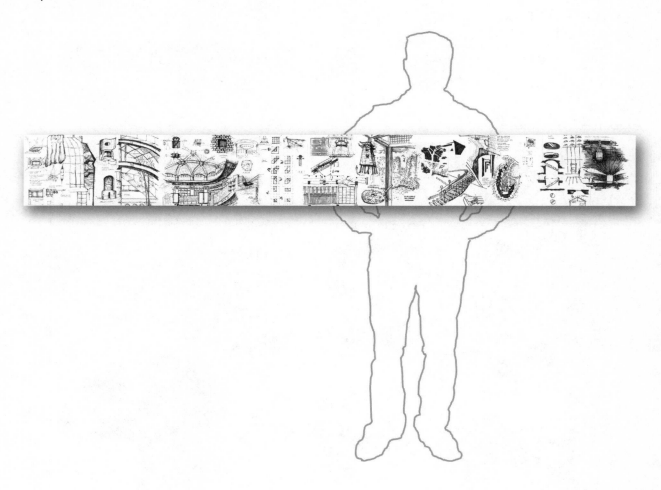

Japan 9: Detail (a)

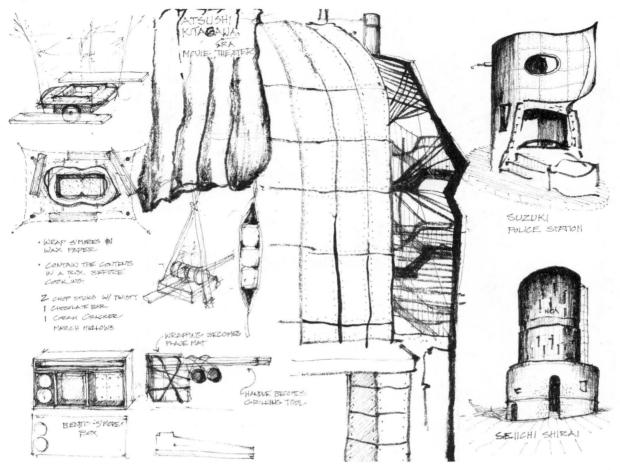

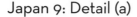

Japan 9: Detail (a) Highlights Relevant to Sustainable Design:

Sustaining security for health and happiness promotes stronger communities.

The architecture of Tokyo includes a rich tapestry of work by contemporary architects. In the upper right corner of this drawing, one police station stands out as distinctive in its "helmet" appearance. Like some of the Japanese castles, the helmet station becomes a symbol of strength and security. As an island in the street, the mouthlike opening shelters the officer who keeps watch over the street.

Sustainable design can embrace people and their communities in new ways. In America, we have challenges in many cities to police neighborhoods that have drug and gang violence. The police in most cases roll in and out with patrol cars and are not always embedded in the neighborhoods with familiarity to the youngest members of the community. Sustaining security and a peace of mind is a tangent to traditional perceptions of sustainable design. If we can't live and work without fear, then the materials, energy, and emissions are a distant priority. This example from Japan may not be the stylistic solution, but the idea of localized support from trusted officers is worthy of questioning alternatives to our current policing systems.

Japan 9: Detail (b)

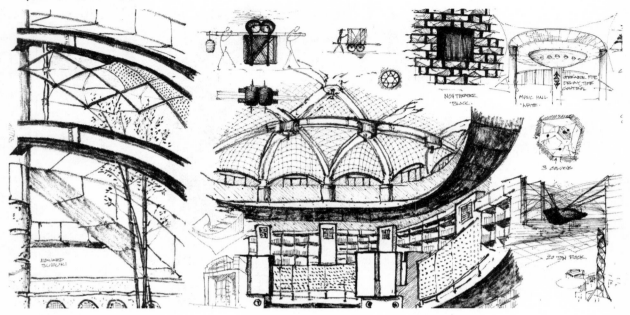

Japan 9: Detail (b) Highlights Relevant to Sustainable Design:

There are multiple opportunities to rethink natural light and materials.

The domed interior of a contemporary library allows light to enter through a diffused grid of steel rebar. The rebar is typically used as structural support inside of reinforced concrete. The exposed industrial rebar takes on a surprising light and elegant quality as it bends and curves along the contours of the ceiling. We can simply use materials in ways that they were not intended. The right side of this sketch shows a small drawing of a large rock. The rock is suspended off the ground and must weigh several tons. The thin steel cables holding it up are visible more clearly in the drawing than in reality, because water sprays out of the walls to mask the cables and give the appearance that the massive rock is floating in air. Sculpture built into architecture elevates the senses to create more dynamic experiences.

This ties into the point in Japan 8: Detail (a). Sustainability is about embracing our connection to the natural world, and the rock in its natural uncut form is a powerful reminder of the source of many construction building blocks.

Japan 9: Detail (c)

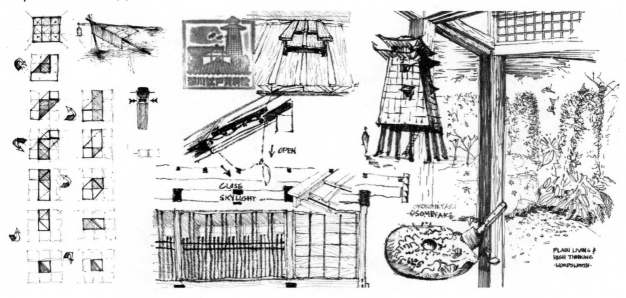

Japan 9: Detail (c) Highlights Relevant to Sustainable Design:

Science, technology, engineering, and math (STEM) count.

Knowledge of science, technology, engineering, and math (STEM) is most likely a key driver for gainful employment in the twenty-first century. Unfortunately, America has slipped in education when it comes to STEM. Every three years, the Program for International Student Assessment (PISA) measures reading ability, math and science literacy, and other key skills among fifteen-year-olds in dozens of developed and developing countries. In 2012, the PISA placed the United States at thirty-fifth out of sixty-four countries in math and twenty-seventh in science.[27] We can do better!

The left side of this sketch includes a diagram of a folding process for a three-by-three grid. For children, math can become interesting in multiple ways other than memorizing multiplication tables. This folding process is one way to conceptually understand the relationship that 3 x 3 = 9 and how pairs of adjacent geometric shapes relate to each other both as triangles and squares. Gaming is a fundamental early development tool for math, and if it is done with physical materials like folded paper in addition to digital gaming, the odds of absorption may increase. The part 3, "Commercial Impact," section of this book includes a chapter on the Perpetual Food Machine that can ignite multiple pistons in the STEM engine for students. Sustainable design requires innovative engineering, and STEM will help people create numerous innovations beyond what we can imagine today.

Japan 9: Detail (d)

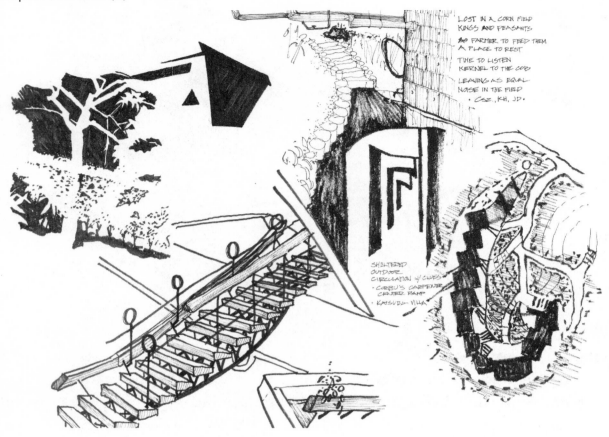

LOST IN A CORN FIELD
KINGS AND PEASANTS
NO FARMER TO FEED THEM
A PLACE TO REST
TIME TO LISTEN
KERNEL TO THE COB
LEAVING AS EQUAL
NOISE IN THE FIELD
• CSZ., KH, JD•

SHELTERED
OUTDOOR
CIRCULATION W/ CURBS
• CORBU'S CARPENTER
CENTER RAMP
• KATSURA VILLA

Japan 9: Detail (d) Highlights Relevant to Sustainable Design:

Step up and challenge preconceptions.

This railing detail has four circular handholds on each side. The railing design is based on aesthetics and function, with the ergonomics of "pulling" up a stair. Above the stair drawing, an inverted pyramid building sits comfortably in shadow. The building gets bigger as it goes up.

Japan: Bonus Insights—The Teahouse and General Observations

We have a lot to learn from each other in the global economy.

The Japanese teahouse is a place where the Skia style is often the most understandable. When we were building a teahouse with Kinya, I remember him asking me, "Charlie, why do you make the column so straight?" Followed by, "Perhaps you make it a little curved!" The teahouse is also a place to understand the quality of Japanese community. A low door always greets visitors. (See the drawing in Japan 4: Detail (d).) Regardless of social status or wealth, all people as they enter must bow to humble themselves in respect for the tea ceremony. The door is not only low but also narrow. Even the mighty shogun must remove their swords and leave them outside. The result is that the teahouse is a special place for people to come together on equal ground.

The hearth is another example of Japanese community. Rather than a fireplace, traditional houses have a fire pit in the middle of the house as a place to gather and share tea. For meals, food is often brought in boxes and bowls that are shared rather than plates and courses for the individual. As well, an empty glass is never filled by the person who is thirsty for more. An observant and sympathetic tablemate takes the bottle or pitcher to fill their friend's glass. The tradition of sharing beverages is still alive even among the teenage community. Community bicycles were an eye-opener for me in Japan. The idea was pretty simple. If you needed to get from a train station to a restaurant across town, then you would just take one of the bikes that was left unlocked near the station. At the restaurant, someone else might need a bike to get somewhere else, so he or she would take it. The bikes would literally make their way around the smaller towns, and this spirit of sharing unlocked bikes was initially foreign to me. I quickly embraced it and rode a lot of different bikes! Thirty years later, I saw the Citi Bike "rental share" program in New York City, and I could not help but smile.

Negative observations from my early 1990s experience in Japan came hand in hand with the positive. I saw a selfish culture that has done nothing short of fished almost every giant tuna from the Sea of Japan. I remember going to the fish markets at five in the morning to watch the seafood come in for sushi merchants and restaurateurs. Some of the boats would come from as far as Madagascar laden with their prized catch on dry ice. Imagine fish so big that circular saws had to cut through them and fish so precious that dockside auctions looked like the floor of the Chicago commodities exchange. Natural resources on and around an island with a population the size of Japan inevitably dwindle, but the Japanese have a pension for the best and the most exotic.

I worked on the construction of a house for a member of the feared Yakuza, the Japanese mob. This man had so many big-game hunting trophies from around the world that he wanted to build a house for display alone. Since the largest and the best wood is now gone from the island, like the giant tuna, he had shipped from Oregon beams that were a foot and a half wide, three feet tall, and over twenty feet long. A culture that wants the best often also wants the best companies from other countries. The Japanese had started ramping up their interest in buying American assets like the Beverly Hills Palm, Rockefeller Center, and a few film studios.

Children have a far different life in Japan than in America. At an early age, they wear matching hats and backpacks and march off to school in a straight line. The very root of American creativity comes from our individualism, which is such an awesome resource. Foreign buyers of American companies and film studios quickly learn that they must not only buy the hardware but also retain the people to brew up the ideas. In Tokyo, the Americans like me, working in the community, were primarily involved in creative work: architecture, fashion, and automotive design along with advertising and marketing. We are very good at inventing things and selling. The Japanese are very good at manufacturing. They are smart enough to buy our talent, knowing that their culture has more difficulty cultivating original ideas from their young people than the discipline of executing the ideas. See the appendix for more on young professionals in Tokyo.

Closing Perspective on the Japanese Experience

Embrace the old and the new. As the Japanese are increasingly using digital technology such as smartphones, they may also increasingly learn that money cannot buy creativity. Ironically they cannot buy the very best asset that we cultivate in America—invention and the spirit of the new. They have much to learn from us, but there is room for us to learn about restraint and discipline from their ancient culture as we charge into the twenty-first century.

6 EUROPE

HUNGARY

The news periodically includes discussions of emerging markets, and Hungary, as part of Eastern Europe, is one area to watch. My fascination with both Hungary and Japan stems from similar interests in change. Both cultures have over a thousand-year history, both are stereotyped in a large degree by Americans, and both may have changed more dramatically in the past few decades than in the past century. The Soviet Union for all its negative impact provided an unintentional research service. The Soviets kept Eastern Europe in something of a time capsule up until the end of the Cold War in the early 1990s, when I was in Hungary making the sketches on the following pages.

I had the good fortune of gaining some added perspective of a unique chapter in modern history by getting inside the Iron Curtain to Budapest over the summer of 1989, before the fall of the Berlin Wall. My father, who was born and raised in Budapest, escaped in 1957 and came to America. We celebrated the fiftieth anniversary of his arrival in 2007, but at the end of the eighties he was very concerned about the status of his parents' gravesite. He was naturally anxious about returning himself. As his oldest son, he asked me to return, find the cemetery, and pay the recurring service fee to maintain the gravesite for the next twenty-five years. My experience in Soviet-controlled Hungary was truly like traveling back in time. The lack of street signage and outdoor advertising was just the tip of the iceberg, and cities like Budapest looked almost the same as they may have if Mozart were to visit back in the second half of the 1700s.

Four years after my first trip, I returned with pen in hand and spent multiple months researching and living in cities and small villages across Eastern Europe.

Please note that the physical sketchbooks that I took to Europe were much longer than ones that I have used over my travels, so in many cases the first set of details are a portion of the larger books.

From Austria to Hungary 1

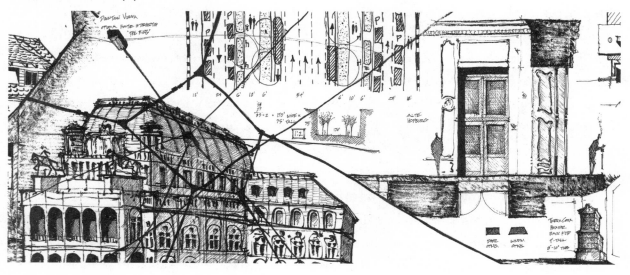

Austria 1: Detail (a)

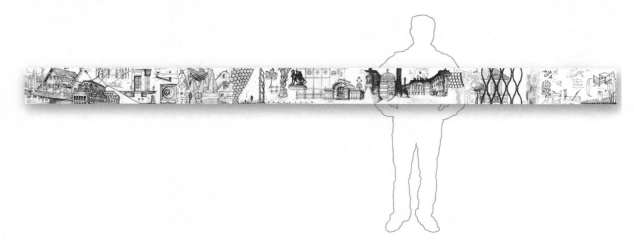

Austria 1: Detail (b)

Austria 1: Detail (b) Highlights Relevant to Sustainable Design:

Effective public transportation with pedestrian integration increases the ease of urban motion and decreases the need for automobiles and the resulting CO_2 emissions.

My research in Hungary started after arrival in Vienna, Austria. This is a view of the Vienna

Opera House looking up through the web of cables for the cable cars at a busy intersection. The upper center is an overhead view of the parallel paths of primary auto traffic in the center flanked by cable cars, pedestrian walkways, parallel parking, one-directional secondary traffic, another layer of parallel parking, sidewalks, and finally the retail shops on the outside edges. This system of urban planning worked well to encourage efficiency, safety, and the integration of public transportation, private transportation, and pedestrians. In America, a version of this without the trolley cars is on K Street in Washington, DC. Prior to the interstate highway construction in America following WW II, major cities and towns across the country had electric streetcar systems that successfully provided transportation options. The US systems were purchased by corporations like General Motors, and some believe literally put out to pasture to create more demand for buses and automobiles.[28]

Austria 1: Detail (c)

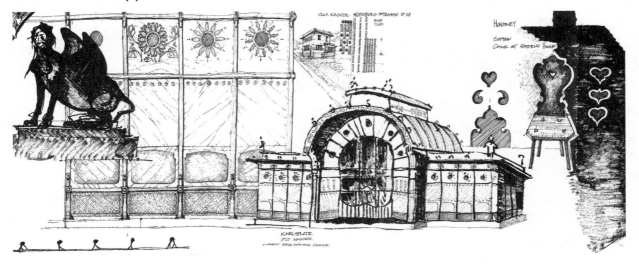

Austria 1: Detail (c) Highlights Relevant to Sustainable Design:

Visually inviting entrances to underground subway systems increase the use of the systems.

This entrance to one of the many Vienna subway system stations was designed by celebrated Austro-Hungarian architect and urban planner Otto Wagner (1841–1918). The structure is made of glass and metal with intricate details and sunflower ornamentation. During the day, it glistens in the sun, and at night, it glows like a lantern.

In America, we are moving increasingly toward what I have started calling the "Uber age." With the ease of Uber car service, individuality and immediacy trump the collective and the scheduled. Think of the difference between single-passenger transportation that is on-demand with the simple push of a button on our smartphones versus group transportation on a local train with a schedule of arrivals and departures. The freedom of on-demand transportation dramatically changes how we think about moving around and has implications on fuel consumption. There are certainly places for individual and collective transportation when it comes to commuting and socializing, and improved mass transit could help encourage more options both above and below ground. On the social front, Uber provides a convenient and safe way to travel for a night out, without the need for a designated driver within the traveling party. Here are multiple ways that my wife and I travel from the suburban town, Wayne, to Philadelphia for dinners or parties in the city. The distance is approximately eighteen miles each way, and we targeted the Main Line area in part because of the convenient access to local train transportation as well as great schools and other advantages. We can walk to the train station that is about a quarter mile from our house. This breakdown is ranked from most energy-efficient to least (Note: the train travels about seventeen miles versus driving which covers eighteen miles):

Round-Trip—Miles Impact for Two Couples:

1: We take the train down and back. *Most energy-efficient.*   34 miles
2: We take the train into town and get a ride home with friends.   35 miles
3: We pick up another couple, or they pick us up for ride sharing both ways.   40 miles
4: We share an Uber car service with one or more other couples both ways.   48 miles
5: We drive in our own cars down and back—two couples.   72 miles
6: We each take an Uber car service both ways. *Least energy-efficient.*   80 miles

(Depending on the time of day, in-city Ubers may be close to the pick-up location, decreasing the distance by four miles. However, if the drivers do not get called for rides back into the city, there could be an added return to the city trips, bringing the life-cycle cost up to 116 miles, more than three times the train or ride sharing trip.)

The Uber fuel impact is larger than you might think given the distance to pick you up. The average wait time for Uber in our area has been about six to ten minutes. At an average of thirty miles per hour on suburban streets, in eight minutes Uber can cover four miles. So this adds four miles of fuel to an eighteen-mile trip. This is a 22 percent increase in fuel consumption, and while the riders don't pay for the gas, the fuel cost is accounted for in the service cost. When I have taken an Uber from one suburban town to another with a distance of only two miles, the same wait time applies. If the driver takes four miles to get to me, this means that the fuel consumption is 200 percent greater than the trip itself for me to get from A to B. At an extreme level, if everyone took a car service instead of going from point A to B through other means, the added connection times would increase our US transportation fuel consumption by 20 percent to 200 percent. The increase in development of autonomous self-driving cars may help reduce the burden of the extra miles incurred with driving services.

I was pleased to see in a 2015 interview, on the *Late Show with Stephen Colbert*, that Uber's CEO, Travis Kalanick, has plans to increase the number of electric cars, perhaps through a fleet of Tesla cars produced by Elon Musk. Electric cars still create life-cycle source emissions given the generation of electricity in coal-fired power plants. However, the emissions are significantly lower. According to the US Department of Energy, for a hundred-mile trip, a conventional combustion engine car emits ninety-nine pounds of CO_2 and costs \$9.96, while electric cars only emit fifty-four pounds of CO_2 and cost \$3.56.[29] This emissions savings of almost 50 percent is meaningful as is the cost reduction, given the growing number of Uber miles and the ongoing volume of transportation miles across America each year. The cost ranking for the round-trips addressed here are almost an exact reflection of the energy-efficiency rankings. The train is the least expensive and the Uber single-couple ride is the most expensive. The advantage of ride sharing is reduced parking costs as well as the reduced fuel-cost-per-passenger relative to single-couple car rides. We have strength in numbers!

Hungary 1: Detail (d)

Hungary 1: Detail (d) Highlights Relevant to Sustainable Design:

Embrace long life and cultural tradition.

One of my first experiences in Hungary was seeing everyday objects like this chair that were built with a high degree of attention to detail in structure and aesthetic. These traditional

Hungarian chairs, with heart-shaped cutouts in the backrest, sit comfortably in many kitchens. Across different regions of the country, I learned that villagers carve out a slightly different variation on the theme. In each case, the chairs are solid wood versus veneer or composite, and they will most likely get repaired before they are tossed out. In fact, these chairs probably never end up in the trash, because at the end of their useful life serving as a place to sit, they probably become firewood. Europe does not have the land space that we have in America for landfills, so reuse and recycling are more of a requirement than an option. I imagine that there are more than a few broken plastic and bent metal folding chairs in American landfills.

At the end of this chapter, I having included a chair that I saw in the Czech Republic that has similar cutouts but turns symmetry on its head. See Czech Republic 6: Detail (d).

Hungary 1: Detail (e)

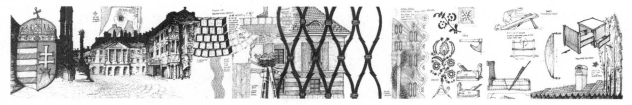

Hungary 1: Detail (f)

Hungary 1: Detail (f) Highlights Relevant to Sustainable Design:

Town squares are significantly more prevalent in Europe than in America, and they may serve as a social asset as well as a means to reduce automobile transportation.

Our "Main Street" versus the town square may have come from the frontier and colonial horse and carriages riding into town. The follow-on is the auto culture that drove modern America. The European town square with a central monument, statue, or fountain is a rich gathering place for outside eating, recreation, entertainment, and enjoying a cup of coffee or a local wine. See chapter 9, Big City 2: Los Angeles for a comparison to the Sixteenth Street Mall solution in Denver, Colorado.

The Hungarian crest or shield is loaded with many symbols like alternating stripes, double cross, and the jeweled crown, worn by Saint Stephen, the first Christian king of Hungary in 1001. Only when the Iron Curtain fell did the crest legally appear on anything from buildings to flags.

The link between the town square and the crest is about pride and brand identity. When the Soviet Union occupied Eastern Europe over the second half of the twentieth century, they denied the residents of countries like Hungary their identity. The town squares would typically have crests and flags visible, given that important civic buildings like city hall were part of the squares. We have been fortunate in America to maintain our identity, and bringing life back to main streets and town squares over shopping malls could further reinforce our sense of community.

Hungary 1: Detail (g)

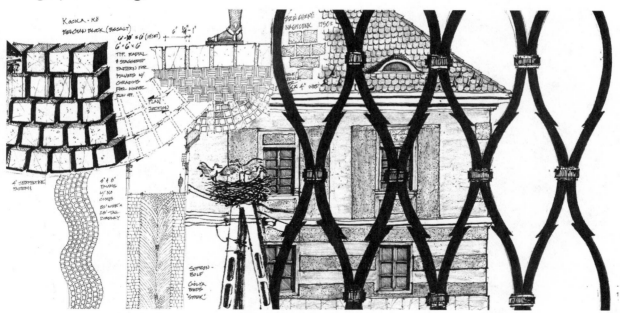

Hungary 1: Detail (g) Highlights Relevant to Sustainable Design:

Permanence over disposability is reflected in paving and fences.

This sketch includes a paving pattern of thick six-inch cube Belgian blocks typically cut from basalt stone. They look like granite and convey a feeling of Roman permanence. The patterns in the street range from radial and serpentine to fan shapes, and the cross section is curved with a slightly higher elevation at the center than the sides to facilitate water runoff. I am burned out on potholes, and in the winter of 2015, I had to pay over $300 to have a new "run flat" tire put on my car. Every winter outside of Philadelphia, enough moisture makes its way into the asphalt that it freezes, expands, and starts to degrade the roads. The result is potholes. While stone roads are certainly too costly, there may be a better way to pave our roads today.

The fence outside one of the Szechenyi palaces sends a signal of elegant restraint and permanence. Sustainability is about reducing waste, so materials like stone and thick iron last significantly longer than twenty-first-century asphalt roads and chain-link fences. The Hungarian aristocratic Szechenyi family has built or endowed everything from schools and hospitals to the famous suspension bridge in Budapest. The fence in this drawing is an example of something that is built to last. The sketch also includes a large nest for birds called Golya, pronounced "Goya," living on chimneys, roofs, or in this case a telephone pole. The birds look something like storks, and the same ones often return every year to the same nests. They become favorite town mascots. There is a superstition that when the birds return each year they bring good luck.

Hungary 1: Detail (h)

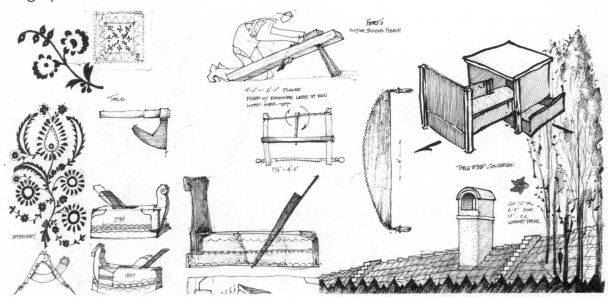

Hungary 1: Detail (h) Highlights Relevant to Sustainable Design:

Organic inspiration drives textile patterns.

This sketch includes samples of the textile patterns, which are typical of a culture that uses organic plant material as a springboard for pattern design.

Highlights Relevant to Sustainable Design:

Sleepover parties are not just for kids in Europe.

The wooden box in this sketch is a table that has two pullout drawers. The smaller one is for storage, and the larger one with the vertical panel is a pullout bed for guests. This design is for friends who want to stay over, like a trundle bed but with a headboard. We don't tolerate drunk driving in America, but the Hungarians, like the Romanians, take it to a whole other level. They have a zero-tolerance system. The penalties are so severe that if you have even a glass or two of wine with dinner and get caught driving, you could end up with very expensive fines and a revoked driver's license. Sleepovers are a logical alternative. From the sustainability side, this is about saving space and sustaining life of the drivers and the potential victims of accidents.

Hungary 2

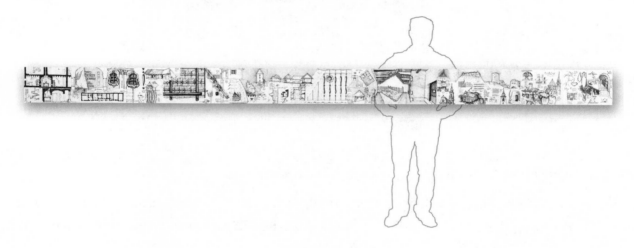

Hungary 2: Detail (a)

Hungary 2: Detail (b)

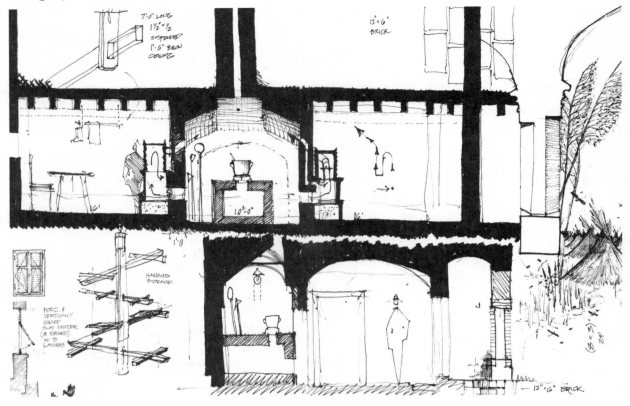

Hungary 2: Detail (b) Highlights Relevant to Sustainable Design:

We can learn to save energy on heating from countries with fewer natural resources than America.

This cross section of a turn-of-the-century house shows a sophisticated heating system. The hearth is unique in that it is open for cooking but channeled to let hot smoke vent into adjacent cavities that serve as ceramic heaters. They are called Bubos Kemence, pronounced "Boob-a-come-ense," and serve as radiators. The traditional wood-burning stove is similar in that chambers take the smoke on an arduous path curving through the masonry as it leaves the house. This path forces the hot, smoky air to heat the masonry along the journey up and out of the house. Even several hours after the fire is out, the masonry still radiates heat. Several New England fireplace makers now offer airtight designs that leverage this thermal advantage.

Years later, I leveraged this thermal advantage in the radiant floors of our solar home. We have both solar photovoltaic (PV) panels for electricity as well as solar water heating panels. The PV panels run the pumps to move the water, and the thermal panels heat the water. By running water coils instead of smoke through the gypcrete under the floor tiles, we are able to continue benefitting from the heat emitted by the masonry floors well after the sun has set. For details, see the chapter "Sustainable Smart House" in part 3, "Commercial Impact."

Hungary 2: Detail (c)

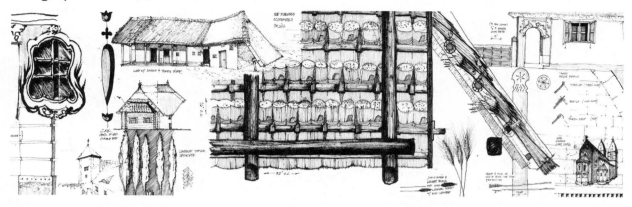

Hungary 2: Detail (c) Highlights Relevant to Sustainable Design:

Natural material roofs have surprising durability after centuries of design refinements.

Thatch roof drawings are on the right side of this sketch. The thatch roof construction techniques in Hungary are similar in many ways to the Japanese-type thatch construction. These roofs last for thirty or more years, which is often longer than asphalt roofs. The straw used for the thatch is grown locally, and farmers bundle it into clusters before layering it into the roof system. The material is plentiful, fast growing, and renewable. We are probably not going to ever go back to thatch roofs, but the idea of a locally grown or locally sourced renewable construction material is appealing. Plus, the idea of trapping "tubes" of air for insulation is worth exploring with the latest fire-resistant materials.

Some companies offer roof shingles made from recycled waste materials, such as plastic, rubber, or wood fiber. While the source material is not grown locally, it certainly can be sourced locally, given that every community in America produces waste materials. Composite wood and plastic materials like Trex are also alternatives to wood. The materials are made from by-products like sawdust, wood pallets, wood chips, and wood fiber mixed with polyethylene plastic, like recycled stretch wrap, packaging films, grocery and retail bags. Trex claims to keep 200,000 tons of plastic and hardwood scraps out of American landfills each year. Pigment and preservative are added in the production process before heat is applied to create the finished wood-thermoplastic boards. Rethinking construction materials based on local and renewable or recycled materials is central to sustainable design.

Aesthetics count. To the left of the thatch roofs, this sketch includes the curved windows on a palace wall and flower-shaped cutouts on a farmhouse gabble, which may have evolved from the popular tulip flower profile. The tall trees called Jegenye, pronounced "Yea-gan-yi," mark the horizon and provide a unique sense of scale. Some of these trees are more than eighty feet tall and can be seen from miles away.

Hungary 2: Detail (d)

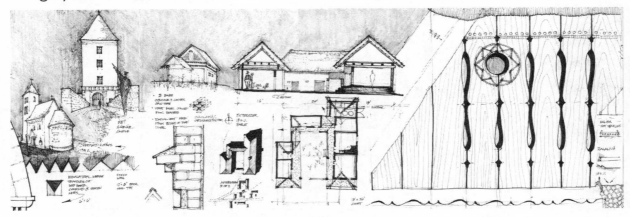

Hungary 2: Detail (d) Highlights Relevant to Sustainable Design:

Think outside of the square box house and look at the U plan.

This drawing includes a U house, which frames three sides of its yard and garden. Instead of a front and backyard, it has an inset courtyard. This level of residential density may have a place to consider in America between the city and the suburbs to create safe, comfortable, and convenient places for children to play and parents to BBQ. Cities typically have the denser population with apartments and row homes, while suburbs often have the single-family box on a plot that is set back from the street or on a cul-de-sac. With trends toward developing mixed-use town centers, this U-plan approach would take up more land space than a row home but less space than a suburban home. The clues for modern pedestrian-accessible town centers could come from towns that were created in a world where pedestrian access was at the forefront. See Hungary 4: Detail (c) for other house plan configurations.

Hungary 2: Detail (e)

Hungary 2: Detail (f)

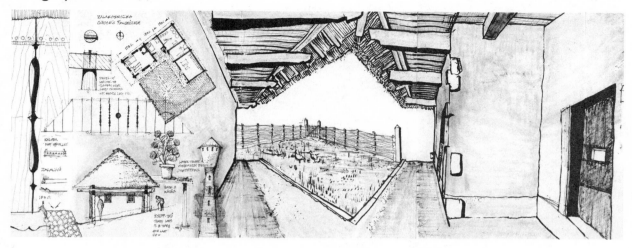

Hungary 2: Detail (f) Highlights Relevant to Sustainable Design:

Think outside of the square box house and look at the L plan.

This drawing illustrates an L house, which frames two sides of its yard and garden. Instead of a front yard and a backyard, it has a partially framed courtyard with the fence completing the perimeter. This design approach has similar advantages as the U house illustrated and described in the previous sketch. Both the U and the L strategies could help reduce suburban sprawl and auto-dependency. By better utilizing the yard space, the density can increase without sacrificing convenience and aesthetics. Closer proximity means less distance to travel. One of the key advantages of mid-density home design is the ability to walk to see a friend in town, get a drink, enjoy a meal, or shop. Having enough yard space to relax or even grow vegetables is also appealing when it is more than the space behind a row home or condominium but not so much yard space that its dominates weekends with mowing or costs more than expected to maintain. See Hungary 4: Detail (c) for other house plan configurations.

Hungary 2: Detail (g)

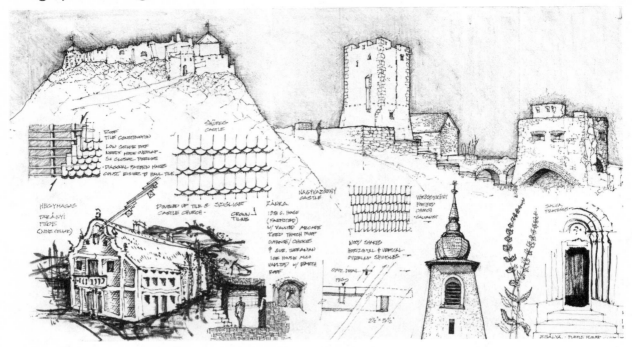

Hungary 2: Detail (g) Highlights Relevant to Sustainable Design:

We can learn about saving waste and energy on building envelopes from roof systems.

Roof tile patterns range from single to double layers and from curved to straight cuts. All are terra-cotta red. Unlike the Japanese tiles, they are also flat and overlap much more of the individual length. Long-lasting tiles prevent the disposal waste of asphalt shingles in landfills. If the asphalt shingles are recycled, the environmental impact is still higher than the clay tiles, because of the energy cost to transport asphalt to the recycling plant, the energy of the processing and remanufacturing, and the energy used to ship them to supply houses and then to the final construction site. The roof tiles that are made from waste materials from the start, referenced in Hungary 2: Detail (c), could be engineered for even longer life as well as future recycling "cradle to cradle" instead of cradle to grave.

This sketch also includes drawings of castles, an onion-like top to a church tower, and fortifications that look something like a hungry face.

Hungary 3

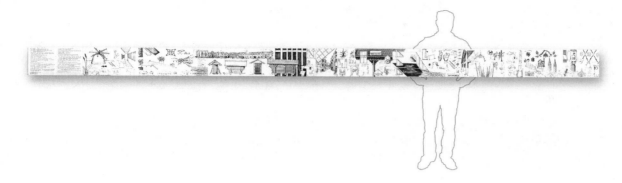

Hungary 3: Detail (a)

Hungary 3: Detail (a) Highlights Relevant to Sustainable Design:

Country pickles may inspire rethinking modern food processes.

In America, vegetables and other food often travel hundreds of miles from farm to table. The distance increases the fuel consumption, the emissions, and the cost. This sketchbook includes many daily sightings in Hungary. The sightings are unique in the country and have little to do with architecture. Examples range from traffic lights that turn yellow before they turn both red and green to geraniums, which typically appear on windowsills at both village houses and high-rise apartment balconies. Along with geraniums, pickle jars often sit on windowsills in the villages. I learned the low-tech trick to make pickles from a local farmwoman selling linens. Take cucumbers from the garden and stick them in a mason jar. Add water, salt, white vinegar, and dill. Put the jar on a sunny windowsill during the day and bring it in at night. After about three days, the cucumbers start fermenting, and you should see tiny bubbles. After about five days when the bubbles have stopped rising, transfer the jar to your refrigerator. When refrigerated, the pickles should keep for a couple of weeks. While cold-packed pickles may have a risk of bacteria, modern processes and technology could provide solutions. This village observation is more about rethinking how we process food than the actual production of any given item. Imagine the production reduction in energy consumption with localized farming over commercial corporate processes. Also see the chapter titled "Perpetual Food Machine" in part 3, "Commercial Impact," that talks about reducing the distance from farm to table by providing a means to grow indoors in cities and towns that do not have year-round favorable climates for outdoor farming.

These Hungarian villagers literally walk from the garden to the windowsill rather than having to expend energy and incur the waste of industrial production.

- Tractors help grow cucumbers.
- Trucks transport them to pickling plants.
- Machines produce single-use jars, labels, and case boxes.
- Energy is used to produce and package the pickles.
- Trucks take the palettes of cased jars to distribution centers.
- Trucks take cases of jars to grocery stores.
- We drive over and back to the grocery store in our cars and SUVs.
- We enjoy the pickles over whatever period of time they are in our refrigerator.
- We throw away the pickle jar or recycle it, which uses more energy than reusing it.

Hungary 3: Detail (b)

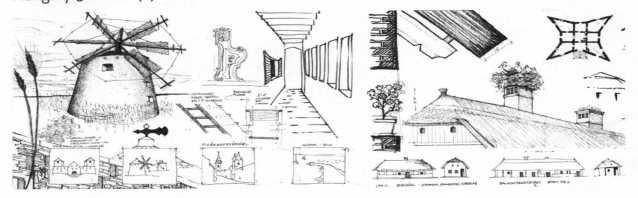

Hungary 3: Detail (b) Highlights Relevant to Sustainable Design:

We can rethink wind power.

Across my travels, all summer long I would see windmills sitting comfortably on the hills. My father and I enjoyed seeing this particular windmill as we ate our picnic lunch. Since there were few restaurants on the road between villages, he would buy fresh bread in the morning along with fruit and vegetables. We carried leftover salami that was salted to the point where it didn't need refrigeration. A summer picnic came to be quite the normal lunchtime activity for us. Using wind power to make electricity is a lot harder than using it to grind grain. I saw that the Amish back in Pennsylvania use wind power to pump water, which is also easier than making electricity. The efficiency of generating electricity from the wind is improving, but the return on investment (ROI) without subsidies is still not high enough in many markets to attract buyers. Vertical-axis wind turbines for commercial and residential applications may offer a more cost-effective micro-power production option than the macro-power of the huge offshore windmills in areas like the North Sea that help power Denmark.

This sequence of images, like many of the drawings, includes multiple illustrations. In this sketch, the chimneys of many village homes have Golya bird nests when the chimneys are dormant. This is just one of many examples of how animals embrace "adaptive reuse." The act of reusing something versus discarding it is central to sustainable design, given that reduce, reuse, and recycle are the three anchor Rs of the early green movement.

Hungary 3: Detail (c)

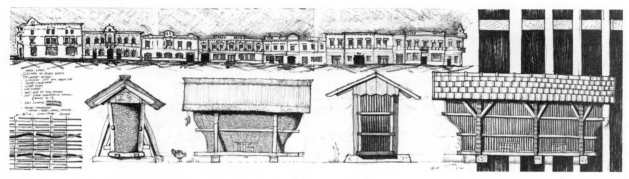

Hungary 3: Detail (c) Highlights Relevant to Sustainable Design:

Form follows function.

This corncrib is one that particularly struck me as interesting. The quality of light inside is totally unique in that it creates some sort of cage effect. These small buildings are simply intended to dry corn, but they may provide a larger architectural inspiration. The one on the left is made of sticks and vines like a large basket. Like the pattern design for the sunflowers by Otto Wagner in sketchbook Austria 1: Detail (c), the weave of the corncrib appears to be simple, but on closer inspection, it is more complex with alternating sizes and then a double twist every seventh row. For roofs, one is thatched, while the other is tiled. The bentwood details along each post elevate this structure from shed to craft and from craft to art. Both are something of a piece of sculpture rather than a farm building.

The question of time must be addressed. Why would someone spend the time to decorate a corncrib? The only thing I can imagine is that part of human nature drives us to make something our own. We have history dating back to cavemen where we would personalize the caves with cave paintings. Since this farmer does not have either a sports car to customize or even a TV to watch, why not spend the time to decorate the shed?

Across the Atlantic on the Amish farms in Pennsylvania, I saw a similar attention to detail in storage buildings like corncribs. See sketchbook USA 5: Detail (a). The idea of building something that lasts out of locally available materials is central to sustainable design.

Hungary 3: Detail (d)

Hungary 3: Detail (d) Highlights Relevant to Sustainable Design:

Simple things count.

The center of this sketchbook includes three examples of brick walls that are all varied slightly in configuration in the design of the top portion. The walls run alongside sidewalks in this small town to keep animals out of flowerbeds and vegetable gardens. Wooden fences require painting and replacement as slats rot out over time, while brick walls last significantly longer. The lifetime total cost of ownership (TCO) of masonry walls is worth considering relative to the initial investment of time and materials. Plastics have largely replaced wood fences, and the by-product of plastic production is also worth considering relative to the job creation through masonry work that has certainly dropped off with the rise of oil-based construction materials.

Hungary 3: Detail (e)

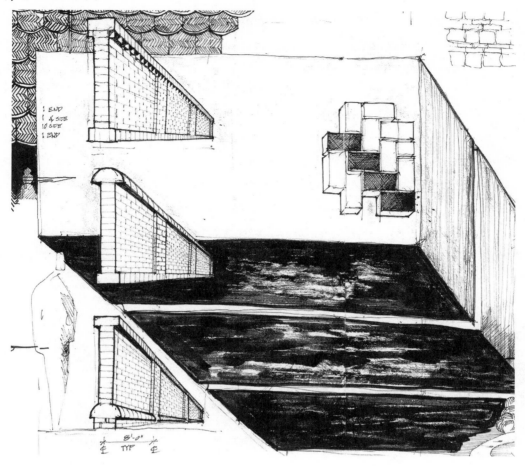

Hungary 3: Detail (f)

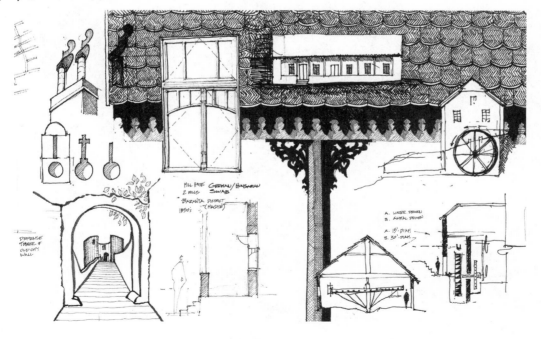

Hungary 3: Detail (f) Highlights Relevant to Sustainable Design:

We can look into reducing energy with natural light and ventilation from window transoms.

The window sketch shows an upper rectangle with three panes of glass and a lower pair of panes with three small glass inserts in each. The upper portion opens up and out to allow for natural ventilation. Plus it prevents the rain from coming in if you need a breeze on a hot summer day when it starts to rain. Each of the two lower portions also opens out as casement windows versus the more common double-hung windows in America. With high-efficiency air-conditioning, the use of natural ventilation is less of a concern now than it was in America before WW II. A significant portion of the world does not have central air-conditioning, so they have had to innovate to maximize natural on-site conditions such as breeze. In 2007, only 2 percent of households in India and 11 percent of households in Brazil had air-conditioning, compared with 87 percent of households in the United States.[30] For other ventilation, like removing smoke, the chimney vents in the upper corner help the wind draft the smoke.

For our solar home outside of Philadelphia, I made the case to my wife that we could use casement windows to take advantage of the natural breezes and still maintain a stylistic look that matched the context of our more traditional "double-hung" neighborhood. The results are that we have significant more natural ventilation, use the air-conditioning in the spring, summer, and fall much less than our neighbors, and save on energy and home operating costs. Plus, new reports on "sick building syndrome" indicate that there are more toxins than we might have imagined in the carpet, furniture glue, and so on. This makes natural ventilation an asset for health rather than just for energy savings.

Hungary 3: Detail (g)

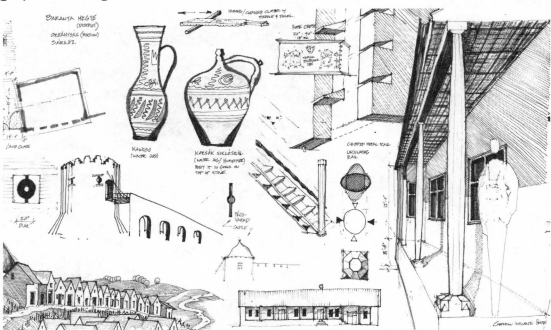

Hungary 3: Detail (g) Highlights Relevant to Sustainable Design:

Geothermal applications have multiple advantages.

Along the bottom of the sketchbook, you will see what appear to be small houses. They are actually *pince,* pronounced "pin-sir," or wine storage houses. The houses are only the front of much larger structures and storage processes. Each one is merely a door with one room for tasting, and then the wine cellar extends back into the hillside, sometimes as far as a hundred feet. By extending into the hill, the tunnellike cellars take advantage of the cool and constant ground temperature below the freezing point of the frost line. The underground space is always about fifty to fifty-five degrees Fahrenheit, depending on the latitude, as long as it is at least three and a half to five feet below the ground surface. Indigenous people around the world have taken advantage of this free and constant temperature well before air-conditioning and heating. The passive geothermal advantage, in this case, keeps the wine at the right temperature year-round.

The greatest thing about the pince is that if you knock on one of the doors and the winemaker happens to be inside, he will gladly sit you down and proudly serve you a taste of his wine. We had quite a few lunches in the pince rows scattered around the wine country. The hillside behind the cellars has a few clustered trees, and I drew them like balls in the style of medieval etchings.

Hungary 3: Detail (h)

Hungary 3: Detail (h) Highlights Relevant to Sustainable Design:

Rethink life on the river.

At the top of this drawing, a third of the way over from the left, I drew a fish net with a circular set of rings and a small boat. The net design works for carrying the fish, which you've caught from the mighty Danube River, fresh and alive on a long day trip. Just below, there is a diagram of a boat that doubles as a mill. The Danube moves through Hungary, and this boat design takes advantage of the movement by weighing anchor and setting up a mill to grind grain, using a similar system as if there were a combination waterfall and steamboat. The innovative nets and boats literally sustain life in simple ways that I had not previously imagined. The river is the source of food with its fish and the source of power with its current. These low-tech solutions are cost-effective and emissions-free.

Decorative textile patterns and stencils straddle the page. Often they are used to decorate not only fabric and furniture but also the sides of buildings. The transformation and metamorphosis of the tulip shape is apparent all over the country. The regionalism within the country is also surprising. The patterns and colors often look quite similar, but I met one old villager who claimed to be able to identify dozens of different folk dress patterns by town. The level of regionalism in fashion, food, furniture, and architecture is surprising considering the country is no larger than the state of Maryland. When I was there in the early 1990s, other than in Budapest, regionalism prevailed over franchising. The twenty-first century may bring untold change that will reduce the charm of regionalism.

Since I do not speak Hungarian, I found that drawing was a key catalyst to capture information. In the evenings, I was able to show people the drawings and learn from the ones who could speak a little bit of English. The Hungarian language is very difficult to learn, because it is rooted in Sanskrit, unlike the romance languages, French, Spanish, and Italian that are rooted in Latin. You may have an easier time learning how to communicate in Japanese than in Hungarian.

Hungary 3: Detail (i)

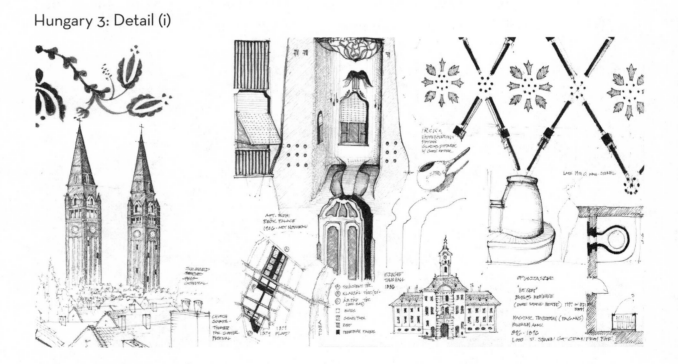

Hungary 3: Detail (i) Highlights Relevant to Sustainable Design:

We can rethink window shading and thermal mass heating systems.

This sketch includes at the upper left of center an illustration of a window that has a window shading system. You can open it out to allow natural ventilation and also benefit from added security when it is closed. In the lower right, a circular home wood-burning furnace is built with masonry to hold the heat and emit it back into the room rather than letting the majority of the heat go up the chimney.

Hungary 4

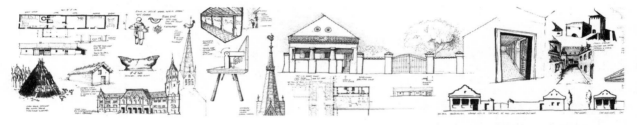

Hungary 4: Detail (a)

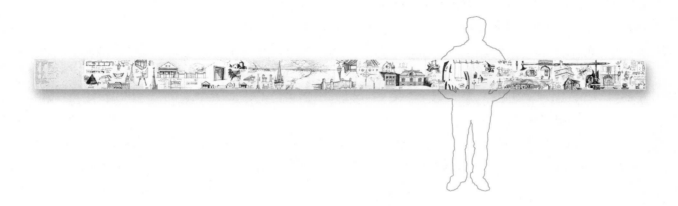

Hungary 4: Detail (b)

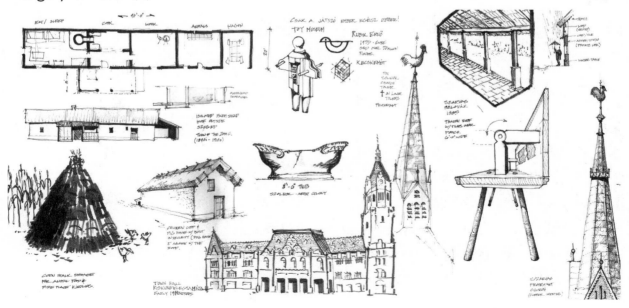

Hungary 4: Detail (b) Highlights Relevant to Sustainable Design:

Look at the side-yard "I" house and cost-effectiveness of protecting chickens from foxes.

The upper left illustrates a row house, which is really a side-yard house, designed to extend as the family grows. If the width between houses is increased, as in some other examples, the yard becomes a private courtyard. The yard is private because there are no windows on the backside of the adjacent house. This creates a balance of privacy and community proximity that works well, especially for families who have young children playing safely in the side yards. Plus, if you want fresh, local, organic eggs for breakfast and poultry for dinner, the enclosed side yard is ideal to contain chickens and also a protected vegetable garden.

The round object in the plan is the heating element in the bedroom. This drawing also includes a rectangular thatch-roofed chicken coop with a very small addition at the far end. The farmer added a doghouse to protect the chickens from foxes, since the right type of dogs cost-effectively scare away foxes. In the lower right, this bench has a hinge to flip the backrest to sit facing the other direction without having to move the bench. See Hungary 4: Detail (c) for other house plan configurations.

Hungary 4: Detail (c)

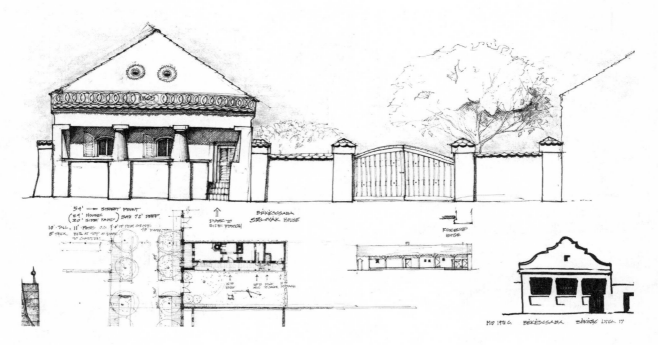

Hungary 4: Detail (c) Highlights Relevant to Sustainable Design:

We can rethink urban versus suburban planning and density for residential properties.

This sketch includes a fine example of a side-yard house. In the United States, we typically have homes with front yards and backyards in the suburbs and apartments and row houses with little or no backyards in our cities. I had never seen a side-yard house in the United States or anywhere else, before my travels to Hungary. This side-yard design has several interesting advantages. First, the porch on the street front side serves several purposes: The porch protects the residents from getting wet when they unlock the front door. It provides a place to sit and watch the passing action of the neighborhood and in so doing strengthens the all-important "public eye"—the monitoring of daily activity, which deters children and criminals from harming themselves and the community. The same can be said for any house in a mid-density American community that has a front porch.

Second, the street-side door is actually not the main entrance to the house. The main entry is from the side porch. The door facing the street opens to the porch colonnade and the garden running parallel down the side of the house. This is a terrific feature, because you can leave the front door open as a clue to invite in neighbors to your side courtyard, while the actual door to the house can stay closed. Vice versa, you can close the street front door and leave the house door open to let children and pets play in the side yard. This design strategy uses two or three times the square footage of a row house footprint but less than half the square footage of a midsize suburban home. The back side (left side of the façade sketch) serves as the privacy wall for the neighbor's home, and each room has a window to the courtyard garden.

The side-yard house has a density appeal similar to other house layouts described in sketchbook:

"I" House: Hungary 4: Detail (b) and (c)
"L" House: Hungary 2: Detail (f)
"U" House: Hungary 2: Detail (d)

Over the course of my travels, I have stayed in homes of varying size and style and seen the potential of mid-density layouts as well as the advantages of high- and low-density planning. These diagrams below may help provide a broad-stroke perspective on the differences.

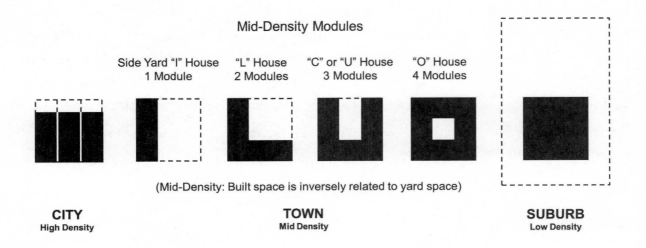

Mid-Density Modules

Side Yard "I" House
1 Module

"L" House
2 Modules

"C" or "U" House
3 Modules

"O" House
4 Modules

(Mid-Density: Built space is inversely related to yard space)

CITY
High Density

TOWN
Mid Density

SUBURB
Low Density

Hungary 4: Detail (d)

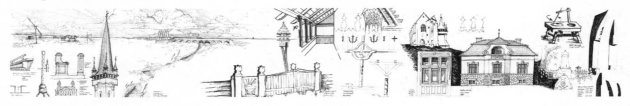

Hungary 4: Detail (e)

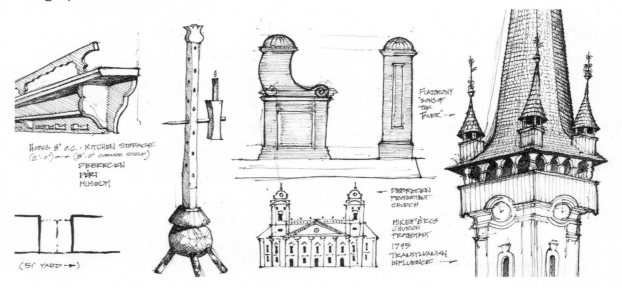

Hungary 4: Detail (e) Highlights Relevant to Sustainable Design:

Smart controls start with bi-level switching for lighting.

One of the keys to current commercial office energy conservation is bi-level switching. "Bi-level" means that you can have ceiling lights on one switch but also task lights such as a desk lamp with a separate switch. By having the dual controls, each individual can use only the light that he or she needs for a particular task. The adjustable candleholder lets someone raise or lower the light according to his or her need to read something in detail or to illuminate a larger portion of a room. The top of this candleholder includes an adaptation of the tulip motif, which is also evident on the top of fence posts, inverted as details on rooflines, and carved into gables of houses as part of the ventilation system. This sketchbook section also includes other examples of where form follows function with aesthetic enhancements: kitchen dish shelf, a church pew, and a church with a Transylvanian influenced steeple.

Hungary 4: Detail (f)

Hungary 4: Detail (f) Highlights Relevant to Sustainable Design:

We can pump water with less energy and learn some cultural history.

The *puszta*, pronounced "poo-staa," is the Hungarian equivalent of the American plains. It is flat with seemingly endless fields of wheat that serve as a backdrop to accent church steeples and tall, spindly trees. The puszta is where the Hungarian cowboys roam, and it is romanticized like our Old West. This detail drawing is of a Gemeskut, pronounced "Game-s-koot." The counterbalance system is designed to get water out of a well without expending the labor to turn anything. The pivot design is clever, and the appearance is unmistakable on the horizon. The pivot design is also time-tested, predating Hungary for thousands of years, in regions where the water table is close enough to the surface that the rope and bucket on the pivot arm can reach down to the water.

Hungary 4: Detail (g)

Hungary 4: Detail (g) Highlights Relevant to Sustainable Design:

Structure can hold memory.

This landscape drawing includes a church tower on the horizon and a famous bridge at the center. The nine-arch Hungarian bridge story goes something like this: A great and vigorous horseman, the leader of a tribe, had ten women all immediately concerned for his well-being. When confronted by a foe and countless warriors, the ten women circled the tribal leader to protect him from insurmountable odds. The nine arches of the bridge represent the space created below their arms. Each vertical section is like their legs and their hands would meet at the keystone of the arch. I'm not sure how this story ends, but let's assume the tribal leader does some heroic gymnastics and saves the day. Regardless, the proportions of the bridge are excellent.

The Hungarian Great Plain, where the bridge is located, is part of a cultural and environmental sustainability story. The World Heritage Hortobágy National Park, the Puszta, is almost 75,000 hectares. A hectare is 10,000 square meters or 2.471 acres, making this area over 185,000 acres. Located in the eastern part of Hungary on the Great Hungarian Plain,[31] the Puszta is protected land like our national parks. The Puszta is an example of how traditional pastoral land use can be harmonious between people and the environment for more than two thousand years. Land-use practices include animal husbandry and grazing for livestock breeds that are adapted to the specific alkaline pastures, meadows, wetlands, and steppes. The grasslands, called the steppe, cover about 5,000 miles from Hungary across the Ukraine and Central Asia to Manchuria at the east. Since horsemen can cross the mountain barriers across the steppe, interaction along the breadth of this Eurasian grassland has occurred for most of recorded history. Attila the Hun led his nomadic horsemen people from the Central Asia steppes to Europe and threatened what was left of the Roman Empire. Early Hungarian ancestors saw the Romans as an occupying force; Attila the Hun was freeing them of an unwanted influence. Attila the Hun died in AD 453, and "Attila" has been a popular name in Hungary since then. History is relative at many levels.

Hungary 4: Detail (h)

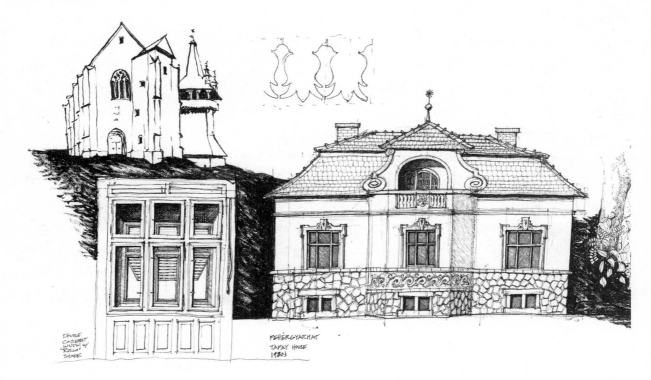

Hungary 4: Detail (h) Highlights Relevant to Sustainable Design

We can rethink natural ventilation and shading.

This sketch includes the house on the right that belonged to one of my relatives, until it was taken over by the Soviets and turned into a retirement home. In previous sketchbook excerpt notes, I have described and illustrated windows that have transoms (windows over windows), and this is another example. The window detail to the left of the façade highlights a double-thick wall and pull chord on the right side to extend and retract the shading devise. Overall, using light intelligently has become a fascination that attracted me to the light-emitting diode (LED) technology and all of its energy-saving potential. Plus, "light harvesting" capabilities recently caught my attention, given available dimming and photo cells that adjust with the balance of available natural light in any given season, month, day, and time of day.

Hungary 4: Detail (i)

Hungary 4: Detail (i) Highlights Relevant to Sustainable Design:

Needs plus regionalism drive simple innovations.

People in different parts of the world have similar needs and solve the same problems in different ways, often based on the available local resources. This sketchbook includes a hand grinding apparatus, our family gravesite, and some grave markers near the Transylvanian border, which used to be part of the Austro-Hungarian Empire. The significance of the grinding machine near the gravesite may have something to do with ashes to ashes and dust to dust. The family graves are on the outskirts of a town called Fehergyasmat, pronounced "Fay-hay-yarm-et." The tomb markers are specific to one particular region. They take on a distinct quality reminiscent of Easter Island. Carved from large local tree logs, the markers stand sometimes over six feet tall and a foot thick.

The V-cut wood roof shingles are an interesting detail to keep water from getting inside the building. The available wood versus clay drive the form, and the V helps prevent the water from resting on the shingle and warping the wood. This drawing also shows another region of wine country. The different sized and shaped presses and the different sized and shaped cellars all contribute to a provincial feeling. Running along the top of the page, the ax-like form actually has a very dull blade. It is called a Fokos, pronounced "Fook-ish." Shepherds use the tools as walking sticks. The curved end piece snags the sheep's collar and directs the sheep on their way.

Hungary 4: Detail (j)

ABAUJSZANTÓ PINCE

Hungary 4: Detail (j) Highlights Relevant to Sustainable Design:

We can leverage passive as well as active geothermal advantages.

The wine cellars built into the hillsides take advantage of the fifty-five degrees Fahrenheit (12.77 degrees Celsius) ground temperature that is typically below the frost line (three feet underground) around the world and around the year. This same approach to consistent temperature control is also illustrated and described in sketchbook Hungary 3: Detail (g). For comparison, here is a detail.

Hungary 4: Detail (k)—From Hungary 3

    In America, the same principles are used in applications such as the Pennsylvania bank barn, built into hillsides to protect the animals during cold winters and hot summers. We took advantage of this passive geothermal advantage to reduce energy costs on the addition to our home, by building the family room and kitchen into the hillside.

Hungary 4: Detail (l)

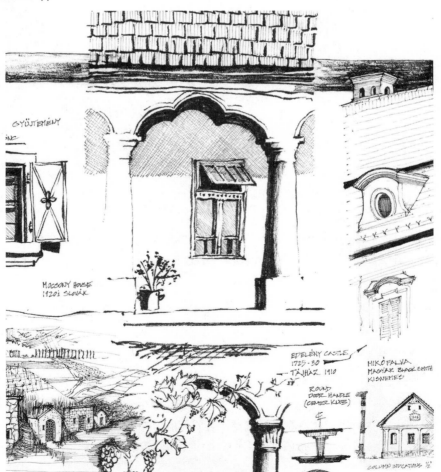

Hungary 4: Detail (l) Highlights Relevant to Sustainable Design:

We can rethink double-hung windows.

Here is another example of an operable transom window that provides natural ventilation and protection on rainy days. This one includes a pair of casement windows below the transom, and it is set back from the façade within a colonnade.

Hungary 4: Detail (m)

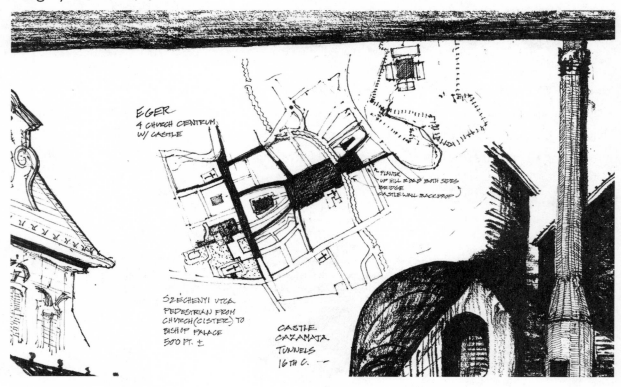

Hungary 4: Detail (m) Highlights Relevant to Sustainable Design:

We can rethink auto-centric suburban sprawl in favor of pedestrian town centers.

This is a diagram of a small-town plan, which is blackened where automobiles are not permitted at certain times of the day. The priority of the pedestrian in cities and towns such as this one is very clear. Like most European cities that evolved prior to the invention of the automobile, the Hungarian ones are no different. The ironic thing is that a city square, which is a great European gathering place for retail commerce and social interaction, has largely been replaced in America by the shopping mall. Perhaps the reason we design malls with double-sided indoor streets, benches, and even trees, is to replicate the pedestrian experience in cities with centers void of cars. The shopping mall is often the last great pedestrian experience for residents of American suburbs.

One difference is that the suburban mall is typically an island surrounded by a parking lot in what probably used to be a cornfield. A European or even an American town square is not surrounded by parking lots but by people and buildings. As Internet technology opens the door even further to working outside of cities, we can revisit the idea of suburban town centers versus strip malls and sprawl.

Hungary 4: Detail (n)

Hungary 4: Detail (n) Highlights Relevant to the Energy Revolution:

We can rethink windows, doors, and car access.

The garage "carriage house" gate, illustrated on the left side, is particularly interesting to me because it has a door within a door. One door is for people, while the larger pair is for a carriage or now a car. All three doors are made of wood, detailed with spaces for air to circulate and draft at the top. Before electricity and roll-up garage-door technology, this was a low-tech solution that integrated two functions in one masonry opening. The air circulation was most likely to ventilate the space for the horses that pulled the carriages. Form follows function and nets out with an aesthetic and lasting result.

Hungary 5

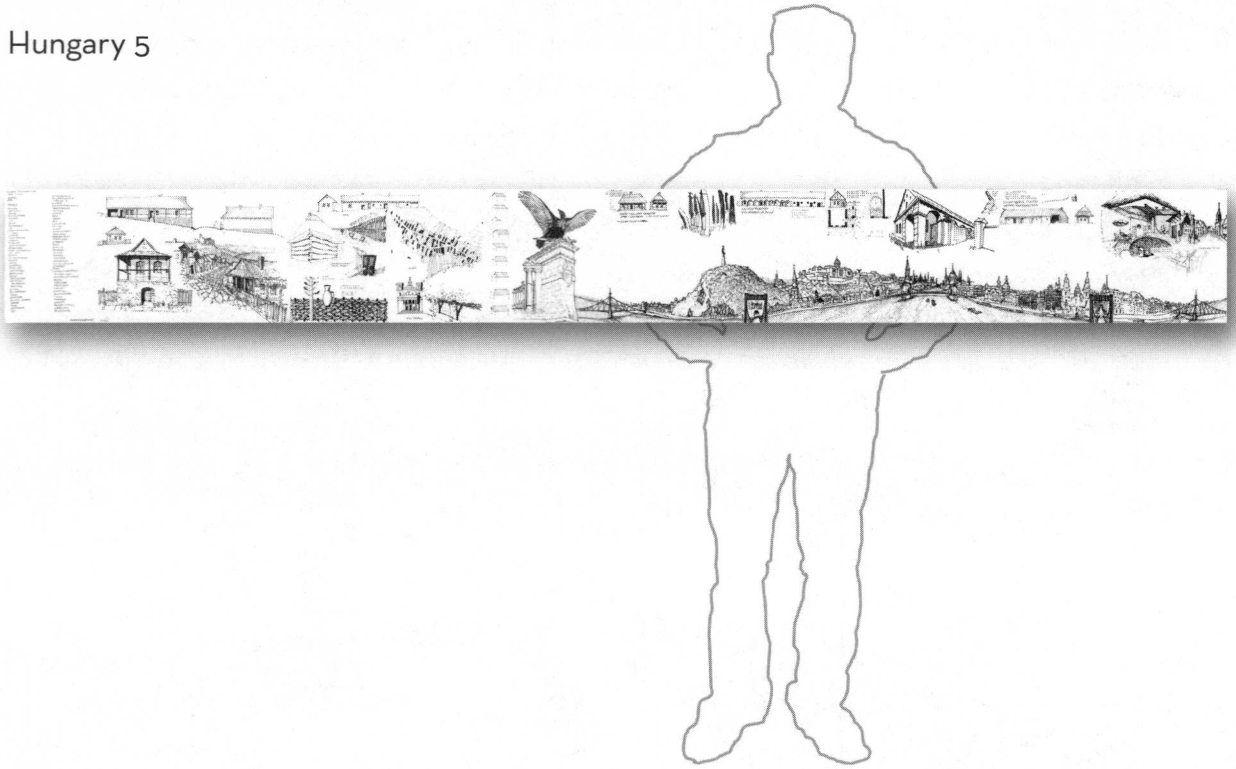

Hungary 5: Highlights Relevant to Sustainable Design:

Cities can give residents collective strength to endure multiple occupations and retain cultural values.

Hungary has weathered occupations from the Turks to the Soviet Union, and their capital city of Budapest has served as a cultural anchor. The density of population in a city helps sustain life through the exchange of goods and services, but that same density may foster a "strength in numbers" resiliency at the cultural level to overcome adversity. For Hungarians, their thousand-year history, tenacity, and resiliency in the face of occupations is a powerful source of cultural pride.

This sketchbook lists the cities and towns that I visited on my Hungarian odyssey. Since Holloko was one of the last stops before going on to the capital of Budapest, the plan on the right hand shows the layout of the town, and the diagram to the right shows the range of roof configurations.

The bird is a large statue that sits on a large castle hill on the side of Budapest. The bird is something of a phoenix, appropriate for a city and people that have risen from ashes several times over the course of a thousand years. The Soviet occupation for fifty years was a small setback relative to that of the Turks, where the occupancy lasted a few hundred years.

Once two cities, Buda and Pest flank the Danube. The city is now joined in name and spirit. This drawing includes a 360-degree panorama of the city with the bird statue anchoring the left.

Hungary 5: Detail (a)

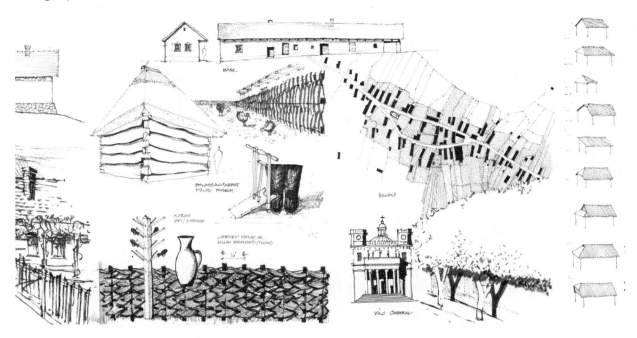

Hungary 5: Detail (a) Highlights Relevant to Sustainable Design:

We can build dynamic towns with a few clues from the past.

The famous town of Holloko, pronounced "Hole-oh-kew," is on a list of the top one hundred historical attractions in the world, determined by an international community of architects. The Egyptian pyramids and Thomas Jefferson's design for the University of Virginia share the acclaim. Holloko is needless to say in good company. The town is comprised entirely of side-yard houses, as previously discussed in previous sketchbook highlights. See Hungary 4: Detail (c) for other house plan configurations. In this town, the low fences convey a welcoming community of trust in a world moving toward the opposite. Many of the houses, like the ones drawn on this page, have a basement entrance that doubles as cold storage for food and wine.

Overall, a few clues about design from the past can inspire the way that we think about the future. As an example, does an active community of residents in a town like this one inspire something like the design for residences for an academic community of graduate students or even an active adult retirement community? We often default to design formulas that may have "sold" recently rather than taking the intellectual risk to at least explore what may have a proven record of success in another country for hundreds of years.

Hungary 5: Detail (b)

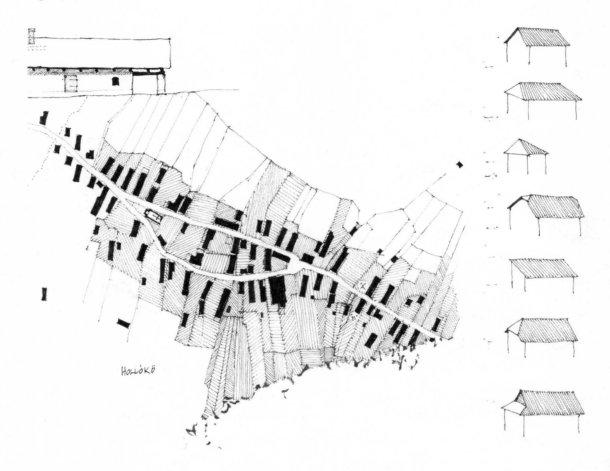

Hungary 5: Detail (b) Highlights Relevant to Sustainable Design:

We can build dynamic towns with a few clues from the past (continued).

The plan shows the layout of the town with each little rectangle of the houses separated by the side yards. The church is at the center of the community, set back from the fork in the road that leads through the town.

The diagrams to the right show the range of roof configurations. Holloko was one of the last places that I visited before moving on to the capital of Budapest.

Hungary 5: Detail (c)

Hungary 5: Detail (c) Highlights Relevant to Sustainable Design:

We can rethink the use of rivers for transit and how our cities meet the edge.

This panoramic view of Budapest is over six feet long and took several hours to complete while standing on one of the bridges. The majestic bird on the left is a large statue that sits on the castle hillside of Budapest. Two city sides, Buda and Pest, flank the Danube River, and this sketch also includes the famous Széchenyi Bridge. Spending the time drawing the city let me look closer at the activity along the river's edge. I realized that industry, roads, and rail have largely dominated the edge of rivers in Philadelphia and other American cities. The "asset" of the river may be something to renew, given that shipping and rail were largely the only games in town up until the advent of airfreight. As the world shifts toward on-demand inventory, the edges of rivers could play an increasing role in the rebirth of American cities for even more enhanced social activity. Many cities have undertaken riverfront redevelopment, and the cleaner river water over the past few decades certainly helps spur the demand to engage near the river's edge.

This bird is a phoenix.

This is appropriate for a city and people who have endured and "risen from ashes" multiple times.

In Greek mythology, a *phoenix* or phenix (Greek: φοῖνιξ phoinix) is a bird that is cyclically regenerated or reborn.

Hungary 5: Detail (d)

Hungary 5: Detail (e)

CARVED WD. POSTS
LOG / MUD / LIME CONST. HAUS
MIN. VENTED GABLE - WD.
STEEP PITCH ROOF

WOOD W/ DIRT INFILL
12" - 18"

FELSÖ - TISZAVIDÉK TÁJEGYSÉG
UPPER TISZA REGION   w/ CALVANIST CEMETARY

⟶ SZENTENDRE ⟶

KISALFÖLD TÁJEGYSÉG
NORTH WESTERN PLAIN REGION

A · BOOT CLEANER
B · WELCOME MAT
C · RAIN SPLASH
D · WINDOW TO COVERED ENTRY

LIMED BRICK PIERS · ARCHED
LIMED BRICK WALLS · DETAILED WDW/CORNER
VENTED/DECORATED GABLE
SIDE GATE/YARD

Hungary 5: Detail (f)

POT AS
THATCH
CAP

· CANTILEVERED BEAM PORCH
· LIMED LOG WALLS
· VENTED/DECORATED WOODEN GABLE
· OVERLAP THATCH CORNERS & COVER BOARD

NYUGAT - DUNÁNTÚL TÁJEGYSÉG
WESTERN TRANSDANUBIAN REGION

ROMANTIKA FAGYLALTOZÓ
COURTYARD WITH ENTRY

SZENTENDRE FÖ TÉR

Czech Republic 6

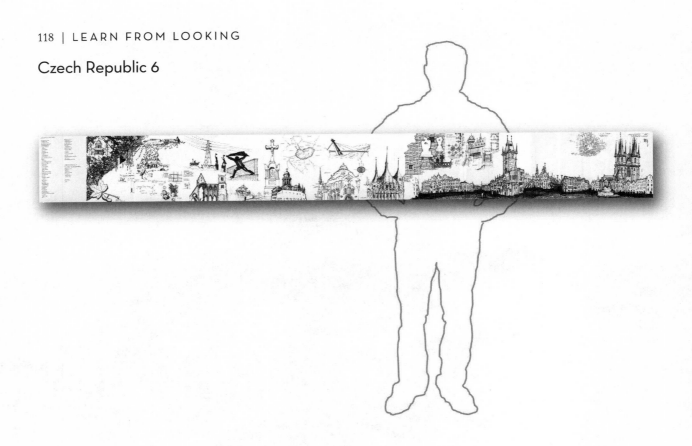

Czech Republic 6: Highlights Relevant to Sustainable Design:

Cultural preservation has a time and place.

This is the last of the Hungary sketchbooks. My travels in Eastern Europe extended beyond Hungary and included Austria, Slovenia, Ukraine, Slovakia, and the Czech Republic. Croatia and Serbia round out the seven nations that border Hungary. One amazing aspect of the Hungarian people is their ability to absorb influences from their neighbors over one thousand years while still maintaining a continuity of their own culture.

In this sketchbook section, the statues drawn in silhouette are from the Soviet occupation. As the Iron Curtain fell, the Hungarian youth vented their frustration over their previously restricted rights by defacing many of the statues. The Hungarian government saw no need to disproportionally preserve the unfortunate chapter in Communist history. However, they set out to build a simple "Monument Park" outside of Budapest for all to view the statues of Communist leaders and remember the dark legacy of a half century. Cultural preservation is important in building any town or city, because people need to remember where they have come from, what they may have endured, and where they are going. This is done in the United States with monuments, but in Hungary, I noticed how these monuments became part of a whole park to secure the memory of occupation.

The cross to the right of the statue sketch is one of thousands of crosses that mark the town border in the rural communities. Sometimes the town had expanded beyond the border, while other times the cross sat quietly in the middle of a cornfield, waiting for the town to expand. I saw different style crosses each day while entering and leaving the towns. Each one served as a sublime reminder of the spiritual base and the individual identity associated with each town. I hope that people so rich in pride and spirit will continue to thrive. The right hand side is from Prague in the Czech Republic. This sketch is an inverted "sister" to the panorama of Budapest. The river view of Budapest was looking in from the Danube, while this one is looking out from inside the city center.

Czech Republic 6: Detail (a)

Czech Republic 6: Detail (b)

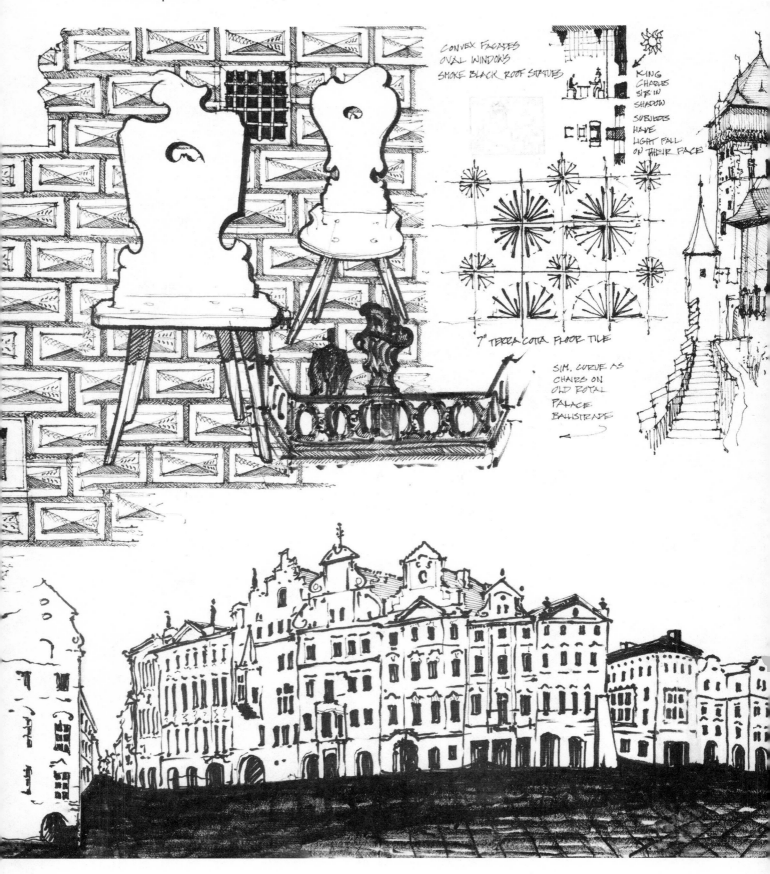

CONVEX FACADES
OVAL WINDOWS
SMOKE BLACK ROOF STATUES

KING
CHARLES
SITS IN
SHADOW

SUBJECTS
HAVE
LIGHT FALL
ON THEIR FACE

7" TERRA COTTA FLOOR TILE

SIM. CURVE AS
CHAIRS ON
OLD ROYAL
PALACE
BALLUSTRADE

KONOPIŠTĚ

Czech Republic 6: Detail (c)

PRAGUE

OLD TOWN SQUARE
STARÉ MĚSTO

CHARLES A. SZOROADY U.S.A.
4321 TURK ST. NW.
WASHINGTON, D.C. 20016
'82

Czech Republic 6: Detail (d)

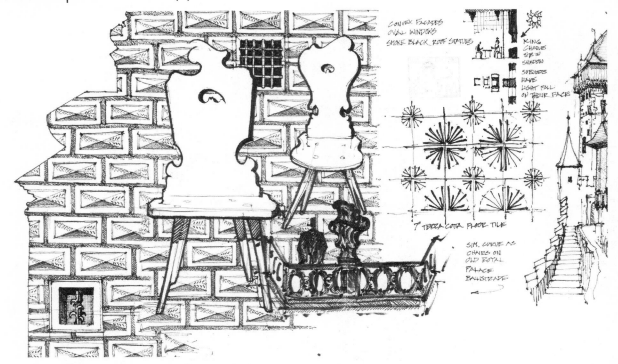

Czech Republic 6: Detail (d) Highlights Relevant to Sustainable Design:

We can rethink symmetry and repair over recycling.

This asymmetrical chair caught my attention. Hungarian chairs that I saw in villages were similar but often had symmetrical tulip shapes or hearts cut into the upper backrest, as in Hungary 1: Detail (d). In my travels, I was able to find local families happy to take boarders. I could see and sit in the chairs at their kitchen tables and also learn more directly about local culture. I have sat in a lot of chairs around the world, and I have never seen one that was asymmetrical. The human body is largely symmetrical, so the standard symmetry makes sense. However, I have added the chair here in this book as a springboard for thinking about what we may take for granted and the opportunities to challenge innovation in our energy consumption and production.

What are we doing symmetrically that could be asymmetrical? The chairs in Hungary and the Czech Republic were carefully made and handed down over generations, with repairs as needed along the way. This is a sharp contrast to a global trend toward disposability. We have the capacity to fix more of what we use when products break down rather than discarding them. In the height of American manufacturing and productivity in the middle of the twentieth century, there were far more furniture and appliance repair stores across the country. Airfreight has reduced many products to thin-gauge materials that in some cases are cheaper to replace than repair. This has added to the trend to discard rather than repair.

Czech Republic 6: Detail (e)

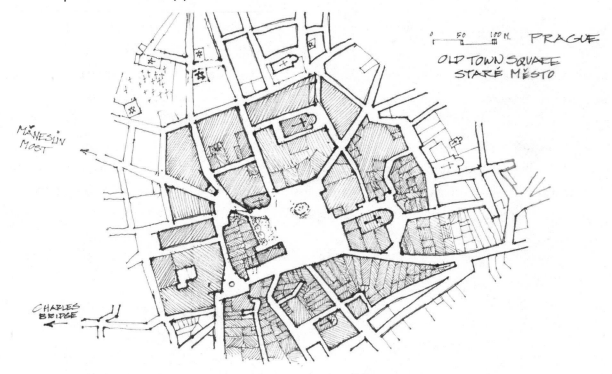

Czech Republic 6: Detail (e) Highlights Relevant to Sustainable Design:

We can rethink city and town centers.

Old Town Square is the historic square in the Old Town quarter of Prague, the capital of the Czech Republic. I spent an afternoon mapping the city and drawing the panoramic view on the previous pages that is about six feet long. I stood at the center of the square and rotated across the scene. You can see that the buildings on the far left and right are the seam of the panorama. I also drew a diagram of the plan with the white space as the open space at the center of the city's dense maze of streets. Like so many European squares, this one restricts auto traffic to make room for pedestrian interaction and bicycles. See chapter 9, Big City 2: Los Angeles for a description of the Sixteenth Street Mall solution in Denver. I referenced my experience with shared bikes in the section "Japan: Bonus Insights—The Teahouse and General Observations." Europe embraces bikes and scooters more than the United States does. Many of the European and Asian cities are so old that the roads are very narrow. Two wheels in line are simply more practical for getting around. Plus, the parking for cars is limited at best. Over the summer of 2015, my wife and I bought single-speed beach cruiser bikes for ourselves and our kids to use at our family New Jersey Shore house. I am now hooked on summer riding around town, between towns, and even just a block to the beach or to visit friends on the bay.

Closing Perspective on the European Experience

We can learn from areas of the world that many Americans cannot identify on a map. Every week from January 2006 through September 2007, my father sent me an e-mail letter with a quote that he felt would inspire or teach me something useful. He included in his communications a hand-drawn sun that came to represent for me his fundamental optimism in the good within the human spirit. My father escaped from Hungary to America in 1957 through the Soviet Iron Curtain, and he appreciated and loved American freedom at his core. This quote gave me perspective, given that Hungary was founded over one thousand years ago. I also particularly loved learning that America secured the iconic Hungarian treasure during WW II, which is such an important symbol of their country, much like the Liberty Bell is for us. My father recognized America's role in his way each summer.

Aug. 20, 2006
Dear Charlie,   For your thought: #31

All those Americans, who cherish their Hungarian origin, honor and celebrate Saint Stephen's Day on August 20th, as they also celebrate the 4th of July as Americans. —Charles Szoradi

Saint Stephen (István), the first king of Hungary (Magyarország), received a magnificent jeweled, gold crown along with an apostolic cross and a letter of blessing from Pope Sylvester II in January 1001, officially recognizing Stephen as a Christian king of Hungary. It was a tradition that the laws passed by the legislators and the sentences ordered by the courts were proclaimed by the name of this Saint Crown. It is now guarded in the House of Parliament in Budapest, when returned from Fort Knox, from safekeeping after WW II. King Stephen in his prayers offered Hungary for Mary, mother of Jesus, and asked her to protect the country from its enemies. I always remember to raise the stars and stripes on my home on August 20, to honor and celebrate Saint Stephen. I hope you and your family will remember to follow this tradition.

Love, Dad

7 NORTH AMERICA

USA

America is simply awesome. We have abundant resources, a foundational spirit of self-reliance, creativity, and the desire to help those in need around the world to the best of our ability. When it comes to sustainable design, we can look in our own backyard for inspiration. This USA sketchbook series looks at our country through the work of some self-reliant Amish farmers, pioneering western ranchers, eighteenth-century builders, and New England homeowners. Plus, other chapters like "Big Cities" cover New York to Los Angeles, and the "Islands" chapter covers Nantucket to Hawaii.

   I have had the great fortune of having terrific friends, many of whom date back to grade school. Beyond the countless interactions, fun over the years, and connections with our children, many of my friends have been gracious to host me as I have traveled across our great country, which has provided the ability for me to record the documentation in this book.

USA 1

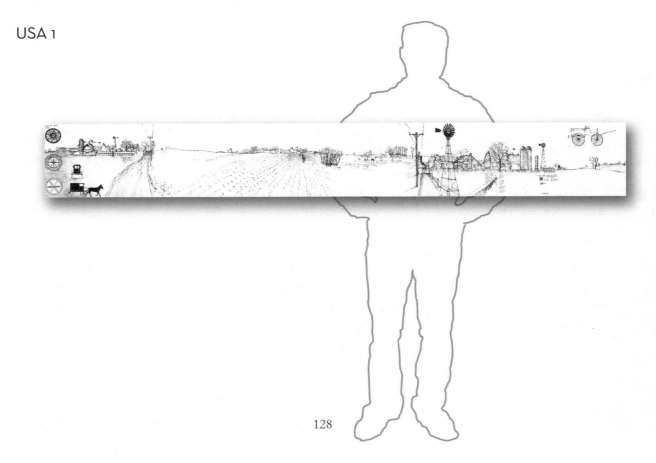

USA 1 Highlights Relevant to Sustainable Design:

We can learn from people who work the land.

The Amish community of the Pennsylvania Dutch is steeped in a low-tech and picturesque tradition. Living without petrol products, they basically live the way that people did more than a hundred years ago. The famous Amish barn raising has come to characterize their lifestyle. Teamwork, family, and materialistic restraint are some of their characteristics along with telltale thrift. A friend from Lancaster County accused me of the latter, using a familiar saying—"You've got deep pockets but short arms."

As I studied the configurations of different farmhouses and their adjacent buildings, I learned that the seemingly arbitrary layout of the complexes actually followed a well-designed sustainability plan. Farm architecture is particularly appealing because it adheres to the underlying sense of the modernist credo "Form follows function." The adjacencies of the farmhouse to the barn, the springhouse to the stable, the smokehouse to the outhouse, and so on, are critical to the success of operations. As well, each farmhouse typically has a large deciduous tree on the southern elevation. The tree serves to shade the house in the summer and welcome the winter sun into the house when the leaves have fallen. This type of attitude is appealing not only from a nostalgic cultural perspective but also as it relates to overall fuel efficiency. Natural heat gain and loss considerations are critical as we continue to burn through our global fossil fuels and increasingly rely on technology to substitute contextual design and seasonal forethought. I adopted this deciduous tree strategy on the south side of our house in Pennsylvania. For more, see the chapter "Sustainable Smart House" in part 3: "Commercial Impact."

USA 1: Detail (a)

USA 1: Detail (a) Highlights Relevant to Sustainable Design:

Build a community of trust.

Here are three examples of rosette hex details. The rosettes are painted two to three feet in diameter on the sides of barns in very vivid colors, and they are intended to deter or ward off evil spirits. These rosettes are one of multiple ways that the Amish build a community of trust where they look out for one another. Sustainability as a concept can go beyond the environment and resource conservation to include community sustainability. The close-knit Amish community has been able to sustain their values for multiple generations and use the resources at hand to maximize the yield from the land. Sustainability includes stewardship and an eye on future generations. From what I saw firsthand and learned about the Amish, they often pass down land from one generation to the next, so caring for their environment has a positive ripple effect for their families and their community.

USA 1: Detail (b)

USA 1: Detail (b) Highlights Relevant to Sustainable Design:

We can rethink power production.

Since the Amish are off the utility gird, they typically use windmills to generate the power to pump water from their wells. Years after preparing this drawing, I started looking into small-scale micro wind power production with residential-scale vertical-axis applications versus the massive blades of the industrial-size wind turbines. The vertical-axis wind turbines are now also available to power streetlights. Plus, localized solar panels are also options on streetlight poles. The combination of wind and solar power often works well, because if it is not a bright sunny day, the chances of increasing wind during inclement weather increase. Today, for traffic monitoring, many locations have poles and speed sensors that are not easily tied to the electric grid. So you will see solar panels on the poles along highways more so than in cities. When you use a navigation app or your smartphone to check to see the traffic congestion, you can thank localized micro power production for the information that we are starting to take for granted.

Highlights Relevant to Sustainable Design:

We can rethink site selection and natural shading assets.

Developers could stop cutting down the trees on subdivision lots. Use deciduous trees on the south side of the houses. Design the site plan by putting the houses to the north of the larger trees. Each major deciduous tree is worth about $60,000 if you had to make a towering machine to shade your house in the summer and collapse it in the winter to let the desirable warmth of the sun heat the home. Saving trees saves energy.

USA 2

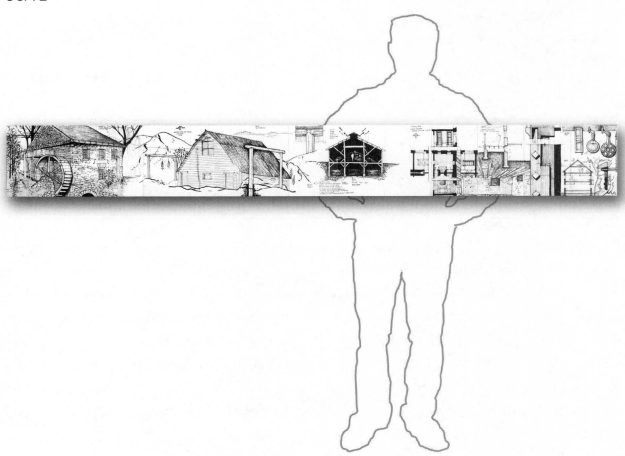

USA 2 Highlights Relevant to Sustainable Design:

Perspective across continents counts.

Various barns in Idaho beg the question, "Why are roof shapes so different within a region and across different regions?" Dairy cows simply have different needs from horses. A barn is never just a barn but a structure designed for its occupants. The simple post gateway reminds me of a gate to a Japanese shrine in sketchbook Japan 6: Detail (a). This instinct to provide a gate is apparently global. A threshold provides something to walk through to distinguish one side from another. The gate itself does not change the land around it, but our perception of being "in" versus "out" becomes meaningful.

A house drawn with its walls folded out gives you a chance to look at the window "jamb" detail on a basement window and study the "shutter dogs" that hold a shutter against a wall. The jamb is the vertical section of the window that supports the frame. Old houses are often loaded with design innovations that come to life on close inspection.

USA 2: Detail (a)

USA 2: Detail (a) Highlights Relevant to Sustainable Design:

Preventive reinforcement is more cost-effective than reconstruction.

Mills have come to symbolize a time in American history that seems simpler. Mills are often painted alongside a picturesque creek partially dilapidated with some mossy stones in the foreground. This particular mill from the 1820s is appealing because of the large S braces on both sides. The S is made of forged iron and serves to support the walls from expanding outward by holding the end of a long iron rod that is connected to the other side. Often star-shaped braces serve the same function to reinforce walls and double as ornamentation.

You can sometimes see the stars in brick structures, such as the last building in a row of town houses. This idea of preventive reinforcement is not unlike preventive medicine. Overall, prevention is key to sustainability in that it helps reduce the burden of replacement and reconstruction, which adds debris to landfills and increases transportation pollution.

The mill wheel itself is perhaps appealing for the same reason as the stars or S curve in that its aesthetic appeal is a by-product of its function. The running water from the stream turns the mill's large exterior wooden water wheel, which in turn moves the smaller interior stone-grinding wheel, which in most cases grinds grain into flour to make bread. The mill wheel has the added advantage of sound and motion to heighten the senses. We largely leave hydropower to the major public works and utility companies, with large-scale projects like the Hoover Dam. However, new technology for tidal power shows some promise where localized power production can yield results in rivers and other areas where water is in motion.

USA 2: Detail (b)

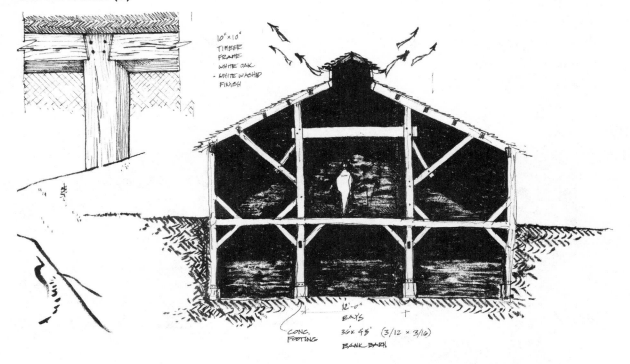

USA 2: Detail (b) Highlights Relevant to Sustainable Design:

We can rethink the form and function of natural ventilation.

For connecting wood, the dovetail joint in the upper left of this sketch is strong and effective. It is time-consuming to produce and requires a high degree of carpentry skill for the angle cuts and pegs, so it has largely been replaced by metal brackets. The diagonal bracing and the roof vents that adorn the top of this barn are common in many regions across the country. Regardless of shape, size, and color, barn components typically serve a function.

Hot air rises up and out through slats along the cupola sides. Often the top also features a weathervane with a directional wind arrow and an animal ranging from a horse to a fish. Not surprisingly, we are so enamored with the look of the familiar barn cupolas that they appear on roofs of buildings across America that have significantly different functions from barns. Some gas stations, banks, and fast-food "country" restaurants have the familiar cupola. Of course the cupolas are never intended to work as they do on countless barns, but the look reminds us of something we like. For better or worse, cultural memory unabashedly takes over reason. We might find that homes and even some commercial and industrial properties would benefit from natural ventilation to reduce their energy consumption on heating, ventilating, and air-conditioning (HVAC), especially in temperate seasons like spring and fall. With the advent of "smart controls" and building automation, the idea of intelligent design could work well with old tech strategies integrated with new tech tactics.

This barn cross section is cut though the ground plane on the walkout side of a hill to also illustrate the passive geothermal advantages of using ground temperature below the frost line to keep the animals cooler in the summer and warmer in the winter than the outside air temperature. Advancements in geothermal active technology make it more affordable now to bury coils underground, but passive geo-strategies are readily applicable and proven to be cost-effective.

USA 2: Detail (c)

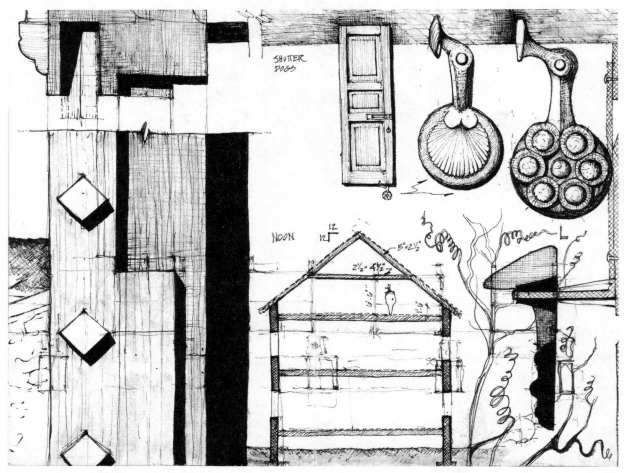

USA 2: Detail (c) Highlights Relevant to Sustainable Design:

We can rethink operable shutters.

Old houses are often loaded with design innovations that come to life on close inspection. These are "shutter dogs" in the upper right, where the metal part above the pivot holds open the shutter against the wall. The lower corner drawing shows the cross section of the dog if you were looking at it from right next to the wall. I like shutter dogs, and I dislike fake shutters that are nailed, screwed, or glued on the side of someone's house. Real shutters feel more substantial when they can swing back and forth with ease and, most important, when they have the functionality to close to protect your house.

USA 3

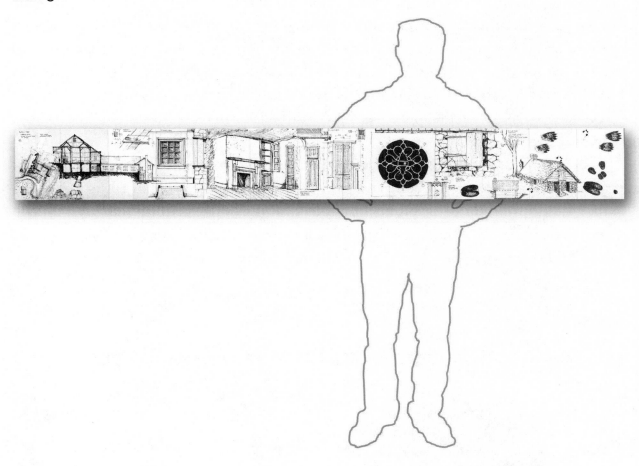

USA 3: Detail (a)

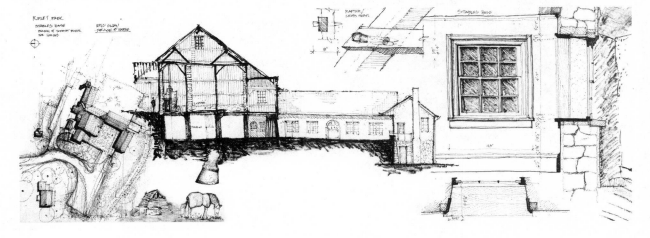

USA 3: Detail (a) Highlights Relevant to Sustainable Design:

We can rethink using hills for efficiency and building thick walls.

This sketch illustrates a Pennsylvania "bank barn," which is typically dug into a hillside. The design allows for animals to freely enter and exit from the bottom level, while the farmer can work upstairs. Whether it is thrashing hay that drops down to feed the animals or wheeling the tractor into the upper-grade level, the farmer can work more efficiently. The bank barns are thus two-story buildings without stairs. As well, the ground temperature below the frost line (typically about three feet) is a constant in the midfifty degrees Fahrenheit (12.7 degrees Celsius), so the animals do not freeze to death in the winter or die of heat stroke in the summer.

The window detail in the center shows the thickness of a stone wall. The level of distinction between inside and outside is "insideness," and the size of the window jamb visually contributes to the condition. The thick wall provides a greater quality of insideness than thin walls. A jamb is the exposed molding or framing around a window or door. This jamb is angled in plan (wider on the inside than the outside edge of the wall) to allow more light to reflect into the room as it bounces off of either side of the jamb.

USA 3: Detail (b)

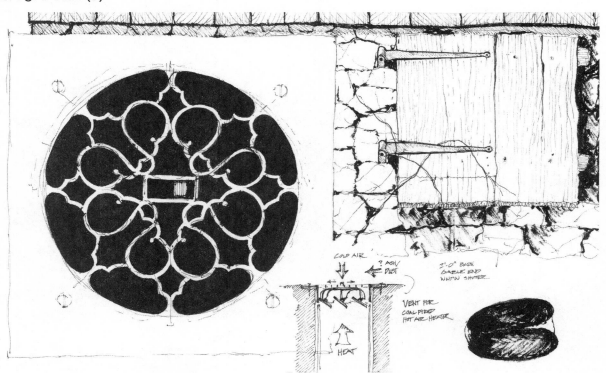

USA 3: Detail (b) Highlights Relevant to Sustainable Design:

We can rethink saving heating fuel by sharing heat between floors.

This floor grate allows the heat from the fireplace on the first floor to rise up through the house. The grate has qualities of function and aesthetic shared by the S braces on the mill, the barn cupolas, and the shutter dogs. They work simply and have an appealing look, versus just one or the other. The bottom of this sketch shows a cross-section drawing of the floor grate. The louvers are moved easily by foot to regulate the amount of air coming up to circulate through the house. This type of design was used before we had ducted central heating and cooling systems, but there is absolutely no reason why sharing climate control between floors does not make sense today. We could take the concept and make it high-tech in a few strategic locations within floors and walls, using smart sensors to balance air temperature and auto closedowns to have separate temperature zones tied to programmable thermostats. Some products are already on the market, for walls, and advancing old ideas with new technology is a theme of sustainable design.

USA 3: Detail (c)

USA 3: Detail (c) Highlights Relevant to Sustainable Design:

Be a good neighbor.

Animal tracks on the snow are often worth following. The distance between the tracks, their size, and their depth are all clues to the animal's weight and shape.

I think it is important to understand the context of where we build architecture, not just relative to other buildings and landscape assets but also to the other animals that are no longer going to feel as welcome once construction starts. Stewardship is a key aspect of sustainability, and thinking about the impact of planting on our neighbors sets the stage for co-habitation. Stewardship is key, because it is about the responsible management of the things that are entrusted to our care. Since humans rank at the top of the food chain, we can lead by example to care for the rest of the links in the chain. As an example of environmental stewardship, we are including indigenous plants at our family beach house that specifically support the depleting habitat of endangered waterfowl. The process of tracking animals is interesting, as a way to learn who lives in the neighborhood and how their brains work. Sometimes a deer or wild turkey will make logical turns around obstacles; other times, they may seemingly roam around aimlessly foraging for lunch. For an amateur tracker like myself, there is no better time to follow animals than after fresh winter snow has fallen.

I had the good fortune of learning from some master trackers on a trip to Africa. We were high in the mountains tracking the silverback gorillas, on a safari through east Africa in Kenya, the Great Rift Valley, and the Aberdare Mountains. The native trackers had the ability to see so many clues in the landscape that it appeared as if they could actually think like the animals. Clues included bent foliage along the gorillas' path through the jungle, broken tree limbs where they had taken down branches to eat the leaves, and matted-down groundcover vegetation where they would rest or sleep. After multiple days of tracking, we found families of gorillas and spent time seeing them with their babies firsthand. It was like being in the Dian Fossey book or the film *Gorillas in the Mist*.

The humanlike expression and curiosity in the eyes of the babies was like seeing into the heart of an ancestor. Personally connecting in the wild with animals that share so much of our DNA is a standing highlight of my travels around the world. The trip was before I got my first foldout sketchbook, so on a future return safari, I will be sure to document the incredible elegance of the landscape, animals, and also the architecture of the Maasai warriors.

USA 4

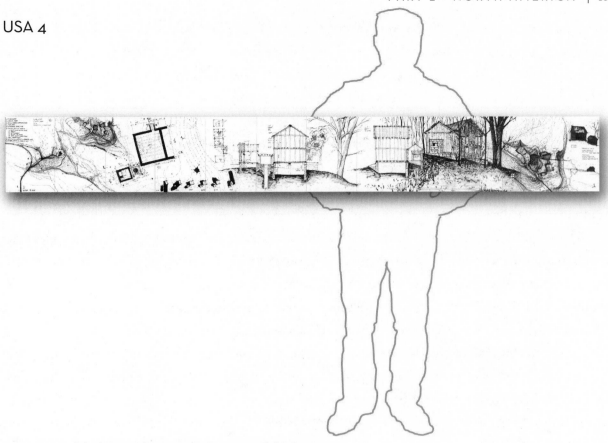

USA 4 Highlights Relevant to Sustainable Design:

Benefit from engaging in a process, with results that may exceed your expectations.

This is an old house on my grandparents' farm that covers a couple of hundred acres near Brickerville, Pennsylvania. Brickerville is past Lititz on the drive out from Lancaster. The area is steeped in American history, in part because the Julius Sturgis Pretzel Bakery in Lititz is the first commercial pretzel bakery in America, founded in 1861. Each year, we would plant some more Christmas trees, and about seven years later, we had an incredible collection of trees that were ready for harvest and display in the living rooms of our house in Washington, DC, my grandparents' house, where we spent Christmas, and my aunt's and uncle's houses. Each year, my uncle would help maintain the trees and clear the underbrush, especially when they were young and more vulnerable. I have a crystal-clear memory of hiking up through the woods to the clearing on the year of the first harvest.

Pennsylvania does not have indigenous evergreen pine trees, so in the fall and winter, the woods are largely devoid of foliage, except for the occasional Pennsylvania mountain laurel that grows no taller than head height. The leaves of the red and white oak trees and the maple, walnut, and birch trees have mostly fallen. Imagine my walk through the brown woods at age twelve, with saw in hand. I am wearing my grandfather's hunting jacket, which was then still too big for me and draped down to my knees. Each year, we have trekked up to check on the tree growth on the day after Thanksgiving. I have waited to see the trees that I had helped plant grow tall enough to cut and bring home. One year, I turned the corner in the woods, and the morning sun had washed across the clearing. I stopped and saw the most beautiful emerald forest of pine, spruce, and fir trees. Bigger than life, the trees unfolded row after row for as far as I can see. Victory! Now, my brother and I had the fun challenge of picking the absolute best, most symmetrical, perfect Christmas tree to bring back to my grandmother. These wild trees were not pruned, so they were mostly asymmetrical.

The tree cutting and transport was an equally fun process. My grandfather had a 1979 Ford Bronco that was bright yellow. It rumbled and roared in four-wheel drive like a military vehicle, and it smelled like fresh-cut firewood … now pine needles. As I prepared these drawings at the woods in my midtwenties, I would see the trees, some of which had grown to over thirty feet tall. We had continued to plant more trees each year so that we staggered the harvests. At the holidays, when I see the first Christmas tree stand setups near our house outside of Philadelphia, I cannot help but remember seeing our emerald forest in the brown woods on the first harvest.

This is an example of a very narrow and seemingly small benefit from engaging in a specific sustainability process, but the memory is large and may last a lifetime. For readers that have school-age children or for educators, this description may inspire projects that build meaningful memories. Even planting a single tree in the backyard or at school has the ability to mark time and enrich the lives of the next generation.

USA 4: Detail (a)

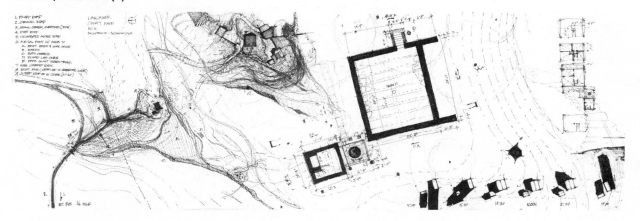

USA 4: Detail (a) Highlights Relevant to Sustainable Design:

We can save energy with the sun without having to install solar panels.

This sketch includes a shadow study at six different times a day. We can optimize the energy efficiency of homes and buildings by understanding when and how the sun is an asset and not a liability. Watching these shadows over multiple times of day and later over multiple seasons and looking at shadows in different regions helped me better understand what people around the world have understood for thousands of years. The seasonal change in the angle of the sun is dramatic and can be used to our advantage with proper building placement and overhang design. As well, the sun's angles change relative to the latitude of the planet, so a house outside of Boston should not look like a house outside of Atlanta. Plus, breakfast rooms should have access to morning eastern light if possible.

If you live in the middle latitudes in America, such as the swatch from the mid-Atlantic states across to upper Central California, you will notice at a Fourth of July picnic that the sun is almost directly overhead. In the summer at around noon, it is almost ninety degrees off of the horizon. By contrast, on New Year's Day at noon, the same sun will be much lower in the sky, closer to twenty-five degrees off of the horizon. This six-month delta is due to the fact that the earth's axis of rotation is not perpendicular to the orbit path around the sun. We can use this to our advantage. For our family's solar home outside of Philadelphia, I oriented the solar portion of the addition to the south, but I also calculated that we needed just over twenty inches of southern overhang to help shade the high summer sun from overheating the house while still allowing the desirable winter sun to shine in and help heat the stone floor. Each latitude on the planet dictates a different overhang distance.

USA 4: Detail (b)

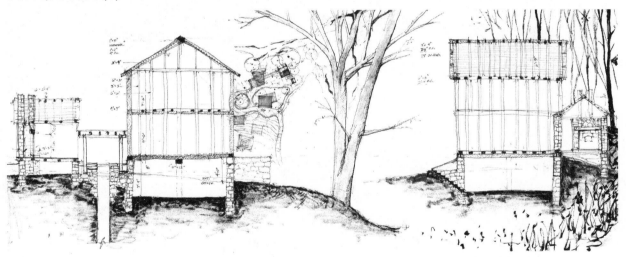

USA 4: Detail (b) Highlights Relevant to Sustainable Design:

Trees count.

Drawing the house and its relation to its immediate environment took much longer than I expected. Identifying the location of the trees rather than cutting them down is the first step toward a respect for the natural context. Siting the trees is time-consuming, and I understand why builders and developers often just cut down all the trees and start from scratch. They do not want to spend time trying to figure out how to work with existing trees and topography. Since the developers make their money selling houses and they do not have to pay the utility bills over the life of each home's occupancy, they are not motivated to build energy-smart houses. When the market starts to ask for smarter homes, the builders may step up to orient the homes to the sun, build calculated overhangs, and leverage the advantages of the existing trees for shading.

USA 4: Detail (c)

USA 4: Detail (c) Highlights Relevant to Sustainable Design:

Overhangs count.

Developers and builders are typically motivated by cost savings and process efficiency over long-term utility cost considerations for the property users. Home builders often work from floor plan templates to reduce design costs, and the templates typically do not have adequate roof overhangs for solar shading purposes. The fix is simple. In many cases, builders trim the rafter overhangs on the job site. By cutting off less of the rafters or buying a slightly longer rafter, they can offer energy-saving advantages for homeowners over the life of the house. Look at overhangs on pre–WW II homes to see the difference in larger overhangs than postwar construction. The same consideration applies to the southern side of commercial buildings. The more we know about the local microclimate, the better, especially when it comes to the location of the sun.

USA 5

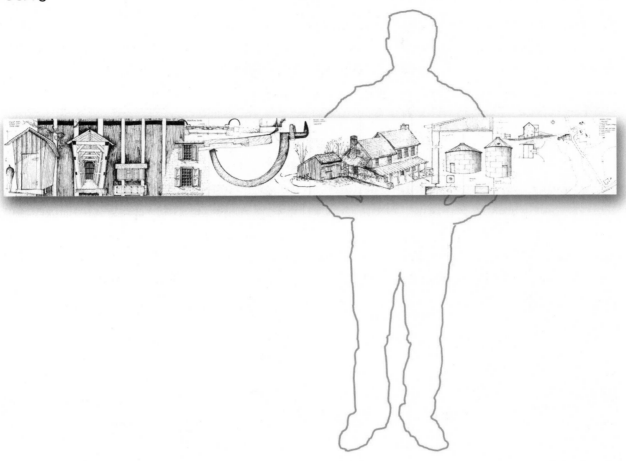

USA 5: Detail (a)

USA 5: Detail (a) Highlights Relevant to Sustainable Design:

Build to last from local materials.

Corncribs are used to store and dry ears of corn for animal feed. Some large-scale commercial corncribs use metal wire or mesh to hold the corn on the cob. This one is built with vertical wooden slats that are spaced with thin gaps to let the air flow through and dry out the corn.

This structure caught my eye for three reasons. First, the level of carpentry detail is impressive for such a utilitarian structure. This one is built with local materials, and it is built to last for many seasons. Second, the shape and proportion are interesting, because very few buildings of any type are wider at the top than at the bottom. This inverted trapezoid allows the farmer to load more corn on a smaller footprint. Third, the quality of light inside is impressive. I was fortunate to see it when it was empty in the off-season. The gaps in the slats let light through in vertical strips that created a unique experience. Overall, regional farm "vernacular" architecture is loaded with design innovation. The surprise of the interior experience, which was so different from the perception from the outside, made me think of other ways to create experiences that challenge preconceptions.

USA 5: Detail (b)

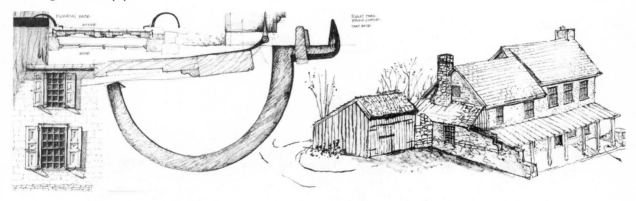

USA 6: Detail (b) Highlights Relevant to Sustainable Design:

We can keep learning more from shutters.

I have drawn and written about shutters multiple times in this book to compare, contrast, and explore paths forward since almost all buildings have window openings. Windows are basically holes in the thermal boundary of a home, given that the insulation value of double-glazed insulating windows is still often only 15 percent of the insulation R value of the walls. So we could rethink shutters as insulation panels to keep the warm air inside in the winter and the cool air inside in the summer. With the latest smart controls, imagine shutters that automatically fold closed or slide across at night to save energy. The lower left corner of this sketch includes windows with a curved shadow at the bottom of each shutter. The large half-circle bracket is not a shutter dog but a traditional solution that accomplishes the goal. These curved brackets hold back the shutters. They are forged from iron and measure about eight to ten inches across.

Additional Highlights Relevant to Sustainable Design:

Rethink the porch.

On the right, the farmhouse with the traditional porch is a great place to relax at the end of the day. The front porch is part of a nostalgic American tradition. Aside from a place to relax, a porch has several advantages. As discussed previously relative to the Hungarian porches and houses in Hungary 4: Detail (c), a mid- to high-density community is strengthened when a porch encourages a "public eye" to help augment the police force. This idea of active and extrovert residency versus passive and introvert residency has not yet been fully explored in an age of increasing technology that focuses our attention internally.

USA 5: Detail (c)

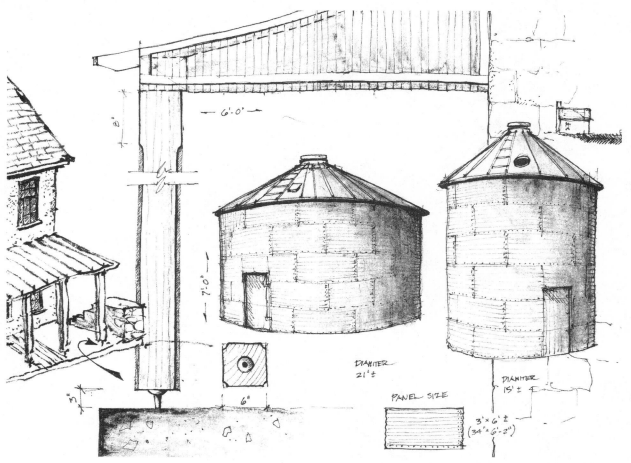

USA 5: Detail (c) Highlights Relevant to Sustainable Design:

We can reduce waste and toxins with smart design.

The post detail on the left of this sketch is an American solution that reminded me of the detail from Asia in a previous sketchbook, Japan 2: Detail (b). The removable section of the Japanese post anticipated that water would eventually damage the wood. This American detail includes a metal "pin" that elevates the wood, so that when it rains the wood does not get wet and wick up the water. Remember that wood is not only porous, but the internal structure is like a set of multiple tiny straws that by natural design draws water up from the ground to feed the leaves in the upper branches. This man-made design simply keeps the rainwater from damaging the bottom of the post, and it eliminates the need for harmful chemical treatments such as pressure-treated lumber.

USA 5: Detail (d)

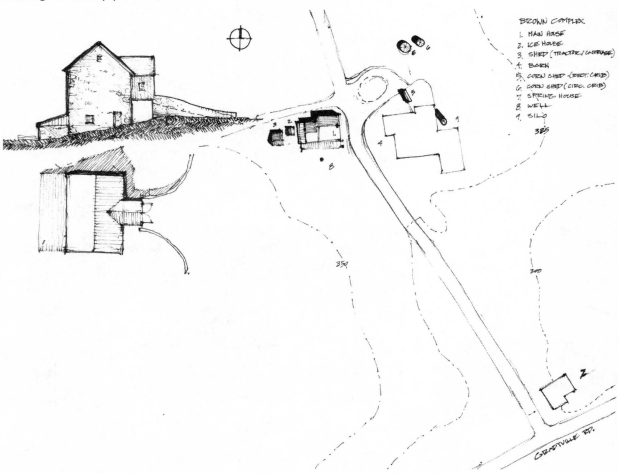

USA 5: Detail (d) Highlights Relevant to Sustainable Design:

Look again at passive geothermal for energy reduction.

I have drawn and written about bank barns multiple times in this book, given that the ground temperature is a beneficial constant and so many areas of the world have hills. This sketch includes at the upper center a small drawing of a bank barn with a curved ramp to a covered bridge that is the entry to the barn on the uphill side. As previously discussed in sketchbooks USA 2: Detail (b) and USA 3: Detail (a), bank barns take excellent advantage of passive geothermal properties of ground temperature.

In the design of our solar home, my wife and I built the lower level of our large family room addition into the hill to take advantage of the passive geothermal properties. The temperature difference in the summer is incredible. One can feel the cooler air inside relative to outside, and the same is true for the warmer ground temperature air in the winter. Our home is included in a documentary series "One Million Acts of Green" and has been featured in magazines, including the cover of *Inventors Digest* magazine. The multiple years of hard work on the strategy, design, and construction have yielded a terrific place to live with very low operating costs, and we hope that our experience inspires others to rethink home design.

USA 6

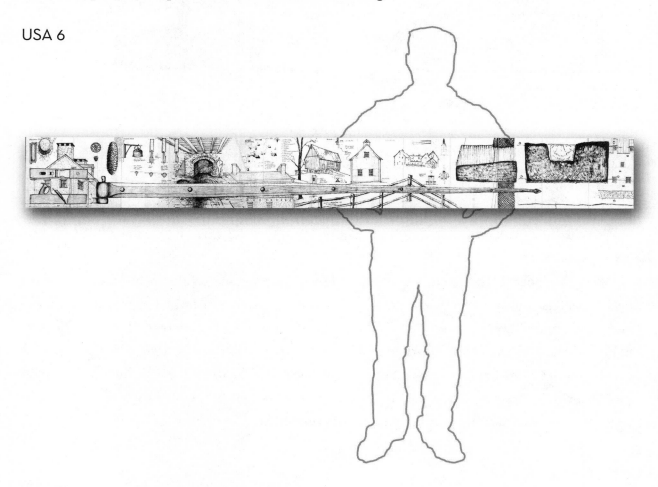

USA 6: Detail (a)

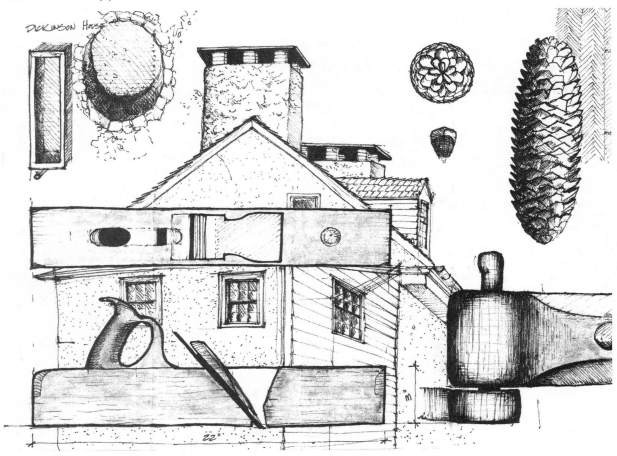

USA 6: Detail (a) Highlights Relevant to Sustainable Design:

We can find inspiration in tools and natural structures.

Over the course of making these drawings in the field, I would occasionally sit down rather than draw standing up. Here are two cases of a hand planer and pinecone, found near where I took a seat. The planer interested me in its simplicity, a block of wood with a metal blade, brace, cavity, and handle.

The pinecone interested me, because I had seen them my whole life, including in the small backyard of our row house in Washington, DC, where I grew up. I had seen many different shapes and sizes, from almost spherical ones to long, skinny ones. I had never really held one up close to look, draw, and take apart. I learned that the seeds are inside, and the flaps or finlike elements protect the seeds. When you see a pinecone that is green and closed, it is holding the seeds and probably still on the tree. If you want to get the seeds out, you may need to heat it up. By the time the pinecone falls from the tree, it is usually dry and open. The natural design is pretty logical.

As the pinecone opens, gravity takes the seeds to the ground, or the wind blows the seeds. Some birds eat the seeds, and some new evergreen trees grow from the cycle.

In this drawing, the plane tool shaves the wood, and the pinecone is a delivery mechanism to produce more future wood. Look closer at things that we may take for granted. Perhaps the storage capacity of the pinecone could inspire the design of cells in a high-efficiency battery design that releases energy on demand in response to a factor such as engine heat in a car.

USA 6: Detail (b)

USA 6: Detail (c)

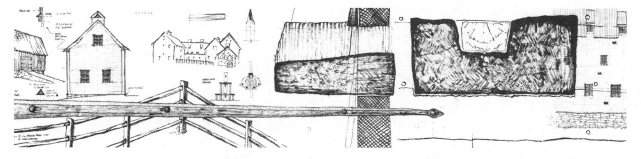

USA 6: Detail (b) and (c) Highlights Relevant to Sustainable Design:

Problem solving through friction reduction.

Friction is the resistance that one surface or object encounters when moving over another. The example of the strap hinge reduces friction by holding the heavy barn door from rubbing along the ground as the farmer opens and closes it. The example of the fence stair and the drains reduces friction at a human energy level by creating efficiencies of motion. Friction reduction is key from farm to business life, and these types of examples demonstrate intelligent approaches to problem solving.

The long strap hinge, about six feet across, is made from wrought iron to support a barn door. I was able to draw it at full scale, given the advantage of the foldout sketchbook structure. In this drawing, the small plan and cross-section drawing of a set of "stairs" in USA 6: Detail (d) illustrates a clever way to get up and over a fence. Rather than building traditional parallel tread and risers on the stairs, this farmer designed and built a stair with as little effort and material as possible. You step once, again, and then cross over, all the more easily than trying to climb over or under a fence.

The drains on the side of a building stick out in odd locations. The story behind the odd façade is that the building is a cloister in Ephrata, Pennsylvania. The residents would regularly clean the floors by washing them down. The dirty water would run to the edge of the room, and then they would push it right out through the wall via the gutter spout. This may have kept them all a little bit more cheerful, because they didn't have to bend over to pick up heavy buckets. The Ephrata Cloister[32] is one of America's earliest religious communities, founded in 1732 by German settlers who placed spirituality over material rewards. This national historic landmark is now administered by the Pennsylvania Historical and Museum Commission.

Beyond friction reduction, the three panel details in the upper left of (b) are from different periods in American history. Restoration architects can study the panel details to identify work from a specific period of time.

USA 6: Detail (d)

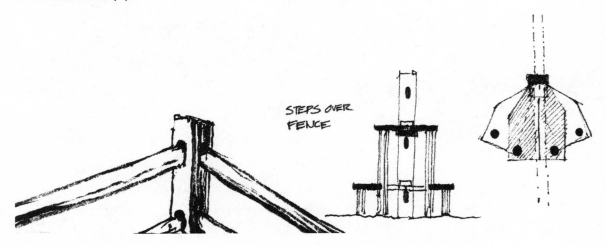

USA 7

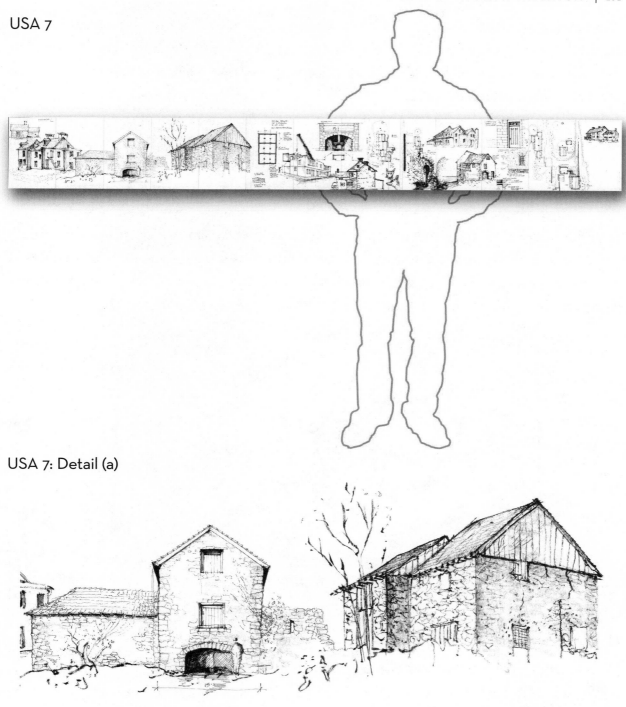

USA 7: Detail (a)

USA 7: Detail (a) Highlights Relevant to Sustainable Design:

We can build structures to last rather than create disposable properties.

Stone construction speaks to more permanence than siding. Material like stone that comes up and out of the earth often has an appealing texture and quality. Some upscale houses have stone façades that are thicker than a veneer, but the applied stone surface is significantly thinner than a load-bearing structural stone wall. The houses look like they have all or partial stone construction. Ironically, many farmers around America and the world have real structural stone houses, but they most likely have a fraction of the annual income of the larger McMansion residents with the fake or nonstructural stone walls.

Builders will make the case that for insulation, the façade stone provides the ability to run stud walls on the inside edge of the stone, and pack the studs with insulation. This is correct, but you could also run stud walls inside a real stone wall. The reality is that the cost of expert masonry craftsman has gone up as the demand has come down. The advantage of a thicker stone wall is that the thermal mass is like a sponge that regulates temperature. By reducing warm and cool temperature peaks from day to night, the walls even out the temperature. Thick walls can reduce fuel costs if designed correctly, in conjunction with interior studs and insulation. We did this in the lower level of our house, which is built into the hill, by filling twelve-inch-thick concrete blocks with concrete and then running the studs with insulation on the interior.

USA 7: Detail (b)

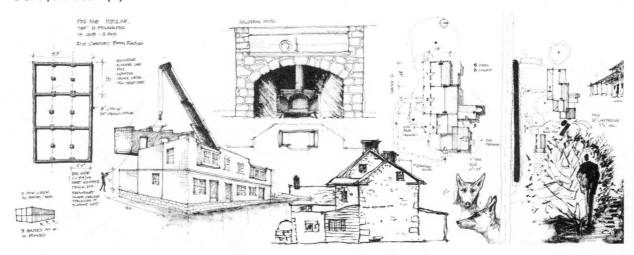

USA 7: Detail (b) Highlights Relevant to Sustainable Design:

We can rethink modular construction as "system built."

We make kitchen cabinets in a controlled workshop or factory environment, so why not make components of homes and buildings versus "stick-built" construction on the job site? This sketch includes a mass-produced prefab unit structure going up in Philadelphia. The process is akin to a modern barn raising in some sense in that the majority of time is spent in preparation before the actual day of construction. In either case, if all goes well, the pieces fit together as planned.

The large, open fireplace is a familiar symbol of Americana that is comforting to us all. Chimneys stick out of pitched roofs. The idea of an architect attempting to design a "complete" house is odd in relation to the history of individual house expansions. Most residences prior to the twentieth century included at least some additions, alterations, and modifications as children came into the world or spouses joined the family. Houses can tell a story about a particular family. A tradition in Vermont dictates planting a pair of poplar trees along the entrance drive for each new birth. Proud grandparents may sit on their porch looking down a long line of sequentially shorter trees. Now, in American culture, we live in a few homes over our lives, leaving less time to set any roots.

USA 7: Detail (c)

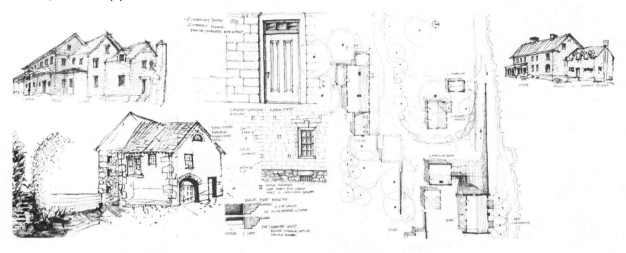

USA 7: Detail (c) Highlights Relevant to Sustainable Design:

Natural light over doors seems like an obvious advantage.

The glass rectangle over the door at the center of this sketch is a transom. In many cases, transom windows are designed so that they are high and narrow enough that they do not pose a security threat. Free light from the sun is certainly more cost-effective than any energy-saving LED light. Our front door has the upper-level glass panes, and during the day, we do not need to turn on the lights in the foyer. Even though the front door is on the north side of the house, the sunlight coming through the earth's atmosphere brings in plenty of light from the north to illuminate the entry. Indirect northern light is an underused asset for many homes.

USA 8

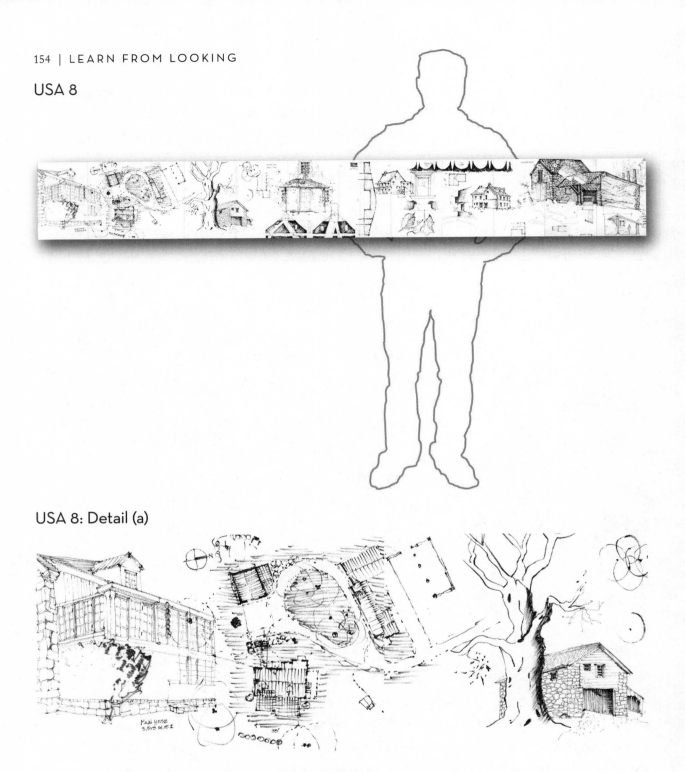

USA 8: Detail (a)

USA 8: Detail (a) Highlights Relevant to Sustainable Design:

Look into solariums for clean air and energy savings.

While northern light is excellent for indirect illumination, southern exposed glass is one critical way to naturally bring heat into a house. Often builders today buy plans and then rotate them around a subdivision to accommodate cul-de-sacs, jogs in the road, or orientation to the street. This *Knots Landing* syndrome is a total disregard for solar orientation and a disservice to the unwary homeowner. The solarium shown here faces southwest to get the maximum exposure during the peak of midday and the afternoon. The builder of this nineteenth-century farmhouse did not have to go to architecture school to learn which way to orient the house.

Solariums are typically great places to grow plants, which help improve air quality. Vegetables also thrive in well-lit areas, and you can reduce heating costs by opening up the doors from a solarium to help passively heat your home. For maximum advantage, tile or stone floors soak up the heat, retain it, and radiate it out into the room. For more information, see the "Sustainable Smart House" chapter in part 3, "Commercial Impact." Make sure to close the doors between the solarium and the main house after the sun goes down in the winter. Plus, to prevent undesirable heat gain in the summer, make sure that the wall between the solarium and the home is adequately insulated. In the evenings, as the outside air cools, you can open the doors to benefit from cross ventilation if the solarium windows are operable. Naturally, it helps to have a large deciduous tree on the southern side of the solarium to shade the summer sun but let the desirable winter sun in to help heat your home. This operation of a home is what I call "active habitation," and it is like operating a sailboat where you need to keep an eye on the weather around you.

USA 8: Detail (b)

USA 8: Detail (b) Highlights Relevant to Sustainable Design:

Look into "green" roofs for energy saving through added insulation.

The center of this sketch shows a roof to a rear entrance of a house that is covered with pine needles. The needles collected over the years because the rear of the house is leeward of the wind. As the needles collected, small weeds and grass shoots began to spring up so that now, the roof is entirely green and mossy. One of the white pine trees that surround the house must have also dropped a pinecone in addition to the needles, because a two-foot sapling is growing on the roof. The sapling is probably three to four years old. This is not a recommended strategy for a green roof, but it reminds me of some flowers growing on the thatch roof ridge of a village hut in Japan.

Apparently the flowers were specially selected to hold the roof together as well as decorate the ridge. The flowers have particularly long roots, which help hold the thatch together. Green roofs are gaining some popularity for commercial properties, given the added insulation value that helps reduce energy costs for climate control. The key is to make sure that the plants selected thrive in the regional microclimate and also are drought tolerant so that there is not an added cost of excessive irrigation.

We usually do not associate live plant material with architecture building systems, but in the case of a trellis or arbor, vines like wisteria can be used effectively. In tropical island climates or states like Florida, arbors with floral vines give off great fragrances and also have the capacity to produce edible berries. The result is an architecture that appeals to three senses in addition to sight: smell, taste, and touch. Sound may even be included if the vine leaves rattle under rain or rustle in the wind.

USA 8: Detail (c)

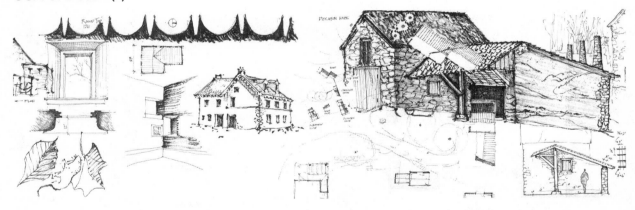

USA 8: Detail (c) Highlights Relevant to Sustainable Design:

Bend the light.

This drawing includes the image of a window and a plan of the thick wall. The wall is curved at the inside edge to allow more natural light to enter the room. One of the great by-products of this functional design move is an appealing aesthetic with the curved plaster and the thick walls. This twelve-inch-thick wall was one of the inspirations for the twelve-inch-thick concrete block walls at our house.

USA 8: Detail (d)

USA 9

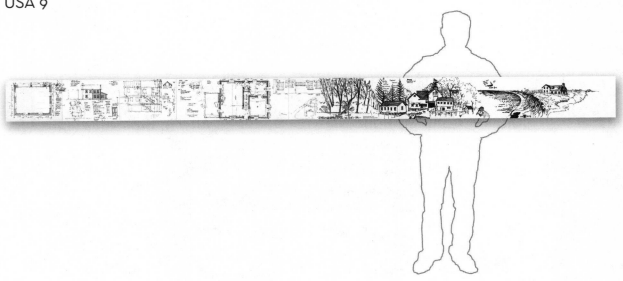

USA 9: Detail (a)

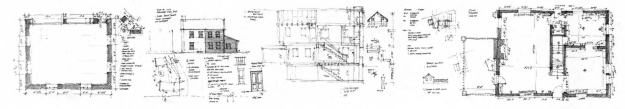

USA 9: Detail (b)

USA 9: Detail (b) Highlights Relevant to Sustainable Design:

Sustainable homesteads speak to American self-reliance and reduce outside energy consumption.

This sketch illustrates a farm complex in Massachusetts. Like the Amish farms, the adjacency of the buildings is critical to the success of the operation. The cupola with the horse weathervane serves the purpose of ventilating the barn, indicating the direction of the wind, and decorating the structure. America was built on self-reliance, and I love staying at properties like this one that embody today the same sense of a work ethic that has made this country so strong.

USA 9: Detail (c)

USA 9: Detail (c) Highlights Relevant to Sustainable Design:

Move with the land.

This is the house that I designed for a friend's parents on a beautiful beachfront property on Nantucket. The challenge in the design was that the land was eroding. So I developed a strategy to have the house built in large components as a system. The system would allow the family or a future homeowner to disengage the large components and literally move the house back on the property away from the eroding vertical sand cliff at the water line.

The American Institute of Architects (AIA) estimates that between 25 and 40 percent of the US solid waste stream is building-related waste. The AIA also estimates that only 20 percent of construction waste or demolition debris is recycled.[33] The component design strategy for the house is intended not only to save money for the homeowner but also to reduce the burden of adding to the waste stream. Reduce, reuse, and recycle starts with reduce and reuse before the more costly recycling efforts. This approach is rooted in waste reduction and material reuse. At a larger scale for residential home construction, builders and developers could take a more focused look at advancing modular and system-built homes. Homeowners, builders, and developers can also add indigenous species of flora around properties to help reduce erosion. Plants that grow well in a specific region are particularly important at shorelines. As an example, beach grass is ideal for sand dunes. In 2012, Hurricane Sandy devastated Seaside Heights in part because of the lack of vegetation on sand dunes.

USA 10: New England

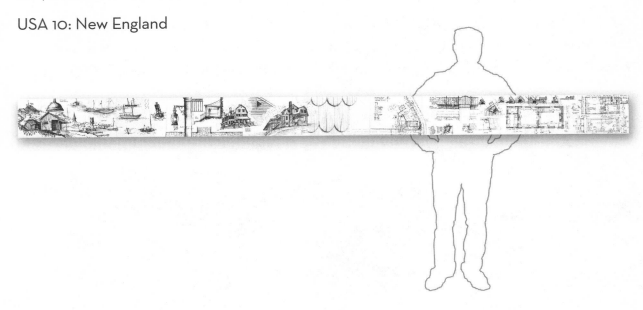

USA 10: New England Detail (a)

USA 10: New England Detail (a) Highlights Relevant to Sustainable Design:

Remote locations often require a keen look at energy, given high costs to deliver each kW.

Martha's Vineyard is an island off Cape Cod, Massachusetts, that is something of a time capsule of cultural memory. Like its neighboring island, Nantucket, these places have preserved the look of their habitat by restricting certain building materials and typical fast-food franchises and overbearing shop signs. The control with the committee approval process is strict to say the least. The intended homogeneity is extreme and potentially stifles an inventive sprit of progress. A beach-side house, with a solarium, facing the water also has an outside shower. An outside shower is the best place to remove the day's sand and think about the evening's activity. The feel of wood grain under foot is more pleasant than a slick tub or tile, and hardwood versus softwood helps reduce splinters. This sketch also shows a few boats as well as a roofline of the largest town on the island, Edgartown. Like many New England towns, Edgartown is distinguished from a distance by its church towers. Churches and school and municipal buildings that play a spiritual and civic role in binding a community are typically the tallest and largest structures.

Only in the last hundred years have commercial buildings and office space overtaken the height of other buildings. In Washington, DC, the federal government restricts the height of commercial buildings. Since office buildings cannot exceed the height of the US Capitol dome, none are taller than about ten stories. In Philadelphia, the same rule was true for the statue of William Penn on top of City Hall. However, in the 1980s, a developer discovered that the law was not actually written down, so he built taller, and others soon followed. Back on the islands of Nantucket and Martha's Vineyard, one of my favorite stories is how cobblestones arrived on the island to pave the streets. Apparently, the trading ships, used in the 1600s and 1700s for whaling, would need ballast weight to steady the empty ships. They used oval river rock stones the size of a grapefruit. Some of the ships traveling from either mainland America or England would empty their ballast prior to loading whale meat, oil, and candles. What better for the town to do with the stones than to roll them out and pave the muddy roads?

USA 10: New England Detail (b)

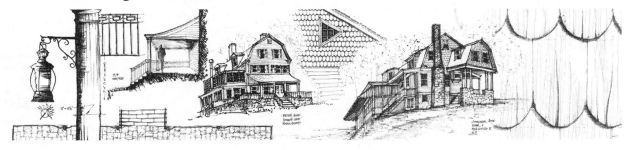

USA 10: New England Detail (b) Highlights Relevant to Sustainable Design:

We can learn from an energy-smart river house.

This sketch illustrates a "fish-scale" house in New Jersey, just south of Manhattan. The house watches over the river and also includes a solarium porch. For the summer, an operable shade protects the glass. I do not understand why today the mass market is so reluctant to use the sun to help heat our houses. Given the increased efficiency of furnaces, we do not have to use the sun, but with rising costs of energy (typically 3 percent per year over the past half century), at some point we may want to use the sun. The fish-scale shingles on this river house are well suited to their context, since this house is on the water, and there are fish in the river. The triangle window is appealing, and it reminds me of a flag on a boat or at a sailing marina or yacht club. This triangle window also reminds me of the geometric-shaped windows in Japan. For comparison, an excerpt from Japan 5: Detail (b) is here:

USA 11: Gauley River, West Virginia

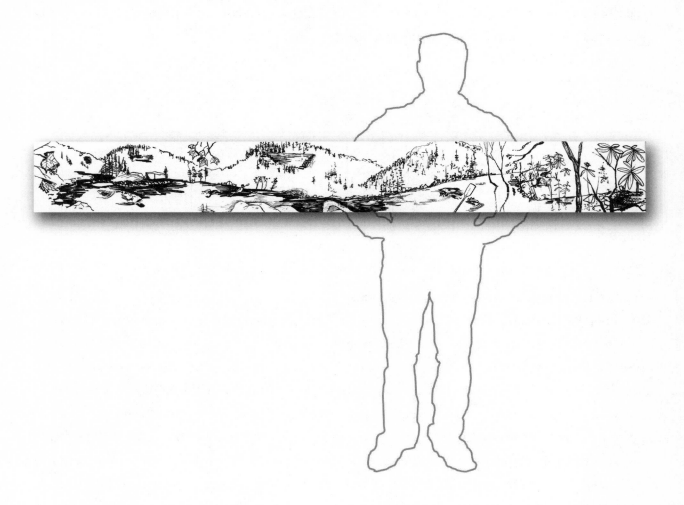

USA 11: Gauley River, West Virginia: Detail (a)

USA 11: Gauley River, West Virginia: Detail (a) Highlights Relevant to Sustainable Design:
Experience the power of nature firsthand.

I was invited on a whitewater rafting trip. The experience was incredible because we scheduled the trip just after the hydroelectric dam on the Gauley River[34] was opened up. So the water created a wild ride. We stopped along the way at a point in the river without all of the rapids, which gave me just enough time to sketch the scene and record some of the vegetation.

Experiencing the power of nature firsthand has helped me become a better steward of the environment. The power is evident in how the water has carved its way through the terrain for so many years. Gauley is one of the most popular whitewater runs in the eastern United States for advanced rafting. The river is the primary feature of the Gauley River National Recreation Area, and my sense of stewardship comes into play for a simple reason. I would like my children and future grandchildren to experience the thrill and awe that I felt.

The water was not always clean. Following the Industrial Revolution up into the first quarter of the twentieth century, Gauley was know as the "River of Ink" due to industrial pollution. The West Virginia State Wild Life League stepped in, and they were successful in obtaining funds to clean up the Gauley River in 1927. This is a positive example of advocacy in support of the common good and protection of natural resources.

The region also has some interesting post-Ice Age history. Dating back to around 10,000 BC, Paleoamericans possibly used the northern valleys leading to the Gauley River for their big-game hunting. Paleoamericans were the first people who entered the Americas during the final glacial episodes of the late Pleistocene period (2,588,000 to 11,700 BC).

Big-Game Hunting for Power: The US Army Corps of Engineers completed the Gauley River Dam in Summersville, West Virginia, in 1966, and in 2001, the power was harnessed for hydroelectricity to generate 80 megawatts (MW). One megawatt is equal to one million watts and powers at least 750 homes. So the Gauley River Dam can power about 60,000 homes. For context, the Hoover Dam is twenty-five times larger, generating over 2,000 MW and powering well over a million homes. According to the Energy Information Administration, hydropower accounted for 7 percent of US electric generation in 2013, representing 52 percent of renewable generation that year.[35]

Natural power along with advocacy, recreation, and historic legacy can all serve as motivators for stewardship and sustainability.

USA 12: Sun Valley, Idaho

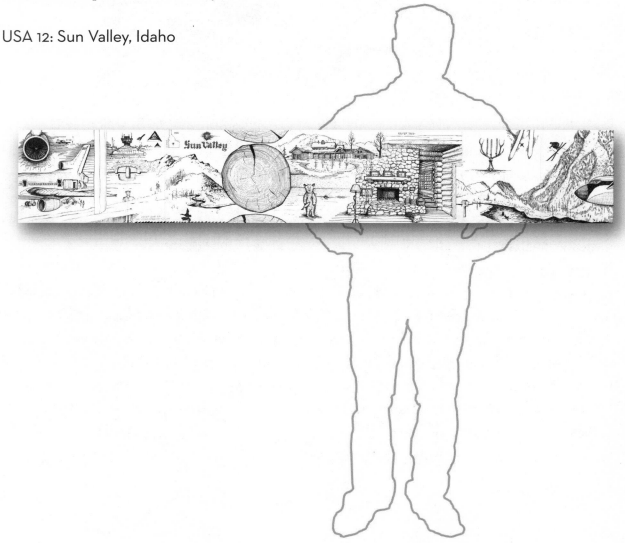

USA 12: Sun Valley, Idaho: Detail (a)

USA 12: Sun Valley, Idaho: Detail (a) Highlights Relevant to Sustainable Design:

Go local with local materials, techniques, and talent.

American settlers built their homes with local wood. Since the early days of the western frontier, pioneers did not have the luxury of sawmills or the big-box home improvement centers that we take for granted today. Log homes were a popular means of building shelter, and the tradition continues today, with the addition of modern trappings such as climate control, Wi-Fi, smart-control lighting, high-definition television, and more. Many of the material preparation and carpentry techniques used on this house are derivative of time-tested processes passed down over multiple generations in the western United States.

One of the key local advantages for Idaho log cabin builders centers around the drying process. If a log is not dry at its core, it may settle, crack, or twist. Many kiln-dried logs are only dry on the outside inch, while the core often remains green with the higher moisture content. Idaho's arid climate helps dry the logs, and seasoned suppliers and builders understand the value of aging the wood for top-quality construction.

The source of the wood is local to the region, with logs often cut from standing dead timbers such as lodgepole pine or Douglas fir. Builders in Idaho have used these species for generations based on durability and also top insulating qualities.

USA 12: Sun Valley, Idaho: Detail (b)

USA 12: Sun Valley, Idaho: Detail (b) Highlights Relevant to Sustainable Design:

Continue to go local with local materials, techniques, and talent.

This house has a stone hearth with the stones sourced from the region. Local river stones were used by early American settlers of the west for creating the critical hearth for cooking and heating. Those two functions are largely replaced with stoves and heating, ventilating, and air-conditioning (HVAC) systems, but the tradition of using local river stones continues today. The stones have thermal mass, which stores and radiates the heat well after the fire is out.

By contrast, the settlements of the East Coast colonies had more brick fireplaces and chimneys than stone, in part because clay was more readily available in those regions than stone. The "Think Global. Act Local." mantra of the green movement, initiated in the 1970s, has many roots, and the advantages of using local materials are numerous. At very least, local material sourcing reduces transportation cost and emissions output.

USA 12: Sun Valley, Idaho: Detail (c)

USA 12: Sun Valley, Idaho: Detail (c) Highlights Relevant to Sustainable Design:

Continue to go local with local materials, techniques, and talent.

This river behind the house is loaded with river rocks as well as fish for fly-fishing. At the local level, the river is the life force. You could literally use the river rocks to build your hearth, then catch the fish and cook them over the fire. This drawing includes a candlestick holder for three candles that is made from the antlers of the local mountain elk. This reminded me of how the Native Americans would intelligently use every part of the bison or deer. I like the idea of the local antlers used for some purpose rather than just a stuffed trophy head mounted on a wall.

USA 13: Adirondack New York—Lake House

USA 13: Adirondack New York—Lake House Highlights Relevant to Sustainable Design:

Engage all of your senses.

Before our daughter, Carter, was born, my wife, Cynthia, and I were fortunate to get invited along with our son, Calvin, to stay with friends at their family retreat on a lake in the Adirondack Mountains. The combination of indoor and outdoor living was completely refreshing along with all of the sports and activities. Calvin also had a blast with the other kids catching frogs, hiking, and canoeing. We engaged all five senses in new ways. Sight, sound, taste, touch, and smell are often taken for granted in our daily digital-centric lives. Seeking out new ways to amplify our senses creates a springboard for also sharing experiences and reinforcing memory. The simple connection with nature void of digital screen time overload is most likely a simple stepping-stone for children as well as adults to move toward sustainable thinking.

USA 14: Annapolis, Maryland—Severn River with Naval Academy beyond the left bridge

USA 14: Annapolis, Maryland—Severn River with Naval Academy beyond the left bridge Highlights Relevant to Sustainable Design:

Learn from sailing.

Sailing is about as ecofriendly as it gets when it comes to transportation over water. I grew up sailing in and around Annapolis decades ago, and I now use the "active awareness" aspect of sailing as an example in describing active awareness for inhabiting homes. We can always default to smart controls that do the work for us, such as lights that turn off automatically when we leave an office-building restroom. However, there are other layers of consideration regarding outdoor influences.

Since winds shift, we designed our house with casement windows and alternated the hinge sides so that we can naturally ventilate the house by opening up a few windows at different times of the day. We have air-conditioning backup, but for a good portion of spring and summer, we do not need to use it. Plus, when we need it, our solar panels help cover the cost of electricity.

Sailors keep an eye on the direction of the wind, and when we moved into our house outside of Philadelphia, I noticed that in the fall the wind would start in the morning coming from the northeast and then often shift in the afternoon to the northwest. The fallen leaves in our backyard would shift slightly from east to west and back again through October and November. Our neighbors would dedicate time or resources to blow the leaves, and I fell in line. I soon realized that the time and carbon emissions output of the leaf blowers was antithetical to the spirit of our sustainable design life. So I used local fieldstones to build multiple planting bed walls along either side of the yard. We were in the process of renovating the house and digging out our "bank barn" family room into the hill, so I used the extra soil to regrade key areas of the yard. This enabled me to set the planting beds from ankle to shin depth. I designed them as leaf traps, stepped down below the grass lines.

Now, between Halloween and Thanksgiving, the wind helps "sweep" the yard clean, and I traded my old carbon-output leaf blower to a neighbor for a carbon-fiber race bicycle.

Closing Perspective on the American Experience

We started America with thirteen colonies that each had varying degrees of sustainability and reliance relative to each other and to England. In 1776 when our founding fathers signed our Declaration of Independence, we fought for autonomy from England but not from each other. We literally teamed up to beat a common foe and in so doing established this great nation that is our United States. With fifty states and almost a quarter millennium of history under our belt, we have the opportunity to increase our prosperity and lead the world in the twenty-first century.

$$13 \quad\quad 1776 \quad\quad 50$$

Some states are rich in natural resources, while others have thriving commercial hubs. Some have more human capital and education resources, while others have harbors, rivers, or other transportation assets. The free market is the best engine to align these resources, and the latest domestic fossil fuel discoveries may shift our dependence on foreign oil. When the colonists opened for business prior to the American Revolution, they did not rely on imported oil. In fact, we were a net exporter, selling more whale oil overseas than we consumed. Over the beginning of the twenty-first century, our dependency on imported oil has been about 40 percent, but the latest discoveries may shift that down to 20 percent.

In the United States, we currently use about 40 percent of our energy for buildings, but the 28 percent of our energy used for transportation drinks up most of the oil.[36] In thinking about transportation, I wanted to share something that most readers may have in common. Before we started driving cars around age sixteen, we each most likely learned to ride a bicycle. The stepping-stone to a two-wheeler is often a tricycle. This may not seem relevant to fossil fuels, but the following insight on rethinking our earliest form of transportation may spark some ideas about challenging preconceptions. I bought a special two-wheel bike for my son when he was just two years old. I was intrigued by the bike design that my mother had seen used in Germany, because it did not have pedals or training wheels. It is now referred to as a children's "run" bike, because the little kids run along and learn to balance before pedaling. This is the opposite of a tricycle that teaches pedaling before balance. The net result is that we never needed to buy tricycles for either of our kids, and they were both riding two-wheeled pedal bikes when they were just three years old. Perhaps we can rethink single-passenger and public transportation at a more aggressive level.

Twenty-First-Century America

Moving forward, we can advance sustainable design and challenge the status quo in sectors ranging from vehicles to buildings and from consumer goods to food production. In this century, America has the ability to eliminate our dependency on foreign oil. We can learn from other countries, and hopefully the drawings that precede and follow this chapter shed some new light on the opportunities at hand.

We can elevate American democratic independence from the eighteenth century to American energy independence in the twenty-first century and build a sustainable future for more generations to come.

8 CENTRAL AMERICA

Mexico 1

Mexico 1: Detail (a)

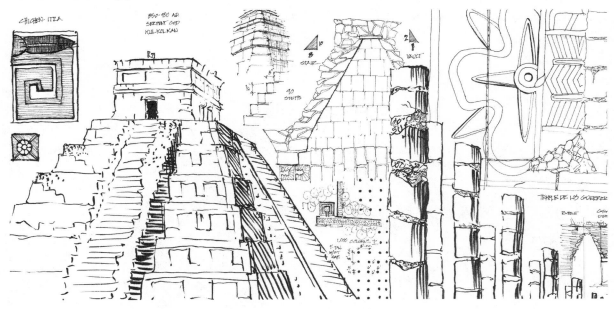

Mexico 1: Detail (a) Highlights Relevant to Sustainable Design:

We can learn from history about how to avoid depleting natural resources and cultural collapse.

The Yucatan Peninsula in Mexico was home to the Mayan people. Two thousand years ago, this highly sophisticated culture not only developed calendars and massive step pyramids but also observatories and major sports venues that rivaled the architecture of Egypt and Rome.

One of the mysteries of the Mayan ruins is why the cities did not continue to flourish. Some research indicates that the large cities had several hundred thousand residents, so it is unusual on the world stage that expansion would not continue. Thermal imaging cameras have revealed foundation stones for structures that sprawled out way beyond what was initially perceived as the city limits. This early example of suburban sprawl also demonstrates a pattern of clear-cutting the indigenous planting and trees to make room for the growing populations. Some further research indicates that the lack of planting may have left the Mayans vulnerable to flooding and mudslides, given that the plants were no longer available to absorb the water. In flooding situations, disease can more quickly contaminate the water system and lead to sickness and death at accelerated levels. The rich Mayan culture may have grown too big too fast and set a fatal path to their own extinction.

Dr. Seuss in his children's book *The Lorax* painted a clear picture of the dangers of cutting down the Truffula trees, and the once thriving business and community built by the Once-ler all but vanished. There are most likely many contributing factors to cultural collapse, but when we talk about "save the planet," we really just need to perhaps "save ourselves." Finding cost-effective ways to slow the depletion of natural resources and fossil fuels makes sense for today and tomorrow.

Mexico 1: Detail (b)

Mexico 2: Detail (b) Highlights Relevant to Sustainable Design:

Answers may lie in front of us to help each other.

In the northern Yucatan, at the pre-Columbian Mayan archeological site of Chichen Itza, I came across this sacred cenote "Well of Sacrifice."[37] Apparently, the Maya sacrificed objects made of gold and other materials as well as humans by throwing them into the well as a means to worship their rain god.

In chapter 3, "Critical Thinking," section with the title, "Moving a Mountain," I wrote about my role interviewing high school seniors for the Jefferson Scholarship at my alma matter, the University of Virginia. The interview students are at the very top of their class, and this cenote inspired a question that I have asked each of them over the past decade.

Here is the question: "Imagine that you and a friend are in a rain forest with all of the trees and the vines, studying deforestation on a field project. Your friend falls into a hole that is thirty feet deep. He/she is strong enough to climb up three feet each day but is so tired at the end of the day that they fall back down two feet. How long does it take your friend to get out of the hole?" The most common answer that comes pretty quickly is thirty days. Out of eight students, about six say thirty days, and only one typically says twenty-seven or twenty-eight days. The fewer days is mathematically correct because on the second or third to last day, the friend is up and out of the hole before falling back down. Each year, one in eight students asks, "Can I help my friend with the vines?" This is the response that I look for, because they listen to the question, which intentionally includes a reference to the "vines." They go beyond the math to think about the context of the situation. Answering a question with a question is harder than people think, because we are often programmed to respond with answers.

Each year, out of the pool of about four boys and four girls, who are in many cases the valedictorians of their high school, the response to help a friend has come from the girls, with only an exception in one year. With a "research" set over about a decade, this is an interesting finding, in that the year-over-year results are so similar. The vast majority of these top-ranking high school students are programmed with a default focus on math to solve problems. Some students have asked great questions like, "How tall is my friend?" "What is the vertical reach of my friend?" or "Does the hole fill up with water to create any floatation?" With each of these questions, the students are probing for the answer that nets out in math versus helping their friend on the first day. This path of student response questions is constructive if it leads to an answer fewer than thirty days, because in so many aspects of life, business, or sustainable design, if you can reach the goal in less time or energy expense, you have created efficiencies.

After seeing the early response pattern from students, I started asking the same question to peers in their forties and other adults. I also asked other students of varying age who were my friends' children or college students who worked as interns at our office. The results held. About 75 percent say thirty days, 12.5 percent say twenty-seven or twenty-eight days, and 12.5 percent ask if they can help their friend with the vine on the first day. Interestingly, beyond the students, the gender results were not as pronounced regarding the "help a friend" response. In particular, a male friend, who is the chief operating officer of a solar company, and another male friend, who is a former US marine with multiple combat tours to the Middle East, both said, "One day or less. I'll get them out with the vines or whatever I can find." They skipped over the question of using the vines and went straight to the declarative response. I asked about why they thought so many other people tried to solve for the math. The energy professional and the soldier both said that they needed to rely on teammates. Ask a colleague or friend the question to see their response.

This idea of teamwork and synergy will become increasingly important in a global energy economy where no one individual, company, political party, or country can get us out of a hole alone.

Mexico 1: Detail (c)

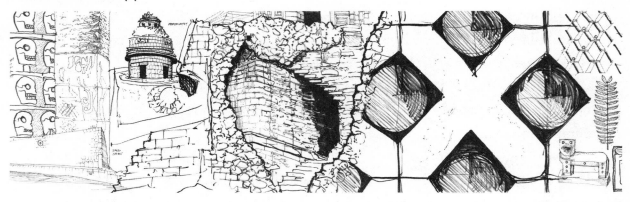

Mexico 1: Detail (d)

Mexico 2

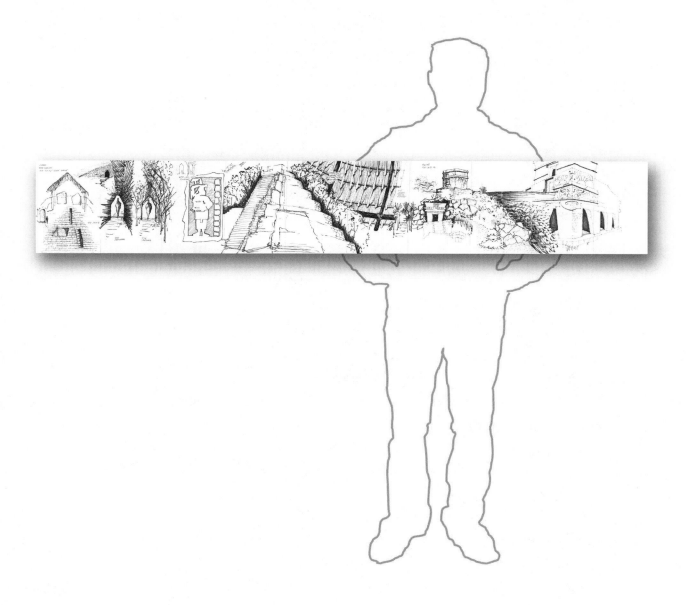

Mexico 2: Detail (a)

Mexico 2: Detail (a) Highlights Relevant to Sustainable Design:

See the influence of your immediate world.

Traveling around the world has provided perspective and the ability to compare and contrast elements that embody sustainability but are often far apart in distance, origin, and initial intent. As I explored the Mayan ruins, I quickly noticed that the architecture was lower and squatter than the verticality of the European cathedrals and church spires. I also noticed that there were not any forests with the same type of tall deciduous trees as in Europe. As I continued to explore the dense jungle of foliage of the Yucatan Peninsula, I found that the leaves were often either directly overhead or very close overhead. In one of the ancient ruins, I found a doorway that reminded me of the opening along the jungle paths.

This sketch illustrates the parallel shape of the opening between the foliage and the architecture. By contrast, the experience of walking in fall or winter in the woods of a deciduous forest is diametrically different due to the verticality.

My experiences as a child hiking and exploring with my brother and parents helped provide the "good" looking skills that I describe in the chapter "Power of Observation." Most people would not connect the dots between foliage and architecture or think to compare a Mayan ruin to a European cathedral. This small example of critical thinking is about questioning the origin of something that many may take for granted. I was looking at what inspired people to build as a *why* versus a *what*.

Mexico 2: Detail (b)

Mexico 2: Detail (b) Highlights Relevant to Sustainable Design:

See the influence of your immediate world (continued).

I do not believe that it is unrealistic to think that the Mayan people a thousand years ago, or the Europeans several hundred years ago, mimicked their natural environment. The Gothic-style pointed arches of great cathedrals and the stained-glass windows convey the feeling of light coming through the woods as you walk down the nave. The Europeans carved biblical stories in stone at various palaces in their religious buildings to teach the people, who in many cases did not have the ability to read. The Mayans carved "glyphs" in their buildings, which like the European carvings told stories, as did the Egyptians with their hieroglyphs.

Without access to see other countries via sea or air travel, let alone print publications, TV, or the Internet, the Mayans did not have a reference as inspiration to build structures that were tall and thin. They created with their own means a form of architecture based on the natural world around them. They did not have the materials and technology at the time to build lean structures, so this observation is more about intent than capacity.

In the twenty-first century, "lean" has become a term for efficiency, used initially by the Massachusetts Institute of Technology (MIT) following studies of Japanese manufacturing processes. Perhaps in the 1970s, we were manufacturing cars in the United States based on what we knew at the time and not the levels of quality assurance and automation that were deployed half a world away. If we look beyond our immediate frame of reference, then we can question what we do and how we do it to decide if there is a different path for consideration.

The gas-guzzling cars of the seventies are largely now extinct, and Detroit had to file bankruptcy. The city became in many ways a ruin. We have the fortitude and savvy to build it back, but we let it slip away in part because we were more inwardly focused than externally conscious. The definition of insanity is doing the same thing over and over and expecting a different result. For too long, we repeated the production of inefficient cars that also did not have the quality assurance and as much reliability as the Japanese imports at that time. We were building cars that were unsustainable, and that led to the economy of a whole city that became unsustainable.

Mexico 2: Detail (c)

Mexico 2: Detail (d)

Closing Perspective on the Mayan Experience

The word "old" is relative to the specific elements of comparison. The Mayan ruins are certainly old relative to all of the architecture in the United States since the founding of the country and most of the standing architecture in Europe, Asia, and around the world. The adage "With age comes wisdom" inspires me to think that the old Mayan ruins have a wise story to tell. Sometimes we just need to pause to look and extract some information from the awesome silence of the millennia.

The wisdom of the ruins may come in the form of lessons in restraint. The successful growth of the Mayan culture and the resulting population increases at urban centers may have contributed to their demise. By clearing so much vegetation to expand their cities and suburbs two thousand years ago, they were the first major "sprawl" culture. Their system became unsustainable with a ripple effect: less vegetation, amplified flood damage, increased water contamination, more disease, and death. They simply did not manage their growth. Across the nations of the world, we have doubled our global population in just the last forty years. Sprawl has often replaced regional farming or woodlands, and fresh drinking water is a commodity that we should not take for granted. We have the means to manage our growth sustainably, and looking back often helps guide the path forward.

9 BIG CITIES

Big City 1: New York City

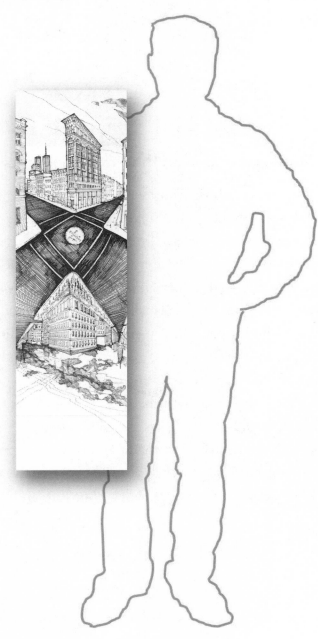

Big City 1: New York City: Detail (a)

Big City 1: New York City: Detail (b)

Big City 1: New York City: Details (a) and (b) Highlights Relevant to Sustainable Design:

We can learn from a vertical city.

This sketch is from Broadway and Broom Street in Lower Manhattan's SoHo looking south toward the World Trade Center, before the tragedy of 9/11, and north toward Midtown's Chrysler Building.

The illustration is several feet tall and is the only one to date that is vertical versus horizontal. This seems only fitting, given that New York is such a vertical city. Having lived and worked in New York, I have profound respect for this engine of urban efficiency. The density of population and the subway system make Manhattan more energy-efficient per capita than any city in America. The logic is relatively simple. If you live in a high-rise apartment, condo, or co-op, the shared walls reduce the loss of heat and air-conditioning to the exterior climate. The same is true for a high-rise office building versus a single-story office park with climate control lost through the walls and roof. In addition to this urban "huddling," if you walk to work or take the subway or bus, then you are dramatically reducing your individual energy consumption over auto commutes.

Even if you take a taxi, a car service, or Uber, the island of Manhattan and the surrounding boroughs are geographically small relative to the distances that average Americans commute. The net transportation residential and commercial energy consumption pales in comparison to less dense planning configurations.

People think of California as the "green" and "ecofriendly" hub of the United States, but Manhattan may be the greenest place to live in America when it comes to transportation impact per capita, by the extent of the subway system and the sheer density and proximity from home to work. In sprawling horizontal cities like Los Angeles, there is probably not a number of hybrid, plug-in, hydrogen, or future cold fusion "flux capacitor" cars that would bring the carbon footprint level down to the per-capita level relative to residents of Manhattan in New York City and other vertical cities around America and the world.

Big City 2: Los Angeles

Big City 2: Los Angeles Highlights Relevant to Sustainable Design:

We can learn from a horizontal vehicle-centric city.

This sketchbook is over six feet long and includes a 360-degree panorama from the rooftop of Le Montrose Hotel in West Hollywood. In 1996 when I captured this scene, hybrid cars did not exist. The city had the burden of a sprawl of freeways and cars bumper to bumper. While home and business owners can do little at this point about the lack of viable public transportation, the community of Los Angeles, like a significant portion of California, has embraced energy efficiency. Hybrid cars adorn the freeways, and residents of LA are turning lemons into lemonade. I lived and worked in California and applaud the appetite for sustainability.

Los Angeles, like many US cities, had electric streetcars during the first half of the twentieth century. From the late 1930s up to about 1950, companies like National City Lines (NCL) took control of the electric streetcar systems in about two dozen cities. NCL's investors included the top US companies with an interest in fossil fuel and automobile transportation, such as Standard Oil, General Motors, and Firestone Tire. Over about a decade, NCL converted many of the electric streetcars to buses. In 1949, most of the companies were convicted of conspiracy to monopolize interstate commerce due to the sale of buses, fossil fuel, and supplies to NCL. However, they were acquitted of conspiring to monopolize the transit. While conspiracy theorists blame the companies for the decline of electric public transit, there are many other factors that were involved such as fixed-rate streetcar fares and the Great Depression.[38] Regardless of the conspiracy theories, the reduction in the number of electric streetcars and the increase in the roads and automobiles changed the transportation system in American cities, and the companies may have just accelerated the decline.

Big City 2: Los Angeles: Detail (a)

Big City 2: Los Angeles: Detail (b)

Big City 2: Los Angeles: Detail (c)

Closing Perspective on the Big-City Experience

Cities are a rich concentration of information. New York and Los Angeles anchor the East and West Coasts as extreme examples of tall and sprawl, while most cities are less extreme with a combination of density and surrounding suburbs.

It is not too late to reconsider electric streetcars or green energy city buses. Over the fall of 2015, I was in one of the combination cities that is an example of tall and sprawl, with advanced transportation. When visiting Denver, Colorado, for a family wedding, I was delighted to see the Sixteenth Street Mall[39] in action. The city permanently closed the street to cars in favor of pedestrians and free buses that run on ecofriendly compressed natural gas. The 1.25-mile "mall" has over three hundred stores and fifty restaurants. Denver also offers shared transportation via car2go smart cars throughout the city. People register to drive the cars for a fee, reducing the parking clutter in so many cities. I have written about European town centers in this book, and the Sixteenth Street Mall along with the shared transportation embody the principles that add value to the urban experience. Hopefully, the outdoor pedestrian mall in Denver serves as a model for other cities.

 ISLANDS

Islands 1: Hawaii

Islands 1: Hawaii: Detail (a)

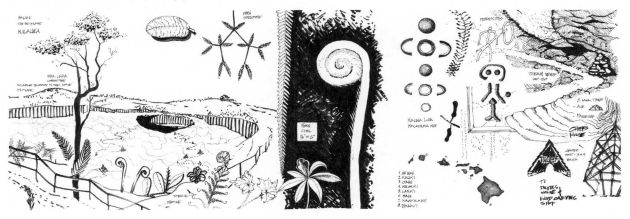

Islands 1: Hawaii: Detail (a) Highlights Relevant to Sustainable Design:

We can learn from natural form.

On my first trip to Hawaii, in my late twenties during the second half of the 1990s, I was focused more on finding the best surf and windsurfing spots than sketchbook documentation. However, I did record a range of organic structures. The coil of the ferns caught my eye, mostly due to the geometric elegance of how the fern uncoils as it grows. The simple compact nature of its structure is highly efficient. As the seemingly simple organic form uncoils, the complexity and sophistication is revealed with each of the flanking members and internal structure to distribute nutrients and photosynthesis. Years later, I thought of this fern when I read one of the letters from my father.

As I mentioned at the end of chapter 6 on Hungary, every week from January 2006 through September 2007, my father sent me an e-mail letter with a quote that he felt would inspire or teach me something useful. He included in his communications a hand-drawn sun that came to represent for me his fundamental optimism in the good within the human spirit. I believe that he provided this ongoing set of letters for me to also share with my children.

Here is the letter that reminded me of the fern in Hawaii.

May 22, 2006

Dear Charlie,   For your thought #18

Simplicity is the ultimate sophistication.

Unknown source (multiples: Leonardo da Vinci, Clare Boothe Luce, Leonard Thiessen +
Used in 1977 by Apple Computer for its Apple II brochure)

More things get complicated than get simple. Making a telephone call, finding an insurance company with affordable medicine, filing a tax form, or eating healthy things has become more complex and contradictory than ever before. Even in art and architecture, complexity and contradiction are still the dominating factors. Venturi is historical, but look at the work of Calatrava or Gehry.

Technology increased our overall efficiency and productivity, but the average person's knowledge has fallen behind. The computer, the Internet, and mobile phones have helped a lot. Many simple people learned and took advantage of it, but many more fell behind. Now a girl in China can call her boyfriend to chat with him about love or about a rainy day, but millions are still dying of hunger or AIDS in Africa without any hope.

The gaps between those who know how and those who don't know how are getting bigger every day, and we still don't know how to reduce this gap.

Love, Dad

Islands 1: Hawaii: Detail (b)

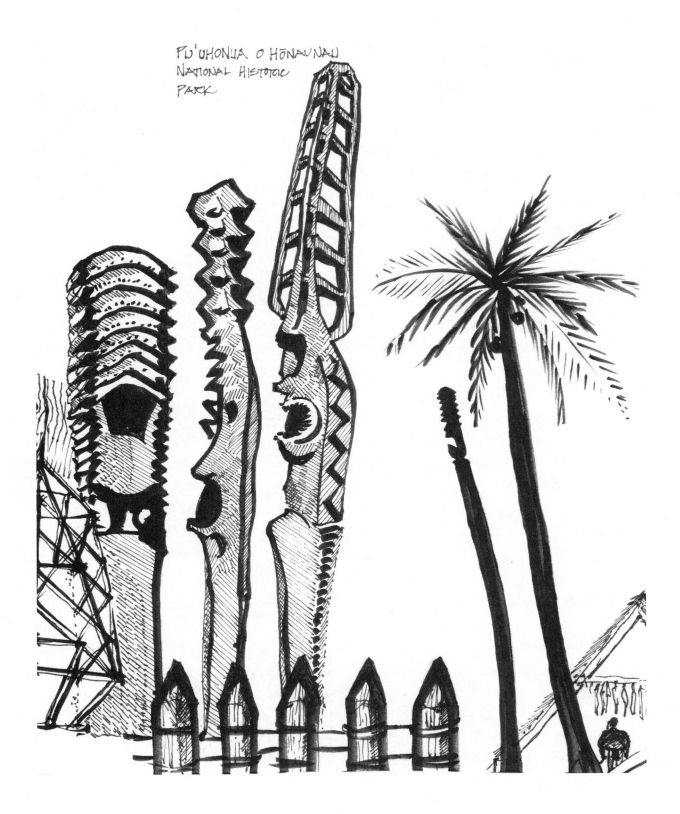

Islands 1: Hawaii: Detail (c)

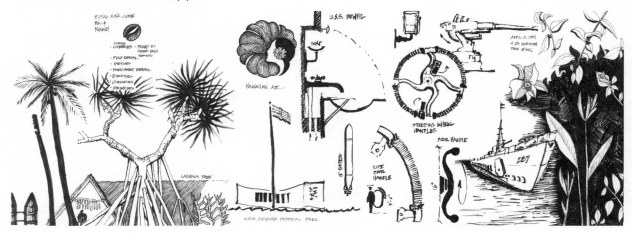

Islands 1: Hawaii: Detail (c) Highlights Relevant to Sustainable Design:

Our military sustains our freedom with an eye on efficiency.

The tragic bombing of Pearl Harbor was a defining moment in American history, when we experienced a vulnerability that would not resurface until 9/11. I have the ultimate respect for the men and women who serve in our US Armed Forces; 1 percent of our population defends the other 99 percent. Our US military not only defends the freedoms that we civilians too often take for granted, but the military is also one of the greatest catalysts for innovation that has a ripple effect to the private sector. The military also often takes a first-mover position for inventions. Certainly, in our case with the LED technology, we were pleased to see that the US Navy saw the advantages of our energy savings before so many others. They led by example.

Two decades after my visit to Pearl Harbor, we started providing our LED lights for the US Navy Military Sealift Command (MSC). The USNS *Comfort* (T-AH-20), the Mercy-class hospital ship, was the first to install our made-in-America technology. Walking the 894-foot length of this massive ship reminded me of my first experience on US Navy vessels in Hawaii.

The US Navy and the Department of Defense consume a lot of energy. The US Navy uses massive amounts of diesel fuel to power the ships that are not nuclear, and in many cases, the ships have duel generators for propulsion and onboard power consumption. The generators are basically like floating power plants that drink up diesel fuel at high levels. Lighting is a major percentage of the nonpropulsion energy consumption. So by cutting the demand for energy by 50 percent or more with LEDs, we are able to reduce the consumption of diesel fuel by the same ratio as the lighting.

- lower operating cost for the US Navy
- lower taxpayer burden on supporting the US Navy

- lower stress and maintenance cost impact on the older ships' generators
- lower CO_2 emissions from the ships
- more resource allocation to the war fighter instead of to diesel fuel
- more American jobs to make the LED lights

Islands 1: Hawaii: Detail (d)

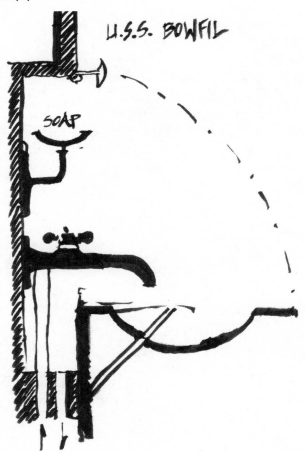

Islands 1: Hawaii: Detail (d) Highlights Relevant to Sustainable Design:

We can learn from military courage and efficiency.

In Hawaii, as I toured the Pearl Harbor memorial, several design features caught my attention. On the USS *Bowfin* submarine, I drew a sink that folds down in front of the faucet. This design dates back to 1942, and the efficiency is very clear. Space is a precious commodity on a submarine or ship, so this design is about efficiency of the area used. Notice that even the soap dish holder is designed to fit into the recessed cavity. As the sink basin folds up, the curvature leaves room for the protruding faucet. Space conservation and efficiency at every turn are very important for the US Navy.

Islands 2: Hawaii

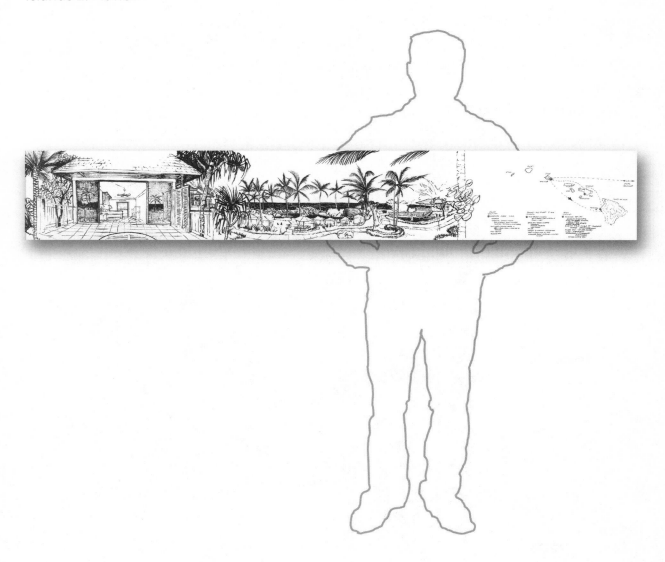

Islands 2: Hawaii: Detail (a)

Islands 2: Hawaii: Detail (a) Highlights Relevant to the Sustainable Design:

We can learn from the ultimate in natural light and ventilation.

This sketchbook is from my second trip to Hawaii. The island of Hawaii, also called the Big Island, is home to the Four Seasons Resort Hualalai at historic Ka'upulehu. My wife and I were fortunate to spend our honeymoon on the exclusive Kona-Kohala coast, at this incredible resort.

I drew this sketch sitting on our villa terrace, with the ocean to my back, and the reflection in the sliding glass doors includes the ocean views. The ceiling fan at center inspired me years later to put five-speed, reversible Energy Star–rated fans in our home. The idea is to be able to create airflow to cool the house in the summer by lifting the warm air up and then reverse the blades on winter days to push the heat down. The indoor-outdoor living experience in Hawaii is extraordinary, and it frees up design opportunities as well to integrate indigenous natural materials.

Locally sourced materials are key to sustainability. On remote islands, going local is often more of a requirement than an option due to the high cost of importing materials from the mainland. As an example, palm trees have served as local sources of construction material, food, and drink since the first islanders set foot on the beach. The meat and the milk from coconuts also come with a convenient drinking vessel when you slice off the top. Plus, the palm fronds work for roofing as well as woven carrying bags and clothing in survival mode. This "use it all" capability reminds me of the way that Native Americans leveraged every element of the bison.

Islands 3: Hawaii

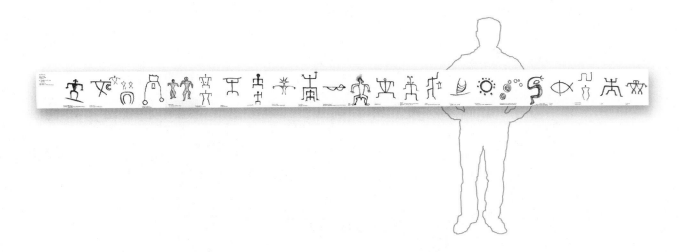

Islands 3: Hawaii: Detail (a)

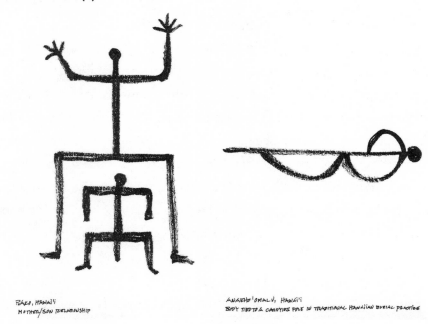

PUAKO, HAWAI'I
MOTHER/SON RELATIONSHIP

ANAEHO'OMALU, HAWAI'I
BODY TIED TO A CARRYING POLE IN TRADITIONAL HAWAIIAN BURIAL PRACTICE

Islands 3: Hawaii: Detail (a) Highlights Relevant to the Sustainable Design:

Make your mark.

These are examples of carvings in the lava. A mother and son are depicted next to a body that is tied to a carrying pole for a traditional Hawaiian burial practice. The simplicity of the figures is an example of early iconography from the native island people. They had sustainable design at the center of their coexistence with nature, more from necessity than environmental philosophy. As an example, the conservation of resources is illustrated with the carrying pole versus a more material-intensive coffin.

Islands 3: Hawaii: Detail (b)

ANAEHO'OMALU

PUAKO
SEMI-CIRCLES ON EITHER SIDE OF THE FIGURE NECK IS INDICATION OF A LEI A'I OR NECK LEI

PUAKO
UNUSUAL LINE TURN TO WEIGHT PROFILE IN MOTION

Islands 4: Spring Island, South Carolina

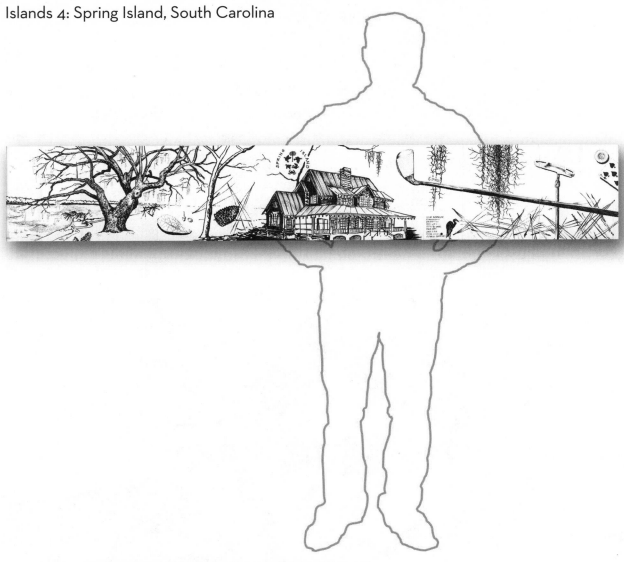

Islands 4: Spring Island, South Carolina: Detail (a)

Islands 4: Spring Island, South Carolina: Detail (a)

Highlights Relevant to Sustainable Design:

Respect interconnectivity.

I was fortunate to join an outstanding group of friends for a retreat weekend and golf outing on Spring Island in South Carolina. The pine trees, Spanish moss, and the diversity of the waterfowl all create a picturesque backdrop. The interconnection of natural life on islands appeals to me. Islands are by definition pieces of land surrounded by water. They are isolated and detached, which makes them an excellent study point for sustainability. The idea of islands standing "free" on their own is key in the balance of resource dependency and the cycles of life.

Islands 4: Spring Island, South Carolina: Detail (b)

Islands 4: Spring Island, South Carolina: Detail (b)

Highlights Relevant to Sustainable Design:

Respect interconnectivity (continued).

When a water bird dies, we may take for granted that a scavenger like a crab may eat its remains. As the counterpart, some water birds eat crabs. Waterfowl eat a surprising range of foods. We might expect that they eat fish, but here are the things that they eat that don't typically move around: algae, grasses, roots, weeds, seeds, grain, small berries, fruits, nuts, and fish eggs. The food on the move includes insects, small crustaceans, snails, worms, mollusks, frogs, and salamanders. Surprisingly, some waterfowl, like ducks, will seek out sand and small stones to eat for the grit that helps their digestion. These clearly nonmoving components of their diet typically include very small amounts of minerals that help balance their overall diet.[40] This idea of interconnectivity is key when we understand the complexity of the ecosystem and our ability to unintentionally disrupt the balance.

Islands 5: Nantucket, Massachusetts

Content Note: Sketches of the neighboring island of Martha's Vineyard are included in the book USA 10: New England, since that sketchbook also includes mainland documentation.

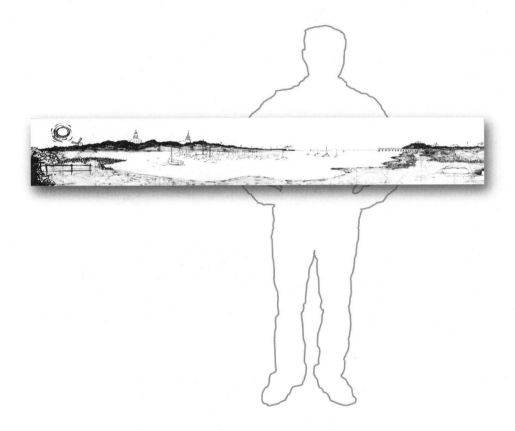

Islands 5: Nantucket, Massachusetts: Detail (a)

Islands 5: Nantucket, Massachusetts: Detail (b)

Islands 6: Nantucket House Design

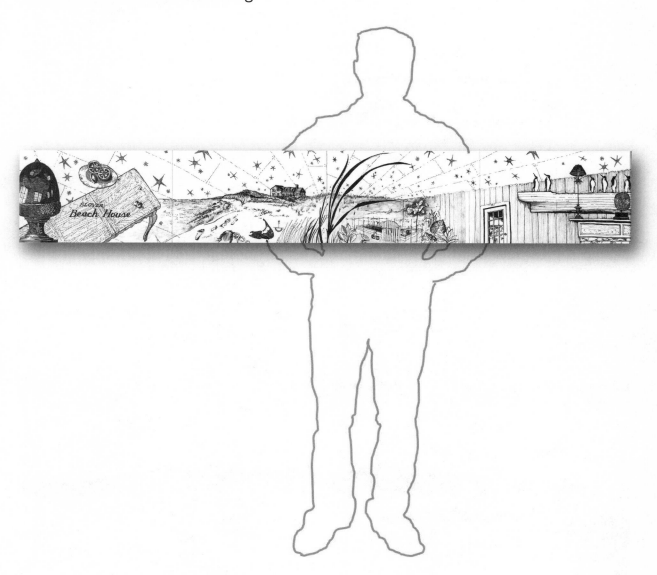

Islands 6: Nantucket House Design: Detail (a)

Islands 6: Nantucket House Design: Detail (b)

Islands 6: Nantucket House Design: Detail (c)

Islands 6: Nantucket House Design: Detail (d)

Islands 6: Nantucket House Design: Detail (e)

Islands 6: Nantucket House Design: Details (e) Highlights Relevant to Sustainable Design:
Note that this sketchbook has supporting information in USA 9: Detail (c).

Grow something, anything.

For this vacation home that I designed in Nantucket for a high school friend's parents, I was particularly impressed when I visited the family after the house was completed to see something that was not in the plans. The father had built a vegetable garden on the property. He simply liked the idea of having fresh produce at hand all summer.

In the 1940s, during World War II, "victory gardens" were part of the American residential landscape, more out of necessity than anything else. We were literally sending so much food overseas to support our war fighters that American families started planting their own food. In this case on Nantucket, in the mid-1990s, the affluent family certainly had the means to stock their vacation home with produce from the local stores. However, the father chose a path of enhanced self-reliance. The joy of eating fresh homegrown tomatoes on a sandwich or in a salad trumped survival requirements and became part of the simple joys of life.

Twenty years later, my daughter, at about age three, refused to eat tomatoes. So, with her help and the support from my son who was then about seven years old, we planted a victory garden at our home outside of Philadelphia. I was hoping that she would get to see the tomatoes grow, experience the satisfaction of having a hand in the cultivation, and enjoy harvesting the fruits of her labor. I also really liked the idea of one more spoke on the wheel of sustainability at our home after my wife and I deployed over one hundred eco-smart initiatives in the renovation and addition construction process.

The results exceeded my expectations. As the large-size tomatoes started to turn red, we saw that the cherry tomato plant reached harvest status more quickly. On summer evenings after work, I would come home to an excited young girl who would run to the door and ask, "Dad, are they ready to pick today?" For a week in August, I would say "Let's take a look," and then after inspection and her help watering the plans from our rain barrel, I would let her know that we would need to wait another day to two. The build-up created great expectations, and the anticipation was exciting for all of us. I remember the smile on Carter's face at harvest day. She got to go first. Her tiny little hands reached out into the cherry tomato bush that was taller than she was. Her little fingers touched a few of them before she found a nice plump one. It was bright red, and she turned to me with a nervous look and said, "This one?" I gave her the go, "Yes!" and she popped it right in her mouth, faster than a blink. Sweet and crisp to the bite, it yielded a huge smile and "Yummy!" to follow.

The produce ended up exceeding our family consumption capacity, and we were able to bring tomatoes and cucumbers to many friends as house gifts that season. We still brought wine, but the added personal garden-fresh vegetables were always welcomed. I attribute the high output and great taste in part to the nutrient-rich soil that we used from our compost bin. The cherry tomato yield was so strong that our son, Calvin, set up a garden stand at the end of our driveway instead of a lemonade stand. At age seven, his first dollar ever earned came from his efforts: ten cherry tomatoes for one dollar. Sustainability and environmental stewardship can come with some family fun, great memories, and profit.

Islands 7: Virgin Gorda

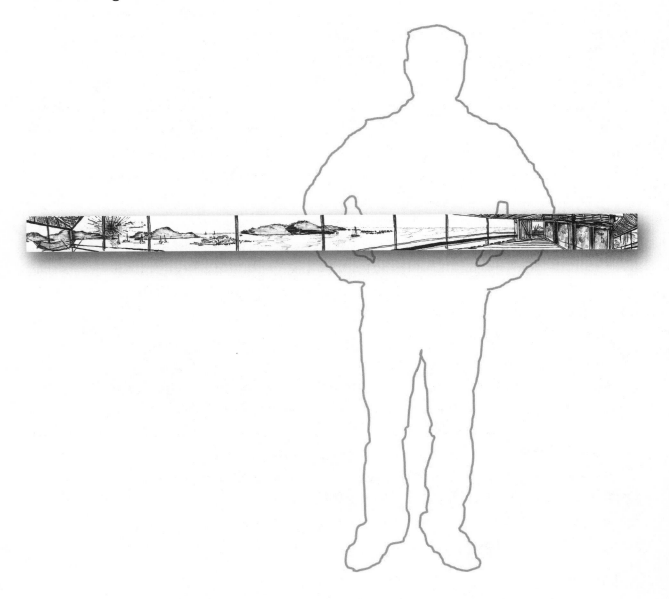

Islands 7: Virgin Gorda Highlights Relevant to Sustainable Design:

We can learn more from the ultimate natural light and ventilation.

The shape of Virgin Gorda apparently reminded explorer Christopher Columbus of a reclining woman, so he named it Virgin Gorda, the "Fat Virgin." It is the third-largest island of the British Virgin Islands (BVI). Years ago, I was on vacation at the Bitter End Yacht Club. Since I love sailing, it was a real treat to stay at the resort that is, side by side with Hawaii, one of the most picturesque places on earth.

The indoor-outdoor living is wonderful and reduces the burden on fossil fuels, given the comfortable ambient temperatures year-round. We stayed on the side of the hill overlooking the water. Instead of windows as holes in the walls, the walls opened up from floor to ceiling with sliding window screens leading out to the wraparound porch. This provided terrific views of the sunset but also brought in more natural light and the breezes for natural ventilation.

Islands 7: Virgin Gorda: Detail (a)

Islands 7: Virgin Gorda: Detail (b)

Islands 7: Virgin Gorda: Detail (c)

Islands 8: John's Island Club—Vero Beach, Florida

Islands 8: John's Island Club—Vero Beach, Florida, Highlights Relevant to Sustainable Design:

Embrace indoor and outdoor living connections.

This is the entrance to a strikingly beautiful beach club. The facility includes multiple indoor and outdoor dining and entertainment areas. In many locations, large hinged doors open up to create the transition where you can sit under the cover of the roof but feel connected to the outside. These tempered zones are neither indoors nor outdoors but a combination of both. The spaces are inviting as well as dynamic in that the members and guests experience firsthand both subtle and dramatic changes in the immediate and the distant environments. This connection with nature in transition spaces circles back to themes from earlier sketchbooks like Japan 6: Detail (b).

Closing Perspective on the Island Experience

Less is more on islands. The cost difference between indigenous and imported materials is often dramatic and means that design decisions have a higher economic impact than on the mainland. Less is more, because you often find more integration between interior and exterior space with less building materials. The walls may be thinner, the windows may be larger, and the overall weight may be less given that so many inhabited islands are in temperate climates.

Pulling together the drawings and notes for this book created some welcomed parallel observations across continents and decades. Time was a surprising asset in the process of documentation, because the learning has built up and will hopefully continue for decades more of work in the field with pen in hand.

3 COMMERCIAL IMPACT

11 SUSTAINABLE SMART HOUSE

The Sustainable Smart House Design described in this chapter is a prototype with ten years of operation at high-efficiency that serves as a model for residential construction. The home that I designed based on information gained around the world is profiled on www.GREENandSAVE.com.

Challenges often spark inspiration. In many cases, the process of finding solutions yields results that are far different than expected.

I set out with a challenge to design a home that was aesthetic, functional, and energy-intelligent on a budget that matched the average US home construction costs. In 2006, the average home construction costs for a major city such as Philadelphia were in the $160 to $180 per square foot range.[41] The research included a two-decade journey, including Asia, Eastern Europe, North and Central America, and remote islands. This book chronicles the journey and includes the travel drawings and insights along the way. Over the course of the exploration, I added three sibling challenges related to sustainability. The first was personal, the second was civic, and the third was professional. On the personal front, I wanted to inspire my children to think about sustainability and critical thinking at a foundational level. On the civic front, I wanted to capture successful strategies that reduce suburban sprawl through city and community planning. On the professional front, I wanted to build a business that fostered sustainability through products and services that yielded a high return on investment (ROI) for customers.

Overall, I simply wanted a house to run cost-effectively, kids to grow up with an innate sense of practical environmental stewardship, a sustainable community, and a business that adds value along with generating income. The solutions have come in many forms, and this story captures the interconnected winding path to reach some positive results. The first four chapters and the last one frame the travel drawings and insights from around the world. The intent of the aggregated content in this book is to provide value to different types of readers through the different chapters.

While this is not a call for us all to dramatically change the way that we live and work, it is a means for us to understand that small and local actions have the potential for larger collective impact. Together, we can foster American energy independence and lead by example to build positive global sustainability.

We started with a 1950s house that we added on to versus tearing it down, as other prospective buyers had intended. The renovation and addition included over one hundred sustainability measures, many of which were applied from the lessons learned through the travels documented in this book. My wife and I completed the multiyear project in 2007, and one of the technology cornerstones is the pump room system described on the following pages.

The "Pump Room" Idea: Integration and Innovation

The Challenge: We set out to see if we could use the sun and technology to cost-effectively provide four key advantages:

- heat the house (in the winter)
- heat the water (year-round for all showers, sinks, washing machine, and dishwasher)
- cool the house (in the summer)
- power the house (year-round for all lights, TVs, appliances, and mechanical systems)

The Solution: We developed an innovative system that I started calling SSI (Szoradi Solar Integration). The system was designed as a pilot program, and if someone wants to apply some or all of the principles, the key points are included in this chapter. Here is how our integrated high-performance system works.

1) Heating the House (In the Winter)

To heat the house in the winter, the solar integration system uses rooftop solar hot water panels to heat water that is then used for radiant floor coils via a 350-gallon insulated tank in the basement. All of the electrical needs for the pumps are met by a companion rooftop photovoltaic system that generates the power for the whole house. To put the water tank size in perspective, a typical home hot water tank is fifty or eighty gallons. On even overcast winter days, the sun heats the water in the panels up to over 100°F and in the summer the temperature can exceed 180°F. The hot water is then piped from the basement tank through radiant floor coils that are encased in 1.25 inches of gypcrete that has an additional half inch of stone tile on the upper walking surface. This radiant thermal mass warms your feet and then rises through the rooms. One of the advantages of radiant over forced-air heat is that the heat stays around your body rather than blowing up toward the ceiling. Szoradi Solar Integration also includes multizone in-floor thermostats and Energy Star programmable thermostats. These smart controls provide maximum comfort and energy savings.

One of the advantages of the combined gypcrete and stone tile is that thermal mass holds the heat longer than wood or other materials and then releases it back into the room. So you benefit well after the sun goes down. As well, with the proper southern orientation and the Low-E energy-efficient windows, the sun actually heats up the floor when the light comes through the windows. Solar integration involves calculating the proper overhang so that the sun is well shaded during the summer from heating the house and welcomed in over the winter to warm it. As an example, at the latitude of Philadelphia, Pennsylvania, the angle of the sun is about 85 percent off of the horizon at noon in the summer, but it drops down to an angle that is only about 25 percent off the horizon over the winter. So in this area, overhangs of eighteen inches can effectively shade all of the direct sunlight over the summer peak hours and let all of it in over the winter peak hours. As well, super-insulated walls help hold the heat inside the house. The combination of the double-insulated walls and low-tech passive solar overhang calculations is key to solar integration, and it is often overlooked by home builders and even many architects. An additional feature is a fan system that draws filtered warm air from the walkout lower-level basement up into the living spaces. Since the geothermal ground temperature is typically about 50–55°F, it is often warmer than the outside air in the winter and cooler in the summer. Solar integration involves building basements and, if possible, walkout systems for increased natural light and access to the backyard or side yard.

On very cold winter nights, the sun alone cannot heat the whole house through the radiant floors without some support. So Szoradi Solar Integration includes solar photovoltaic panels (PV) for generating electricity. The electricity not only powers the pumps for moving the water through the radiant floors but also powers the motors in multispeed reversible ceiling fans that are used on slow speed in the winter to gently circulate the warm air that rises to the ceiling back down into the rooms. As well, the electricity powers a backup electric hot water heater for the radiant floor system if there is a particularly overcast or snowy winter day. If the radiant is not enough, then the electricity generated from the PV panels powers dual multizoned high-efficiency heat pumps that work like a furnace to blow warm air throughout the multizoned duct work in the house. Basically, a heat pump works like an air conditioner in reverse, blowing warm air in and cold air out. By using a heat pump, you are also possibly eligible in your region for reduced rates on the cost of electricity from your local electric company. As an example, with PECO in the Philadelphia area, we paid half of the regular market rate for electricity every year, between October and May, just because we used heat pumps. Note that this incentive was changed after a few years, so homeowners need to review all of their options, and we had installed a high-efficiency natural gas furnace in expectation of incentive changes. If the sun does not generate enough electricity to power the heat pumps, the solar integration works with a dual electric meter system. Basically, you sell the power that you create when it is sunny to the local electric company, and you buy it back when you need it. This avoids the additional cost of a battery to store up the electricity, and it creates an efficient billing system with a debit and credit record each month. As a backup to the backup system, Szoradi Solar Integration ensures comfort by including a high-efficiency gas furnace.

2) Heating the Water (Year-Round for Showers, Sinks, Washing Machine, and Dishwasher)
To heat the domestic hot water for the house all year round, the solar integration system uses rooftop solar hot water panels to heat water that is then stored in a 350-gallon insulated tank in the basement with a separate coil from the radiant floor system. On even overcast winter days, the sun heats the water in the panels up to over 100°F, and in the summer the temperature can exceed 180°F. Hot shower water temperature is typically about 110°F, but when you buy the water from the water company, it comes in underground at about 55°F. So most American households have a tank that works pretty hard to raise the water temperature and then keep the water at about 140°F

all day even when it is not being used. This is basically a waste of energy to keep the water hot, and it would be like leaving your oven on hot all day every day, just to cook dinner. Solar integration preheats the water, and if it needs a boost on an overcast day, the Szoradi Solar Integration system includes a backup tankless water heater, also referred to as an on-demand water heater or flash water heater. The hardware basically works rapidly to flash heat the water only when the pressure is released from the shower, sink, washer, dishwasher, and so on. So you typically end up saving 50 percent on hot water utility bills. The European and Asian markets have successfully used these systems for years, and they are only recently gaining traction in America. Solar integration takes the tankless system to a higher level by feeding preheated water through it. If the water going in is over 110°F, the temperature sensor does not fire up the system, and there is no additional power needed.

3) Cooling the House (In the Summer)

To keep the house cool in the summer, Szoradi Solar Integration system uses a combination of systems, including rooftop solar photovoltaic panels (PV) for generating electricity that powers the air-conditioning. The air-conditioning units are multizoned high-efficient heat pumps with Energy Star programmable thermostats that can be set for maximum comfort. By using a heat pump, you may also be eligible for reduced rates on the cost of electricity from your local electric company.

As well, the thermal mass floors hold the cooler temperatures because they are made of 1.25 inches of gypcrete that has an additional half inch of stone tile on the walking surface. One of the advantages of the combined gypcrete and stone tile is that thermal mass holds the "coolth" longer than wood or other materials and then releases it back into the room.

Since solar integration involves calculating the proper overhang so that the sun is well shaded during the summer from heating the house, overhangs of eighteen inches or more can effectively shade all of the direct sunlight over the summer peak hours when it is very high in the sky. As well, super-insulated walls help hold the cool air inside the house. The combination of the double-insulated walls and low-tech passive solar overhang calculations is key to solar integration, and it is often overlooked by home builders and even many architects. An additional feature is a fan system that draws filtered cool air from the basement up into the living spaces. Since the geothermal ground temperature is typically about 50–60°F, it is often cooler than the outside air in the summer. Solar integration involves building basements and, if possible, walkout systems for increased natural light and access to the back or side yard.

The electricity generated from the sun powers the motors in multispeed reversible ceiling fans that are used on moderate speed in the summer to create gentle breezes and lift warm air up in reverse mode. If AC is needed and the sun does not generate enough electricity to power the heat pump and the fans, the solar integration works with a dual electric meter system. Basically, you sell the power that you create when it is sunny to the local electric company, and you buy it back when you need it to avoid the cost of batteries.

One of the key components of the solar integration cooling system is natural and cross ventilation with windows located to capture cross-breezes on days that are not extremely hot or humid. Casement windows allow you to open the full size of the windows versus double-hung windows, which only let you open 50 percent of the viewable area. Since the evening temperature typically drops below the daytime temperature, you can often draft the house after the sun goes down to bring the cooler outside air in to replace the inside air that has built up during the day. As a boost to the cross ventilation, solar integration includes a high-efficiency quad-motor whole-house fan. You may have seen the large propeller of a whole house fan in the second-floor ceiling of your grandparents' house, because before central air-conditioning, these fans were used to literally suck the hot air up and out of the house via the attic.

The concept is very valid, but the old fans used a lot of electricity and were very noisy. The new fans use less than half of the electricity, draw twice the air, and make much less noise, in part because multiple motors do the work instead of one giant blade. They also take up much less space in the ceiling, often just a single sixteen-inch joist bay. The best thing about a whole-house fan is that you can open just one or two windows when you come back from work in the evening, flip the whole-house fan on for about an hour, and let it literally flush the hot air out of all the rooms due to the pressure differential. The whole-house fan that we recommend also has a high and low speed to give you the most flexibility. So instead of running around opening all the windows, you save time and effort. Then you can decide to either use the AC or not, given the day. This preconditioning saves the AC from doing a lot of work to bring the house down in temperature even just a few degrees. Basically, this move is like being on a sailboat rather than a powerboat. On a sailboat, you need to be aware of the conditions and engage with the elements more directly, while on a powerboat you basically just expect it to run. The environmental savings, fuel savings, and the satisfaction of connecting with the elements is part of the Szoradi Solar Integration experience, but the system is also well equipped to go on autopilot at any given moment.

4) Powering the House (Year-Round for Lights, TVs, Appliances, and Mechanical Systems)
Solar integration includes solar photovoltaic panels (PV) for generating electricity. The sun generates more power on the surface of the earth in one day than all of the fossil fuels underground. The size of the appropriate solar panel array for a home is directly related to the amount of roof area that has access to the sun and also the amount of energy needed to supply the house. In some cases, the available roof does not cover the total needs, but a portion of the utility bills is better than nothing. In addition to generating power, solar integration involves creating efficiencies to

actually reduce the power that is used. This all works toward the goal of creating a sustainable residence. To help reduce electricity demand, the solar integration system initially incorporated compact fluorescent lights (CFLs) that were marketed to use 66 percent less energy and last up to ten times as long as incandescent bulbs. At that time, CFLs provided homeowners with choices of different types of light: soft white, bright white, or daylight. As well, some CFL bulbs came with dome casings to mask the spiral and make them look more like traditional incandescent bulbs. The home now includes LED lights, which often save 80 percent or more of the energy over incandescent bulbs and 50 percent over CFLs. Plus, LEDs are dimmable, last longer, and do not have the toxic mercury that is in CFLs. Other energy-reducing aspects of the home include Energy Star appliances, sun tubes, skylights, standby power reduction, translucent interior doors, switches on timers, and switches with motion detectors.

Collectively, the solar integration system reduces energy consumption and cost to save money and the environment while simultaneously increasing the comfort of the home.

Solar Shading Example of Exterior Low-Tech Solution

In 2007, we planted a river birch that grew almost twenty feet from its start at around eight feet to almost thirty feet by 2016. It also now helps with the outdoor living comfort by shading part of our back patio. Overall, make sure to plant trees that will thrive in your specific climate and soil conditions.

Summary of Sustainable Smart House

Integrated high-tech and low-tech systems yield advantages that are more than the sum of their parts. The prototype system described in this chapter has ten years of high-efficiency operation since 2006. See more at www.GREENandSAVE.com.

12 LIGHT IT UP

This "Light It Up" chapter is about an energy-smart lighting business with proven energy-saving results for public and private sector clients (see more at: www.IndependenceLED.com).

As the founder and CEO of Independence LED Lighting, I am extremely proud of our linear lighting system that has external drivers and aircraft-grade aluminum deep fin heat sinks. The modularity of the system allows us to scale to produce over one thousand different commercial lighting product configurations. Our LEDs save 50 percent or more of the energy consumption over traditional lights. Since we moved our manufacturing from China to America in 2010, we have produced lights for over thirty US Navy ships and for leading US Fortune 100 companies from Morgan Stanley to MetLife.

Modularity creates ease and efficiency to produce various lengths, colors, lenses, and so on. LEGOs inspired me with the power of modular construction. LEGOs obviously come in many different shapes and colors. The rectangular "brick" that has four pairs of bumps totaling eight "studs" (two-by-four) is the building block that has a surprising capacity to produce multiple configurations when combined with other bricks. A red brick in construction is a fundamental architectural building block, and so too is the LEGO brick. If you take two of the eight-stud bricks, you can create twenty-four different connection configurations. Three bricks yield 1,560 configurations, and the increase continues. With six LEGOs, the configurations yield almost a billion combinations.

Number of Modules	Number of Configurations
1:	1
2:	24
3:	1,560
4:	119,580
5:	10,166,403
6:	915,103,765

The multiplier effect of configurations is significant relative to lighting, because commercial buildings have so many different shapes, sizes, ceiling heights, and output needs. Lighting is increasingly complicated. The old days of buying a commodity lightbulb are largely over. A modular lighting system enables building owners and managers to have energy-smart lighting solutions that are tailored to meet their needs. The trend toward mass customization is enabled by modular system design. The complexity of lighting is also increased with the introduction of smart controls such as occupancy sensors and light harvesting. Occupancy sensors don't just turn lights off and on when someone is in a room but can lift light levels from default minimum setting in an area like an exit stairwell to higher levels with microwave sensor technology when someone is "seen" evacuating a building, even through thick smoke. Light harvesting is about leveraging natural light in rooms with windows to automatically dim back the LEDs to maintain the target light levels and yield maximum energy savings.

Here are multiple subsets illustrating how Independence LED Lighting manages lighting complexity:

Independence LED Existing Condition Analysis:

- ☐ existing lens condition
- ☐ existing de-lamping potential
- ☐ existing mounting height
- ☐ existing lateral spacing
- ☐ existing foot candles
- ☐ existing hours of operation
- ☐ existing ballast power factors
- ☐ existing natural light integration
- ☐ existing electric utility rates
- ☐ existing metering conditions
- ☐ existing voltage

Independence LED Product Selection Considerations:

- ☐ wattage
- ☐ color and lens
- ☐ beam angle
- ☐ reflectors
- ☐ rated life
- ☐ dimming
- ☐ light harvesting
- ☐ directional lumens

- ☐ occupancy sensors
- ☐ battery backups
- ☐ rebate impact on ROI
- ☐ warranty

Independence LED Performance Analysis:

- ☐ return on investment (ROI)
- ☐ internal rate of return (IRR)
- ☐ net operating income (NOI)
- ☐ total cost of ownership (TCO)
- ☐ greenhouse gas reduction (CO_2)

Independence LED Support Services:

- ☐ lighting audit
- ☐ project management
- ☐ photometric modeling
- ☐ LED product matchmaking
- ☐ multiphase proposals and planning
- ☐ rebate administration
- ☐ tax incentive administration
- ☐ code compliance
- ☐ financing program options
- ☐ installation coordination
- ☐ pre- and post-retrofit measurement and verification

The Domino Effect

In the energy-smart lighting sector, the domino effect may work as a metaphor for a market tipping point to reduce energy waste, starting with one LED at a time. A two-inch domino can tip one that is one and a half times larger than itself. It only takes twenty-three dominos of increasing size to impact a building the size of the Empire State Building.

Entrepreneurs who develop and manufacture products or launch services that are disruptive technologies face the challenge of selling against the incumbents. In the case of lighting, LEDs have taken longer than expected to overcome the traditional fluorescent, compact fluorescent, high-intensity discharge (HID), and incandescent lights. Some of the early LEDs introduced before 2010 failed to meet quality assurance standards. Many of them came from overseas manufacturers. As the efficiency levels have increased and the cost has decreased, the tipping point for LEDs is near.

Summary of Light It Up

Change your lights at home and at work. This is a winnable war on energy waste. By changing the lights to LEDs across the commercial public and private sector in America, we can create the following:

- more than 500,000 new jobs
- a quarter trillion in cost savings
- three trillion pounds of CO_2 emissions reduction

Data Sources[42]

For more information and the calculations, see www.independenceled.com/war-on-energy-waste.

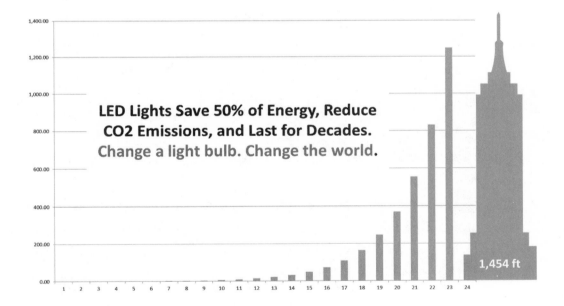

13 KEY TO US ECONOMIC REVIVAL

Key to US Economic Revival

I believe that sustainability also comes when you can pay your bills to keep moving forward, so job creation and economic strength are paramount to both short- and long-term growth. On July 7, 2014, the *Philadelphia Inquirer* published my op-ed focusing on American job creation.

A recent Brookings Institution study found that the United States has become "less entrepreneurial" in recent years: American businesses are dying more rapidly than they are born.

The study, authored by Ian Hathaway and Robert E. Litan, shows that business creation declined by about 50 percent between 1978 and 2011. Frighteningly for the American economy, from 2009 to 2011, the rate of business destruction exceeded the rate of creation.

There are signs of an end to this downward spiral, particularly in the area of technology manufacturing.

My experience may serve as an example: When Independence LED Lighting returned production of light-emitting diode tubes and fixtures to the United States from China in 2010, we discovered that the benefits of the move went far beyond generating more reliable products at a competitive cost. We've also seen a rapid proliferation of jobs.

In relocating manufacturing to the United States, our initial aims were to improve quality control, increase turnaround time on engineering prototypes and testing, and reduce shipping costs for U.S. customers. We improved on all counts by moving stateside. However, what we also discovered was that the move spurred the growth of other businesses. Like any other manufacturer, we need partners, distributors, and suppliers (who have suppliers of their own). As part of the illumination industry, we've hired (directly or indirectly) a legion of energy auditors, a larger army of installers, and a wide variety of support personnel. As we have grown, we have increasingly realized how much power small businesses have in stimulating the creation and growth of U.S. jobs and businesses.

The actual production and assembly process is just the first and most immediate step in job creation. The different phases in manufacturing establish the demand for a wide variety of occupations, ranging from industrial roles to professional positions. In 2011, manufacturing supported about 17.5 million jobs in the United States; 5.5 million of those positions were in sectors not directly related to manufacturing, including transportation, agriculture, accounting, consulting, insurance, and wholesaling.

Independence LED saw first-hand how its manufacturing of more than 1,000 different LED tubes and fixtures created a continuous and growing job cycle not limited to the manufacturing process.

For example, targeted research and development efforts led to job opportunities in system and component engineering, while material sourcing and prototype assembly required both in-house and third-party testing and verification. With the manufacturing occurring in the United States, these high-paying, strategically critical jobs are staying here at home.

A technology manufacturer can create thousands of jobs far outside the company's offices and production facilities. Manufacturers need sales representatives to spread the word about products and authorized resellers to ensure that end users get what they need. In the clean-tech business, our reach extends to hiring at energy service companies, utility rebate inspector firms, electrical contractors, architects, and more. Additionally, because we build in America and sell around the world, "ripple effect" jobs are not limited by proximity to our offices in Southeastern Pennsylvania. From Hawaii to Maine to everywhere in between, hardworking people are counting on an increased demand for American technology manufacturing.

Lighting isn't the only business with an expanding "job glow": Technology manufacturing inherently stimulates the economy through the creation and expansion of support businesses. According to the Bureau of Economic Analysis, manufacturing has the highest multiplier effect of any industry.

That means that in addition to the outright creation of new businesses, technology manufacturers stimulate the growth of other U.S. businesses by providing better training. Once a company is established, it has a better understanding of its own industry and is in a good position to mentor smaller, start-up outfits. And with both manufacturing and technology companies showing 20 percent budgetary increases in employee-training expenditures, companies have an increasing wealth of knowledge to offer their American partner companies.

For example, my company helped in the development of Southern LED Solutions and Round 2 Lighting in Philadelphia. In just two years, their business has grown from a start-up division of a family-run enterprise to a company with major account traction and installed case studies. As a manufacturer always on the lookout for top-quality talent, we have established training programs around the United States, including with minority-, women-, and veteran-owned enterprises. This training leads to high-quality, satisfying jobs that pay great wages.

By itself, the U.S. manufacturing sector would be the eighth-largest economy in the world. It would be smart for America to leverage this economic strength to its advantage. Technology manufacturing fosters job growth, provides training opportunities, and spawns the growth and expansion of other companies. U.S. technology manufacturing is clearly the key to stimulating the reemergence of American entrepreneurialism, and the time to revive the spirit of innovation in this country is now.

Data Sources[43] Plus, see the appendix for more on background notes for the op-ed.

Summary of Key to US Economic Revival

Let's build more things in America. Sustainability and self-reliance are siblings. It is crazy to think that with all of the threats in the world, such as terrorism and economic uncertainty with trade partners like China, we would not want to make at least 10 percent of the things that we use every day in our own country.

14 PERPETUAL FOOD MACHINE

The Perpetual Food Machine is a system to feed the world cost-effective organic food.

What is it? The Perpetual Food Machine is a system that I have designed by aggregating multiple technologies to deliver a sustainable food supply chain. Once it is set in motion, it produces fresh vegetables and fish for over a decade.

The Perpetual Food Machine was inspired in part by the poem "Invention" by Shel Silverstein. When my son was six years old, we memorized this poem together. It is particularly relevant in the context of our lighting work since we have filed multiple patents and secured major industry firsts. As an example, we designed and manufactured the LEDs for a massive distribution center, and the solar panel system on the roof feeds our LEDs to produce the first "net zero" cost of lighting facility in America. Our lights plug into the sun.

INVENTION
by Shel Silverstein

I've done it, I've done it!

Guess what I've done!

Invented a light that plugs into the sun.

The sun is bright enough,

The bulb is strong enough,

But, oh, there's only one thing wrong …

The cord ain't long enough.

Why now? We face several socioeconomic challenges:

- Global population has doubled to over seven billion since the first Earth Day in 1970.
- We may deplete fresh water resources before running out of fossil fuels.
- In many parts of America, food travels hundreds of miles from farm to table.
- America faces increasing health challenges from childhood obesity and an overweight population.
- Low-income households are at the highest risk, given limited access to affordable fresh produce.
- The developing world faces increasing food challenges, given droughts and extreme weather.

Farm to Table Data Sources[44]

Technology solutions: Leverage the advantages of light-emitting diode (LED) technology with an integration of hydroponic (water) and aquaculture (fish) to provide cost-effective, fresh, and organic vegetables at local levels through indoor aquaponics.

Results: Fresh and cost-effective food for the world. The intended deployment of this system goes beyond local indoor and greenhouse farming to include installations at corporate campuses and in restaurants that have an interest in serving local organic salads. Deployment also includes K–12 schools, colleges, and graduate programs where the students would have active participation and learn science, technology, engineering, and math (STEM) along the way. Deployment could also include prison correctional facilities, where inmates participate in the growing process and learn technology and support trades to better prepare for work after serving their term, to help reduce recidivism rates.

Perpetual Food Machine

FIG. 1

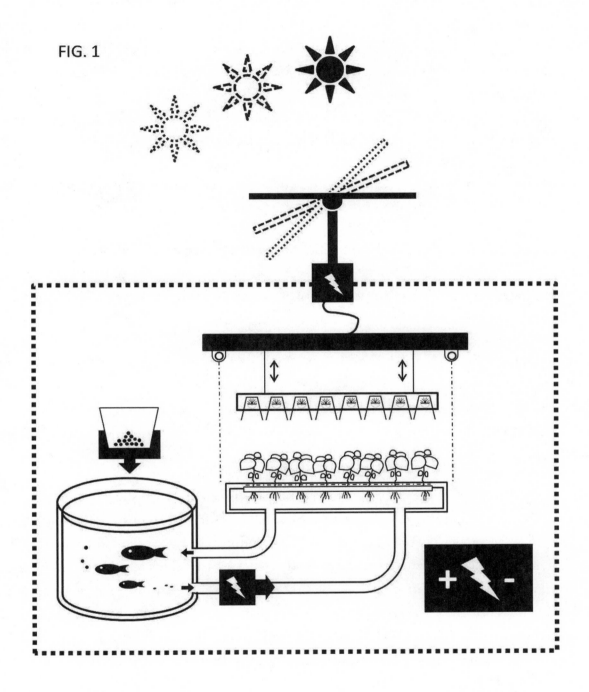

How it works: This system is based on a closed loop where the sun produces the electricity to power the LED grow lights, the plants' roots are fed by the waste nutrients from the fish, and the herbivore fish eat algae and dill weed that is grown on a portion of the grow racks. The mature fish and plants are harvested, and spawning tanks and seed cultivation are the next generation in the repeating cycle. The machine will produce organic fish protein and vegetables with 90 percent less water than traditional farming and no draw on the electricity grid for a net-zero carbon footprint. In addition to greenhouse and indoor farming, this system is designed for the developing world, inner-city schools, and corporate and campus cafeterias.

Advanced power system: Solar photovoltaic panels optimized with sun tracking, direct current (DC) power to the LEDs, and high-efficiency battery backup for nightshift growth.

Advanced lighting system: Light-emitting diode (LED) linear modules optimized for high photosynthetic photon flux density (PPFD) red and blue wavelengths plus infrared diodes, reflectors integrated at modules, base and side of plants, and smart controls for simulating sunrise and sunset, plus fixture elevation tracking with plant growth.

Advanced ecosystem: Nutrient-rich fish waste feeds plant roots through hydroponics and aquaponics optimized with nitrifying bacteria, biochar nutrients, fish to plant compatibility alignment, fish spawning via green wavelength LEDs, smart controls for water temperature and fish-feeding cycles tailored to metabolisms relative to growth phases, and rain barrels for water collection.

Sustainable life advantage: Beyond feeding people on earth, this system is also applicable for the space station and use in long-distance space travel or for colonizing another planet such as Mars. If we choose to pursue life beyond our own atmosphere, a closed-loop ecosystem will require resource efficiency, renewable energy, and in this case the added advantage of the balance of oxygen production and carbon dioxide (CO_2) emission. Since we breathe in oxygen and exhale CO_2 and plants emit $CO2$ and "breathe" oxygen, humans become an integral component as well as a beneficiary of the system. We literally help feed the plants every time we exhale, and they give us the oxygen and the nutrients to survive. This codependency is at the core for sustainable design where $1 + 1 = 3$. Three is life.

Summary of the Perpetual Food Machine

We can rethink the food chain and stop shipping food hundreds of miles from farm to table. Beyond the inspiration from Shel Silverstein's poem, "Invention," I was also inspired by:

- Hungarian village pickles—their use of water, sunlight, and locally grown vegetables
- Judy Wicks—her focus on the advantages of organic produce and a local economy
- Independence LED Lighting—our recent research and development into LED grow lights
- Children—the excitement my kids had harvesting vegetables that they helped grow
- Innovation—my overall joy in exploring how to advance sustainable technology

CONCLUSIONS

WE CAN ALL TAKE ACTION

Information is only as good as what you choose to do with it.

My travel and observations over the past twenty years have generated some actionable intelligence. The lessons learned across multiple continents have yielded many of the results described in this book and specifically in part 3, "Commercial Impact." In my personal and professional life, I have tried to walk the talk with critical thinking and sustainable design. This final chapter of conclusions is about a path forward.

15 LOCAL FUTURE

This chapter on local future describes a path to American job creation and economic growth by localizing key aspects of our lives.

On June 29, 1956, President Dwight D. Eisenhower signed Law 84-627, known as the National Interstate and Defense Highways Act. At that time, it was the largest public works project in American history, with $25 billion dedicated for the construction of 41,000 miles of highways. In addition to major roads, across US cities, the trolley systems were replaced by buses. This massive initiative literally paved the way for our auto-centric lifestyle that has become the envy of the world. We not only have the personal freedom to drive wherever we want in our communities and across the country, but we also use the roads in commerce to move everything from apples to zucchinis. The network of roads connects us but also shifts the way that we source local products and use resources. With countries like China that are dramatically increasing their adoption of automobiles, there is no end in sight to the increasing demand for fuel.

Imagine an America that is not as dependent on foreign oil. Henry Ford had thought that alcohol-based fuel was the ideal resource to power automobiles, in part because it burns cleaner than fossil fuels but also because biofuel can be made locally from so many different types of organic matter. We might have gone further down the alcohol path to fuel vehicles if it were not for massive and influential corporate oil interests before the early twentieth-century alcohol prohibition. The powerhouses, Standard Oil, run by John D. Rockefeller, wanted to make more money by expanding the refining process to include vehicle fuel "gasoline" as well as kerosene, which they were already piping and selling to illuminate homes and offices. Now, instead of just relying on massive refineries that require trucks, trains, ships, or pipelines to move the gasoline to where it is used, regional biofuel plants could add a choice for consumers by leveraging what grows well in regional areas as the source of vehicle fuel. Ethanol got a bad reputation for wasting food, when in fact the by-product is often feed for animals. Overall, local choices give us many benefits.

Local choice at the pump: Choice creates competition, and Brazil has now eliminated its dependence on foreign oil by developing flex-fuel programs that give drivers choices at the pump. Brazil leveraged its sugar cane production to offer biofuels, and the production facilities are localized across the country rather than centralized. The local facilities and supporting jobs help spread the employment lift across the country.

Local power production: Homes and offices can use passive and active solar as well as hydrogen fuel cells to augment the electricity grid. This not only adds spokes to the wheel of power diversity but also helps hedge against potential terror threats to the energy grid.

Local power distribution: Plug-in electric cars draw the "juice" right out of the wall, making each home and office a potential local filling station. The companion fast-charge stations on the road would add an additional choice at rest stops: gasoline, diesel, biofuel, and electricity.

Local food production: Instead of the majority of food that is trucked in from across state lines, we could have localized indoor organic vegetable farms in the numerous abandoned industrial buildings, warehouses, and other empty structures across the country. Real estate is only as good as the activities that it houses. In addition to local commercial food production, the latest grow-light technology is applicable for installations in homes, schools, and office parks. This local focus could even apply to restaurants that could literally offer a "house" salad from vegetables grown on site.

Local town centers: Mixed-use zoning fosters community interaction as well as a pedestrian choice over the strip mall alternative. For thousands of years, town centers with marketplaces were the sociocultural hub of human interaction. Outside of Philadelphia, we have the King of Prussia Mall, which is one of the largest in the country. Next to the mall, the recently built Wegmans Food Market is so large that it has become its own town center with multiple dining options. Right next to the Wegmans, the latest mixed-use development is an example of the growing pattern of integration of residential, commercial, and retail zoning.

Local energy-smart buildings: The latest technology enables us to increase the efficiency of the built world all around us. The efficiency factors have increased, and the costs have decreased on so many building-related products. This creates a tipping point for adoption of what was previously disruptive new technology. The installation of the products creates demand for local employment.

Local manufacturing and job creation: Local opportunities increase the need for primary and support jobs that cannot all be outsourced overseas. The very nature of the local need for human resources creates the employment lift. Over the history of America and even across the history of humankind, local jobs were the key to community success.

Local business structure: Up until the nineteenth-century American Industrial Revolution, almost everything was local. As an elected board member of the Sustainable Business Network (SBN)[45] for six years, I have seen the early twenty-first-century reinterest and traction in local initiatives firsthand. SBN is a founding member of North America's Business Alliance for Local Living Economics (BALLE),[46] pronounced "bah-lee." BALLE was founded in 2001 by Judy Wicks and Laury Hammel. It is now the fastest-growing national alliance of socially responsible businesses in North America, with over eighty community networks in thirty US states. Another example of momentum is B Lab and the community of B Corporations (B Corps)[47] that have synergy to help fuel the advancement of socially responsible businesses. B Lab was founded in 2006 by Jay Coen Gilbert, Bart Houlahan, and Andrew Kassoy. As of 2015, B Corps have grown to a community of over 1,400 companies across forty-three countries and 130 industries.

I have known the B Corp team and Judy Wicks since 2007 when we were founding signers of the B Corp Declaration of Interdependence, which was held at Judy's celebrated White Dog Café in Philadelphia. Since Judy founded the Sustainable Business Network, I also welcomed connecting with her through my board role. In her 2013 book, *Good Morning, Beautiful Business,*[48] she reinforced the value of a local economy that I had learned from her many years earlier. In the preface to her inspiring book, she describes seeing an image of a girl in Haiti looking for food in a garbage dump. She writes, "The year was 2007, and by then it had become clear to me that to rescue that vulnerable little girl from hunger or, worse yet, abuse and exploitation, we would need to do far more than examine a few episodic causes here and there. We would need to change our failed economic system from one dominated by transnational corporations to one based on local self-reliance—one in which the inevitable fluctuation of prices in the global marketplace would have little effect." Judy was one of the many inspirations for the Perpetual Food Machine, given the local advantages of providing fresh organic produce to the developing world, as well as to the underserved communities in America and the general market.

Now, business leaders have the inspiration, tools, and support resources to leverage the best of global technology while focusing on local products, local jobs, and responsible stewardship in a new American economy. We can lead by example in the twenty-first century.

16   ENERGY FITNESS

Energy Fitness is a communications strategy to inspire meaningful change in how we think about energy consumption and sustainability. This communications strategy is designed to inspire meaningful change in how America thinks about energy consumption and sustainability. We should be able to put politics aside and focus on meaningful solutions with a sustainable ROI.

Energy "savings" is about less of something, but America does not typically like to reduce things when we can increase them. We like big burgers and big cars. We like big hats and big boots. We like big sky country, big houses, big boats, and big buildings. We like it when stock prices increase in the market, and we like to increase our national gross domestic product (GDP). We like to increase our military authority, and we overall like to increase the spread of democracy. We are an undeniable force to be reckoned with around the world. Simply, we like to increase our output and impact.

Energy Fitness helps *increase* homeowner strength.

Energy Fitness helps *increase* business profitability.

Energy Fitness helps *increase* government capacity.

Energy Fitness helps *increase* American energy independence.

Energy Fitness = National Strength

When people, businesses, and the government carry less debt through effective waste reduction, they are all economically stronger. You may think of "fitness" for your body and not your home, business, or a government agency. Now, think of the buildings as the body for the activities, and optimize those structures for maximum performance. Well-trained athletes use less energy than the general population, given their lower body fat-to-weight ratios—body mass index (BMI). Buildings are still energy fat. Over 40 percent of US energy is consumed by buildings, and over 25 percent of electricity costs are for lighting.

Fitness trainers help cut the fat to help people grow stronger, and there are thousands of proven energy professionals, tools, and tactics ready and waiting to help out.

Weigh in: Fitness often starts with a scale to see where you stand. Measurement is the key to management, and energy-smart trainers start by counting everything from watts to air-conditioning efficiency factors in order to calculate the waste in your current energy consumption—building mass index (BMI). Then they show you what you'll look like with less fat. Some tactics like LED lighting cut the fat by 50 percent or more, and some new vehicles cut the fuel consumption fat by 25 percent or more. Less operating costs equals *increased* net operating income (NOI) for businesses and more disposable income for homeowners. More money in the economy spurs growth.

Win

If we get behind the concept of American Energy Fitness, we can create hundreds of thousands of new American jobs right now and gain more strength and agility to compete in a global economy for generations to come. This is the sustainable triple bottom line: people, planet, and profit.

17 EYES OPEN

Our eyes are open when we increasingly look at the world through the screens on our smartphones. However, we may sometimes miss seeing the forest from the trees or some detail in the three-dimensional world that is right in front of us. The application of the word "screen" on our devices is interesting to me, because the flat panel on our electronics is the second definition of the word. The first definition of screen is about partitioning, such as in a screen door that divides space and has a filtering impact. I have titled this final chapter "Eyes Open" to simply reinforce the theme that we can all take a little bit more time to look around and see aspects of the world that may inspire us in ways that we never expected. If we have more open eyes, we may also have more open minds.

The act of looking *well* takes time and training to focus attention, just as an athlete improves with training and practice. The reward for opening your eyes is strength of intellect and contribution to others if you choose to share what you see. In my case, critical thinking and sustainability yield more than the sum of their parts. When you embrace moves to rethink ways to save energy or conserve resources, the initiatives often create jobs that help people. Time-tested sustainability practices and innovative new technology can cost-effectively reinforce ecosystem interconnections that help us and the planet. The financial result, in many cases, is increased profit from the return on investment (ROI) for individuals, businesses, and governments. This triple bottom line approach to people, planet, and profit is counter to some common perceptions that environmental stewardship is a cost versus a profit center.

Success is manifested in short- and long-term gains with payback periods subject to the type of sustainability initiative. Sustainable energy is not only important in the twenty-first century as the population of the planet increases and thirsts for fuel, but it is a catalyst for direct employment, a ripple effect for support jobs, and a key spoke in the wheel of American energy security. Some sustainability moves make sense today, while others are not applicable in every circumstance until efficiency levels increase and costs decrease. This book has identified many opportunities that may have merit at different places and times, from the power of observation and critical thinking through the travel drawings up to the potential commercial impacts.

Moving forward, measurement is the key to management. Here are five ways to constructively move forward.

First, look around and learn about existing conditions in your home, school, or workplace. Ask why something is done one way versus another. It never hurts to count things as well along the way. Measurement could be as simple as counting the lights or watts to assess your current electricity costs or as complex as taking on a comprehensive business process and logistics analysis.

Second, review your choices. In addition to looking at new technology, look back to successful precedents that may generate new ideas. This book has included many examples of inspiring and sustainability practices that are time tested.

Third, review the total cost of ownership (TCO) over the life of a product purchase or process change decision. TCO is often underused relative to return on investment (ROI) based only on upfront cost analysis. TCO is a key guiding metric for cost-effective sustainability.

Fourth, go together. An African proverb frames it well: "If you want to go fast, go alone. If you want to go far, go together." Embrace the fundamental concept of teaming up. Consider engaging with people or companies that may be competitors at one level but strategic partners at another. Charles Darwin weighed in on teaming as follows: "In the long history of humankind (and animal kind too) those who learned to collaborate and improvise most effectively have prevailed." We have strength in numbers, and the need to improvise often leads to innovation and prosperity.

Fifth, take action. Make a move no matter how small to start advancing along a path of improvements. Innovation and connectivity, with each other and the natural world, have positive advantages at personal, regional, national, and global levels.

This book has reviewed many examples, in America and around the world, of innovations and the type of sustainable design where one plus one equals three. The sum of thoughtful initiatives is often greater than the parts.

Thank you for taking the time to see what I have seen. Now, open your eyes and open your mind to embrace what you see and what you think in a world with untold opportunities for innovation.

5 SUPPORT INFORMATION

APPENDIX

The following content is additional information in support of some of the chapters in this book.

Addition to Chapter 2: Power of Observation—Section 4: Invention
One Hundred Years of Family Innovation
Spouse and Children—Fostering Critical Thinking at the Earliest Ages

Addition to Chapter 3: Critical Thinking
Pens and Pencils—Situational Awareness for Writing Implements

Addition to Chapter 5: Asia—Japan: Bonus Insights
Young Professionals in Tokyo

Addition to Chapter 13: Key to US Economic Revival
Background Notes for the Op-Ed

Addition to Chapter 2: Power of Observation—Section 4: Invention
One Hundred Years of Family Innovation

Great-Grandparents

Growing up, I heard stories about my great-grandfather, Carl Zwermann, who had secured over a dozen patents on his engineering designs for what we all use and take for granted today in indoor plumbing. He invented key aspects of the "water closet" with the bowl, tank, and interior mechanics that we now call the modern toilet. His manufacturing facilities in Michigan and Illinois became key cornerstones of production in the early decades of the 1900s. The production plants also used innovative thermal management to increase efficiency in the porcelain kiln and drying processes. By the end of the 1920s, Carl Zwermann had built the family's US porcelain sanitary plant into one of the largest manufacturing facilities of its kind in the world. During World War II, special plumbing fixtures were made for the US Army and for US Navy ships.

Grandparents

I was fortunate to spend time growing up with my grandfather and grandmother on my mother's side. I never had a chance to meet my father's parents, since they passed away in Hungary before my father immigrated to America. My grandfather Clyde Hill was a mechanical engineer, trained at the University of Pennsylvania, who joined my great-grandfather's business early in his career. In 1942, he launched a sprinkler systems business for commercial and industrial buildings. My grandmother Eva Hill was a strong influence on me as well, since my brother and I were fortunate to spend every Thanksgiving and Christmas with my grandparents and also travel with them.

My grandfather's company, Lancaster Equipment Engineers, helped improve life safety in built structures specifically for commercial and industrial facilities through fire pump safety. As an engineering graduate from the University of Pennsylvania, he also inspired me to attend Penn for my master's studies in architecture.

Parents

My father, Charles Szoradi, passed away in May 2015 at the age of ninety-one after a spirited life. He was an architect who started exploring sustainable design practices and passive solar technology as early as the 1960s. His work helped reduce operating costs for property owners, and he served as an inspiration for me. He also authored the biography of Lewis Mumford for the *Encyclopedia of Architecture*. Lewis Mumford was a twentieth-century American historian, sociologist, philosopher of technology, and influential literary critic, particularly noted for his study of cities and urban architecture. In his early writings on urban life, Mumford was optimistic about human abilities and wrote that the human race would use electricity and mass communication to build a better world for all humankind. This layer of information is one more example of early influences, particularly as it relates to my work in energy-saving lighting and demand-response integration with electrical utility companies.

My mother, Barbara Szoradi, is an absolute inspiration to me on so many levels. She is in her midseventies, thriving and still working part-time in education as of the date of this publication. She was younger than my father when they met, after he came to America. My mother has been a sought-after third-grade teacher at Sidwell Friends School in Washington, DC, for multiple decades. She has traveled the world on professional and personal adventures from Machu Picchu to Angkor Wat. As a reflection of her innovative thinking, she was inspired by her joy of amateur archeology to dig pits in the schoolyard to bury artifacts and let her students literally dig down through the yard to discover for themselves American history. One of her most recent endeavors is to collect eighteenth- and nineteenth-century tools and create projects that challenge the student to invent. As an example, imagine a simple challenge to take a large block of ice and come up with a means to move it. She then shares with the young students that the century-old hinged double-prong ice hook is a great answer. She has been collecting tools from auction houses, junk shops, and eBay for the past few years to assemble a collection that may be the envy of the Smithsonian.

My mother has an enduring creative spirit. Back in the 1960s and early 1970s, I remember at a very young age that she would make the groovy wall hangings with her super-sized spinning wheel and loom. She later switched to quilting and took sustainable reuse to a high level, in some cases using my brother's old flannel shirts, my grandfather's old neckties, and special indigo fabric scraps that I brought back from Japan. Teaching and creativity are only a subset of her mojo, because she also won the Marine Corps Marathon twice in her age group, and I always admire her fighting spirit.

One of my mother's oldest friends is a fellow elementary school teacher, Karen Page. Mrs. Page invited me to teach her class about sustainability for Earth Day. She introduced me to the class as her former kindergarten student. Given that I had Mrs. Page as my teacher almost forty years prior, I cherished the moment to reflect on two women who have dedicated their lives to education and their tenacity to stick with it for so many years.

Charlie Szoradi (Author)

Through our work at Independence LED Lighting, I have carried on the innovative and patriotic spirit of my great-grandparents, grandparents, and parents. In the tradition of my great-grandfather who supported our US military, we brought our manufacturing from China to southeastern Pennsylvania in 2010. Within a year, our energy-saving LED products were installed on the first US Navy ship for Military Sealifts Command (MSC), and as of 2016, the installations are on over thirty ships. The Independence LED Lighting products were also chosen for the first US Veteran

Affairs (VA) Hospital retrofit and for the US Marine Corps Base Quantico. We are saving money for taxpayers, creating jobs, and reducing greenhouse gas emission along the way.

My interest in sustainability has come from the seeds of childhood experiences to help build American energy independence. I was granted my first utility patent from the US Patent and Trademark Office in 1993 for a modular construction system, and our home outside of Philadelphia has over one hundred sustainability and energy-reduction innovations that earned it a place in a Cisco Systems, Inc. documentary series "One Million Acts of Green" as one of the most ecofriendly homes in America.

On the business leadership front, I was one of the founding signers of the B Corporation Declaration of Interdependence in 2007. As of 2015, B Corps have grown to a community of over 1,400 companies across forty-three countries and 130 industries. B Corps are certified to meet rigorous standards of social and environmental performance, accountability, and transparency with a single unifying goal to redefine success in business. B Corps are "better companies—better for workers, better for communities and better for the environment." This approach aligns with the triple bottom line and sustainable design. As an elected board member of the Sustainable Business Network for six years, I have also been fortunate to work with countless other companies and organizations that share in an approach to an intelligent balance of business and stewardship.

Spouse and Children

My wife, Cynthia, and I are proud of our son and daughter, as all parents are proud of their children. Cynthia is an interior designer with an incredible eye for innovations. We have been particularly proud of some of the ways that our children have exhibited an interest in invention and critical thinking from an early age. At his fourth birthday party, Calvin was standing near our kitchen island and watched the mother of his friend pull out the trash can drawer. We have two cans, with the front for trash and the rear for recycling. The mother tossed her Diet Coke can in the front trash receptacle, and after seeing this, Calvin said, "Hey, Dad, how about an invention that would automatically sort the recycling?" He then turned to the mom and with a nonjudgmental tone of constructive advice calmly said, "You could probably use something like that."

At night after reading to the kids in bed, I have encouraged a spirit of invention at the end of our prayers. Each night, we start by saying together, "Now I lay me down to sleep. I pray the Lord my soul to keep. If I live another day, I pray the lord to guide my way." We then take turns saying, "Dear Lord, today, I am thankful for …" (The kids come up with something top of mind like a fun bike trip around the neighborhood before dinner, meeting a new friend, a good dinner, or reaching a video game goal.) The next part of the prayer is, "Dear Lord, please keep an eye out for the poor boys and girls so that they have …" (The kids come up with things like plenty of food and families that love them, and Carter at age five had a great one, which was "good balance so that they don't fall down and get hurt.") The closeout to these brief bedtime prayers is something that I started saying that the kids now learned to say on their own. "Last but not least, please give Calvin and Carter super good ideas so that their inventions will help people."

Addition to Chapter 2: Power of Observation—Section 4: Invention
Spouse and Children—Fostering Critical Thinking at the Earliest Ages

One of my earliest memories is of playing on a massive sand pile in our backyard, and I do not know if it is an actual memory or a memory that I have recreated by seeing photographs. I grew up in Washington, DC, in a town house that my parents renovated when I was only a few years old. My brother is two years younger than I am, and he may have been just coming onto the scene as the renovation was completed. As an architect, my father took the opportunity to use the renovation as a means to showcase his design work, and one of the many features was a back patio that would double as a play and entertainment space when the family car was not parked on a portion of it. Many of the neighbors' houses had garages that were accessible from the alley behind the house, and he and my mother opted to use the square footage for the open-air "backup" parking since parallel parking was also available at the front of the house. The sand pile was for the underlayment of the brick pavers used for the dual function patio/parking area, and the sand instead of traditional mortar would allow the rainwater to return to the groundwater rather than creating runoff. Needless to say, a massive sand pile multiple times overhead for a toddler was better than any contained sandbox.

Almost four decades later, when my wife and I embarked on renovating our own home, we made sure to let our son, Calvin, play in what was for him an equally massive sand pile. I take great pride in the fact that our son was able to grow up as a toddler also seeing a construction process firsthand. At age two and three, he enjoyed his super-sized sand pile/pit since we ordered enough extra sand to last for years. His sand world was bordered by a low set of stones that we saved from the excavation process during the construction. Calvin enjoyed digging in the sand as well as moving the sand out of sand world via his numerous hand-me-down trucks from various neighbors and friends with older kids. Years later, he still enjoys digging sand at the beach like so many kids around the world.

A parallel memory from my preschool days is the surprise in seeing the massive volume of coloring books at class and then at a friend's house. We had a few coloring books, but my parents must have thought that a great set of crayons, finger paints, and brushes were some of the key tools to early visual expression and that oversized blank paper was a better canvas than the predetermined outlines of coloring books. We gave our son, Calvin, and his younger sister,

Carter, a few coloring books when they were young, but we also gave them plenty of blank paper and canvases. To date, Calvin and Carter have painted over two dozen canvases, many of which hang in our home and our office. The abstract expressionism also earned Calvin his first paid commission over the fall of 2014.

Once upon a time in a land of disposable plastic toys, a three year old boy said, "STOP."

"Today, I want to paint!"

Creativity for Children

Man-made containers like the plastic sandboxes sold at toy stores are by their very nature going to end up in landfills, and the idea of "play" by its very definition may become more enjoyable and rewarding if perimeter restrictions are not so rigorously defined. The perimeter could simply be the edge of the sand or the lines of a coloring book. Parental directives like "keep the sand in the sandbox" and "stay within the lines" may restrict a generation from "thinking outside of the box." The cost of a few extra bags of sand is only a few dollars at the home supply store, and the backside of copier paper or sheets of recycled paper are plentiful. This observation is by no means an attempt to direct parents to raise a wild child who breaks the rules but more to encourage free thought that may set the foundation for a future generation to discover something as profound as a new form of renewable energy.

Age three, my son, Calvin—first big canvas

Age four, my son, Calvin—first outside painting

My son, Calvin (age eight), and my daughter, Carter (age four), painting together

Age four, my daughter, Carter, in jammies stands proudly with her latest painting on display

Addition to Chapter 3: Critical Thinking

Pens and Pencils: Situational Awareness for Writing Implements

Over the summer of 2015, I was at the New Jersey Shore with some friends and our kids playing on the beach. One friend needed to join a conference call that required entering in a passcode that was over five digits long. Given that so many of us have telephone numbers in the contact data files of our phones, we have largely stopped practicing memorization. My friend asked for a pen so that he could write down the passcode code number. We all looked each other in our board shorts and smiled knowing that there was not a pen on us or anywhere near us. The clock was ticking on the call start time, and I picked up my daughter's beach shovel, held it handle side down to the sand, and said, "What are the numbers?" The results etched in the sand spread about the length of a beach towel, and the conference call started on schedule.

Addition to Chapter 5: Asia—Japan: Bonus Insights

Young Professionals in Tokyo

At the age of about eighteen to twenty-something, before marriage, many young women took part in what looked like a relatively absurd process of opening department stores in the major cities like Tokyo. Hundreds of women in uniform first sang the store's theme song, and then they stood at the ready at every corner of the store. The overstaffing, I believe, was a sort of privatized welfare state, because it existed in other businesses as well. Japan is truly a service society with people to do all sorts of tasks. At every construction site in a city or in the villages, several workers would stand guard to "protect" the entrance. They would wear spotless uniforms and shiny white helmets, looking like plastic LEGO soldiers. Aside from reducing unemployment, I think the overstaffing reduced the risk of liability and lawsuits. For example, if one of the women at the department store happened to prevent someone from slipping on the escalator, or one of the workers at the construction site happened to prevent the wrong machinery from entering the job site, a possible accident and resulting lawsuit could be avoided.

This particular employment theory is speculative and intended to provoke thought. When I arrived in Japan in the early 1990s, young women seemed to get a raw deal by waiting to get married. Once they did, it seemed that the young husbands would go running around drinking and carrying on in the streets like adolescent Dr. Jekylls by day and Mr. Hydes by night. Countless men read pornographic comic books on the subway depicting "super" women with "super" anatomies. The adolescent behavior extended to the socializing. After work, the "salary men" would drink to excess and even urinate along the streets of Tokyo without thinking twice about it. The juxtaposition was most apparent when the salary men facing a Don't Walk sign on a street devoid of traffic would wait instead of jaywalking. This phenomenon is one example of how they strictly follow certain rules learned from childhood. Even the vending machines on the streets selling liquor reflect the strict discipline instilled in the Japanese youth—at least then.

Addition to Chapter 13: Key to US Economic Revival
Background Notes for the Op-Ed

Our company did not set out to create the diverse range of jobs that have unfolded, so the resulting "glow" is largely a happy accident. We have learned that American technology manufacturing is a powerful catalyst for economic strength in areas that are not often considered by business owners, analysts, or politicians. As a Pennsylvania-based small business, we chose to move our light-emitting diode (LED) tube and fixture manufacturing from China to Greater Philadelphia in 2010. We are a subset within global technology manufacturing, and our story may provide some perspective on the power of the private sector. We wanted to improve quality controls, decrease turnaround time on engineering prototypes and testing, and reduce shipping costs to service US customers. We did not have the resources at hand to take on major brands, so we built a network of strategic partners, suppliers, energy auditors, distributors, sales representatives, and installers. We set a goal to beat the largest overseas manufacturers in a race to the top of performance and reliability rather than a race to the bottom of price in the mass market. The results have been a ripple effect of job creation along with Fortune 500 and US military benchmark installations and industry accolades.

Retaining jobs: Our customers are able to use the annual energy savings to retain employees who might otherwise have been at risk of layoffs. As an example, a $100,000 LED retrofit may save $36,000 to $50,000 each year for multiple decades. With a medium US income per capita of $42,693, the savings are meaningful relative to payroll. Plus, utility company rebates in many states cover a portion of the retrofit cost and in some applications all of the cost.

Creating new jobs: Our job creation begins with core products. Targeted research and development leads to system and component engineering. Material sourcing and prototype assembly is then followed by in-house and third-party testing and verification. Each phase is refined, and high-paying jobs are created along the path for each product and seasonal improvements to the line of products. Once released to production, any one product triggers many more jobs, ranging from the product component manufacturing to product assembly and manufacturing management. Plus, packaging design follows each product along with shipping fulfillment and transportation. Our Independence LED Lighting line of LED tubes and fixtures includes over 1,000 different SKUs based on variable size, color, output, and application, so the job-creation cycle is continuous and growing. Making products is just the beginning of the jobs. Each product is like a pebble dropped into a pond, and the ripples run hundreds of times greater than the diameter of the first ring. The ripple of jobs includes sales representatives, authorized resellers, energy auditors, energy service companies, utility rebate inspectors, trainers, electrical contractors, installers, architects, lighting designers, smart-control designers, marketing providers, trade show and exhibition designers and event staff, online and print collateral designers, along with customer service and account managers. Work is also required for professional services such as recruiting, accounting, and legal, ranging from patent filings to partner agreements. The manufacturing "pebble in the pond" ripples across blue- and white-collar jobs.

Creating new businesses: Over multiple years, Independence LED Lighting has developed a network of over 150 signed manufacturer representatives and authorized resellers. Many of these have started new companies or new energy-saving divisions within existing companies. We hold training programs around the United States and LED Boot Camps at our headquarters for a range of minority-owned business enterprises (MBE), women-owned business enterprises (WBE), and service-disabled veteran-owned small businesses (SDVOSB) that are creating jobs through their organizations. Since the energy-efficiency sector is newer than other industries, the playing field is more even, giving opportunities to a more diverse demographic. The total impact is thousands of jobs that are not employees of Independence LED Lighting but part of the expanded glow that comes from American technology manufacturing from Philadelphia to Oahu and from Seattle to Miami.

Economic impact: According to the US Green Building Council's Green Jobs Study, from 2000 to 2008, the green construction market generated $173 billion in GDP, supported over 2.4 million jobs, and provided $123 billion in labor earnings. Moving forward, the growth projections are strong, given the interest from business and property owners in operating-cost reduction. According to the US Department of Energy, nearly 40 percent of total US energy consumption in 2012 was consumed in residential and commercial buildings, and 25 percent of the electricity for buildings is for lighting. Since LEDs can cut the lighting cost by 50 percent or more, the opportunity for national energy savings and job creation is massive.

Summary: US technology manufacturing provides a triple win: 1) more jobs for Americans; 2) low-, middle-, and high-paying jobs for a diverse set of our population; and 3) increased US economic strength. Overall, we can work smarter, not harder. If we don't step up to make more of the products that we consume, we are at risk of becoming just buyers versus builders. This great country was founded on a spirit of innovation, with product creation aligned with consumption. We have the natural resources and the know-how to regain a leadership role across the global technology landscape.

ACKNOWLEDGMENTS

This collection of insights and field drawings would not be possible without the influence and support of the people who I love and admire: my two awesome children, wife, brother, parents, in-laws, and extended family, as well as my colleagues, teachers, and friends dating back to grade school and around the world.

My children share in the joy of creativity, and they energize me every day. My wife, Cynthia, encourages me. She has also displayed some of the field drawing books around our home, and she endures my recounting of travel stories to friends and guests who have come to tour the eco-smart solar home that we built together. My parents set the foundation for observation and critical thinking, and my brother inspires me with his photography, endurance, spirit of adventure, and his lifesaving mountaineering work.

My friends and teachers have served as priceless sounding boards and challenged me to question what we do as a culture and how we do it.

Many authors have influenced me over the years, but in particular I would like to acknowledge Malcolm T. Gladwell and the dynamic duo Steven D. Levitt and Stephen J. Dubner.

The creator and executive producer of *60 Minutes*, Don Hewitt, influenced the storytelling components within this book. The award-winning *CBS News* magazine first aired in 1968, just two years after I was born, and at the time of Hewitt's death in 2009, it was the longest-running prime-time broadcast on American television. I have watched *60 Minutes* my whole adult life, and Hewitt distilled the success of the show down to, "Tell me a story." Hopefully this book captures a balance of statistics and storytelling along with observations and insights.

The archiving of the sketchbooks was provided in part through the expert photography of my friend Amanda Stevenson at her Philadelphia studio. She was a tremendous help in taking high-resolution images and also digitally "stitching" them together given the long accordion-fold formats. Many people took the time to read early manuscript drafts, and Bill Slover, Steven Gewirz, Geremy Connor, Ryan Mitchell, Cormac Dalby, Mitchell Adler, Gary Allen, and my mother, Barbara Szoradi, provided excellent feedback and constructive notes along the way.

To date, I have kept the collection of foldout drawing books private. Now, perhaps through this documentation, you and other readers can share in this spirit of innovation from lessons learned as they apply to individual and collective paths toward a sustainable future.

INDEX

Page numbers: **bold** denotes picture/illustration; *f* denotes figure; n denotes end notes

ABOUT THE AUTHOR

Two Sharp Eyes, a Good Brush Pen, and
a Positive Attitude about Change

Charlie Szoradi is an outspoken champion of sustainability, critical thinking, and American job creation through US innovation and manufacturing. Mr. Szoradi is an architect and the founder of the award-winning company Independence LED Lighting, which moved the manufacturing of its energy-efficient technology from China to southeastern Pennsylvania in 2010. Under his leadership as CEO, Independence LED has since earned the trust of business owners, facility managers, and engineers across the market with installations ranging from Fortune 100 clients to the US military. In 2011, the company won the Green Business of the Year Award by the Main Line Chamber of Commerce, and in 2013 the Independence LED tubes won the Best Lighting Retrofit by the US Green Building Council for the Urban Green Award.

For more than two decades, Mr. Szoradi has focused on clean technology, dating back to his University of Pennsylvania master's of architecture thesis on energy intelligence entitled "Eco-Humanism" in 1993. He received his first patent in that same year, based on his modular construction system, which he initiated as an undergraduate at the University of Virginia several years earlier. Mr. Szoradi is a sought-after speaker on sustainability and the author of works across a broad range of publications. His writings include magazine feature articles as well as op-ed newspaper and white paper content. He is also the author of the biography of the celebrated Italian Renaissance architect, Leon Battista Alberti, for the *Encyclopedia of Architecture*, produced by John Wiley & Sons in collaboration with the American Institute of Architects. Charlie Szoradi and his wife, Cynthia, have two children and live in a solar home outside of Philadelphia, Pennsylvania.

CREDITS

Cover design by Elaine Ward from iUniverse.

Field drawing sketches by Charlie Szoradi.

Photographs and diagrams including the Perpetual Food Machine by Charlie Szoradi.

Author Photo of Charlie Szoradi by Daphne Connor.

ENDNOTES

Introduction

[1]   Triple Bottom Line:

TBL or 3BL are abbreviations for this accounting structure that has three parts: social, environmental, and financial. The three parts are also referred to as the three Ps: people, planet, and profit, or the three pillars of sustainability. Some private sector profit-focused companies as well as nonprofit and public sector organizations have increasingly explored or adopted triple bottom line practices since 1994, when John Elkington coined the phrase. Mr. Elkington is the founder of the British consultancy firm SustainAbility. He is a leading authority on sustainable development and corporate responsibility. Currently, he is the founding partner and executive chairman of Volans, self-described (http://volans.com/about/) as follows, "Volans is a think-tank and advisory firm that aims to stretch the thinking of our clients, partners and particularly leaders toward 'Breakthrough,' that is, to look beyond incremental change and address systemic challenges at scale. Founded in 2008, we have been driving stretch agendas in different ways, ranging from bridging between mainstream business and social enterprise through to engaging innovators in such fields as big data, biomimicry, supply chain management and sustainable lifestyles."

Part 1: The Foundation

Chapter 1: Getting Started

[2]   Charles Darwin:

Charles Darwin is the celebrated author of *On the Origin of Species by Means of Natural Selection.* His work was first published on November 24, 1859, by John Murray, London, England, and it is widely considered to be the foundation of evolutionary biology.

[3]   Kinya Maruyama:

This celebrated architect, author, and educator was born in Tokyo, Japan, in 1939. He earned his master's degree in architecture in 1964 from the Waseda University. He travels to share his insights and conducts lectures at the University of Pennsylvania, the University of Texas, the University of Utah, the University of Washington, and the Kuwasawa Design School. Maruyama also develops his workshops in many other countries such as France, Uganda, and Morocco.

Chapter 2: Power of Observation

This chapter includes biographical accounts and observations by the author on the subsections: Active Selection, Look Closer, Find It, and Invention.

Chapter 3: Critical Thinking

[4]   Definition of Critical Thinking:
Source: the National Council for Excellence in Critical Thinking
http://www.criticalthinking.org.

[5]   Light-Emitting Diodes (LEDs):
General Data Source: Independence LED Lighting, LLC: http://independenceled.com/.

[6]   Fluorescent Tube Data:
US Department of Energy (DOE) Report released January 2012: "Number and Length of Linear Fluorescent Tubes across major U.S. Property Sectors." See: https://web.archive.org/web/20150721184651/http://apps1.eere.energy.gov/buildings/publications/pdfs/ssl/2010-lmc-final-jan-2012.pdf and Appendix #5 of the White Paper: http://independenceled.com/t12_to_led_tube_white_paper/.

[7]   Fisher Space Pen:
Source: *Scientific America* article, "Fact or Fiction? NASA Spent Millions to Develop a Pen that Would Write in Space, whereas the Soviet Cosmonauts Used a Pencil," http://www.scientificamerican.com/article/fact-or-fiction-nasa-spen/.

[8]   Mount Fuji:
William Poundstone, *How Would You Move Mount Fuji?, Microsoft's Cult of the Puzzle, How the World's Smartest Companies Select the Most Creative Thinkers,* chapter "Answers" (Little, Brown and Company, 2003).

Chapter 4: Sustainability and Clean Tech for America

Sustainable Design Approach

[9]   Sustainable Design Philosophy:
See F. McLennan, *The Philosophy of Sustainable Design* (Ecotone, LLC, 2004).
GSA: US General Services Administration—sustainable design principles.
See http://www.gsa.gov/portal/content/104462.

Clean Tech for America

[10]   Tipping Point:
Malcolm Gladwell, *The Tipping Point, How Little Things Can Make a Big Difference,* chapter 8, "Conclusion: Focus, Test, and Believe" (Little, Brown and Company, 2000).

[11]   2010 Midterm Election:
See https://en.wikipedia.org/wiki/United_States_elections,_2010.

Conservative Perspective

[12]   America the Strong:

See William J. Bennett and John T. E. Cribb, *America the Strong: Conservative Ideas to Spark the Next Generation*, part 1: "Free Enterprise" (Tyndale House Publishers, 2015).

[13]   Think Like a Freak, Mexico City Car Rationing:

See Steven D. Levitt and Stephen J. Dubner, *Think Like A Freak*, chapter 6, "Like Giving Candy to a Baby" (William Morrow, 2014).

[14]   Freakonomics:

See Steven D. Levitt and Stephen J. Dubner, *Freakonomics* (William Morrow, 2005).

[15]   SuperFreakonomics:

See Steven D. Levitt and Stephen J. Dubner, *SuperFreakonomics* (William Morrow, 2009).

[16]   Fish Depletion:

Statistics from the World Wildlife Fund Report:
- Between 1970 and 2012, the marine vertebrate population decline is 49 percent.
- Local and commercial fish population reduction is about 50 percent.
- Tropical reef coral decline is about 50 percent.
- Plastic waste in the oceans is about 250,000 metric tons.
- Sea grass reduction around the world is almost 33 percent.
- Population reduction of some commercial fish (e.g., tuna, mackerel, and bonito) is almost 75 percent.

Source: http://www.worldwildlife.org/publications/living-blue-planet-report-2015.

[17]   Think Like a Freak—Think Small:

See Steven D. Levitt and Stephen J. Dubner, *Think Like A Freak*, chapter 5, "Think Like a Child" (William Morrow, 2014).

Sustainable ROI—Seven Insights and Actions:

[18]   **Insight #1: Population**

Daniel Goodkind, Population Division, US Census Bureau: The World Population at 7 Billion: http://blogs.census.gov/2011/10/31/the-world-population-at-7-billion/. The global population only grew from about 250 million in the year 1000 to one billion around 1850. We reached one billion around 1825, two billion around 1925, and 3.6 billion around 1970, on the first Earth Day. The United Nations estimated that the world would reach the seven billion milestone on October 31, 2011. The US Census Bureau estimated the world population will pass seven billion on March 12, 2012. Unsustainable Growth article: http://www.zmescience.com/science/unsustainable-human-population-growth-0534/.

[19]   **Insight #2: Water**

Fresh Water Data: http://water.usgs.gov/edu/earthhowmuch.html.

In the Midwestern United States, the Ogallala aquifer covers over 170,000 square miles and holds over 900 trillion gallons of fresh water. Thirty percent of the water for US agriculture comes from Ogallala, but recent measurement studies indicate that the water formed in the Jurassic period is depleted at alarming levels, and it is being drawn out faster than it is replenished.

Sources: https://en.wikipedia.org/wiki/Ogallala_Aquifer
http://www.geology.iastate.edu/gccourse/issues/society/ogallala/1.gif
and http://hrd.apec.org/index.php/The_Ogallala_Aquifer_and_Its_Role_as_a_Threatened_American_ Resource.

Jurassic Period Notes: The Jurassic period was the second segment of the Mesozoic era. It occurred from 199.6 to 145.5 million years ago, following the Triassic period and preceding the Cretaceous period. During the Jurassic period, the supercontinent Pangaea split apart.

The water needed to produce a hamburger: http://www.livescience.com/32331-how-much-water-is-used-to-grow-a-hamburger-.html. About 1,300 gallons, according to the US Geological Survey. That takes into account irrigation for the vegetation the cow eats, water for the cow to drink, for processing, and other factors. *LA Times* article cites 660 gallons of water for a 1/3 lb burger: http://www.latimes.com/food/dailydish/la-dd-gallons-of-water-to-make-a-burger-20140124-story.html. It takes 1,800 gallons to produce a pound of beef: http://www.gracelinks.org/1361/the-water-footprint-of-food. Consider that the average American eats about 171 pounds of meat a year—three times the international average and twice the amount recommended for good nutritional health!

http://www.huffingtonpost.com/2014/10/13/food-water-footprint_n_5952862.html.
Some will argue that the measurement of gallons per pound isn't fair—we should consider water consumed per gram of protein. In this case, pulses (including beans, lentils, peas, etc.) win out at five gallons per gram of protein, followed by eggs at 7.7 gal./gram, milk at 8.2 gal./gram, and chicken at 9 gal./gram. The numbers only go up from there, with beef topping the scale, requiring 29.6 gallons of water per gram of protein.

[20] **Insight #3: Paper**
If you purchased the e-book version of this publication, you should feel great about the environmental benefits of reduced paper consumption when you see the data below.

Paper Data Source: iD2 Communications Inc.—Communications for Sustainable Communities
http://www.id2.ca/downloads/eco-design-paper-facts.pdf. The United States uses 25 percent of the world's paper products. Source: American Forest and Paper Association. Industry analysts estimate that 95 percent of business information is still stored on paper. Source: International Institute for Environment and Development (IIED) Discussion Paper (IIED, London, September 1996). New York's largest export out of the Port of New York is waste paper. Source: "What About Waste," Cornell Waste Management Institute, 1990. The average American uses more than 748 pounds of paper per year. Source: American Forest and Paper Association. Forty-five percent of paper is recycled in the United States. Source: Worldwatch Institute. The average American attorney uses one ton of paper every year. Source: "Waste Reduction Is a Smart Business Decision," Onondaga Resource Recovery Agency, 1998. Recycling one ton of paper saves 682.5 gallons of oil, 7,000 gallons of water, 3.3 cubic yards of landfill space. Source: "Waste Reduction Is a Smart Business Decision," Onondaga Resource Recovery Agency, 1998. If

offices throughout the United States increased the rate of two-sided photocopying from the 1991 figure of 20 percent to 60 percent, they could save the equivalent of about fifteen million trees. Source: *Choose to Reuse* by Nikki and David Goldbeck, 1995, Earth 911.

[21] **Insight #4: Transportation**

In the United States, we use 28 percent of our energy to move people and goods from one place to another. The transportation sector includes all modes of transportation—from personal vehicles (cars, light trucks) to public transportation (buses, trains) to airplanes, freight trains, barges, and pipelines. One might think that airplanes, trains, and buses would consume most of the energy used in this sector, but, in fact, their percentages are relatively small—about 9 percent for aircraft and about 3 percent for trains and buses. Personal vehicles, on the other hand, consume more than 60 percent of the energy used for transportation. Over the past century, dependence on vehicles burning petroleum-based fuels has become a defining component of American life, bringing countless benefits. In fact, the United States, with less than 5 percent of the world's population, is home to one-third of the world's automobiles. In 2007, automobiles, motorcycles, trucks, and buses drove nearly three trillion miles in our country—about the equivalent of driving to the sun and back 13,440 times. Over the next twenty years, the total number of miles driven by Americans is projected to grow by 40 percent, increasing the demand for fuel. Source: http://needtoknow.nas.edu/energy/energy-use/transportation/.

[22] **Insight #5: Energy**

The United States consumes 25 percent of the world's energy with a share of global GDP at 22 percent and a share of the world population at 4.59 percent. Source: http://en.wikipedia.org/wiki/World_energy_consumption and "World Population Prospects". United Nations. Retrieved February 7, 2011.
In 2014, 41 percent of total US energy consumption was consumed in residential and commercial buildings. Source: US Energy Information Administration: http://www.eia.gov/tools/faqs/faq.cfm?id=86&t=1.

[23] **Insight #6: Agriculture**

Soil Depletion Data: https://www.populationinstitute.org/resources/populationonline/issue/1/8/.

[24] **Insight #7: Suburbanization**

See the sources for the first six of seven in this section, since suburbanization is a challenge that includes each of the other challenges.

Earth Facts: Earth's area of land is 148,326,000 km^2 (57,268,900 square miles), which is 29 percent of the total surface of planet Earth. Area of water is 361,740,000 km^2 (139,668,500 square miles), which is 71 percent of the total surface of the Earth. Ninety-seven percent is saltwater, and only 3 percent is fresh water. Source: Nations Online Project www.nationsonline.org/oneworld/earth.htm
and source: https://www.learner.org/courses/envsci/unit/text.php?unit=7&secNum=2.

As of the year 2000, about 37 percent of Earth's land area was agricultural land. About one-third of this area, or 11 percent of Earth's total land, is used for crops. The balance, roughly one-fourth of Earth's land area, is pastureland, which includes cultivated or wild forage crops for animals and open land used for grazing. Global warming has already affected the ecosystem by changing where some species can survive, the timing of breeding, migration, flowering, and so on. Although it's difficult to predict the future extinction risk, some scientists have found that 18 to 35 percent of plant and animal species will be committed to extinction by 2050 due to climate change. Source: http://www.wunderground.com/climate/facts.asp.

Overall Earth Day Impact: Earth Day is now "the largest secular holiday in the world, celebrated by more than a billion people every year." Environmental groups have sought to make Earth Day into a day of action that changes human behavior and provokes policy changes.
Source: http://en.wikipedia.org/wiki/Earth_Day.

Sustainable Re-view: *What Is Old Is New Again*

25   Construction Debris:
Waste Stream Data—American Institute of Architects (AIA)
http://www.aia.org/aiaucmp/groups/secure/documents/pdf/aiap072739.pdf.

Part 2: Travel Drawings and Observations

Chapter 5: Asia—Japan

26   Construction Debris:
Japan 2: Detail (c)—Tatami mats
Waste Stream Data—American Institute of Architects (AIA)
http://www.aia.org/aiaucmp/groups/secure/documents/pdf/aiap072739.pdf.

27   Student Performance:
Japan 9: Detail (c)—Science and Math Education: http://www.pewresearch.org/fact-tank/2015/02/02/u -s-students-improving-slowly-in-math-and-science-but-still-lagging-internationally/.

Chapter 6: Europe

28   Street Cars:
Austria 1: Detail (b) —General Motors Street Car Conspiracy: https://en.wikipedia.org/wiki/ General_Motors_streetcar_conspiracy.

29   Electric versus Other Cars:
Austria 1: Detail (c), US Department of Energy—Alternative Fuels Data Center: http://www.afdc.energy.gov/ vehicles/electric_emissions.php.

30   Air-Conditioning:
Hungary 3: Detail (f)—*New York Times* article on "The Cost of Cool": http://www.nytimes.com/2012/08/19/ sunday-review/air-conditioning-is-an-environmental-quandary.html?_r=0.

31   Great Hungarian Plain:
Hungary 4: Detail (g)—United Nations Educational, Scientific, and Cultural Organization (U.N.E.S.C.O)— World Heritage Convention: http://whc.unesco.org/en/list/474.

Chapter 7: North America

[32]   Ephrata Cloister: USA 6: Detail (b) and (c):
http://www.ephratacloister.org/history.htm.

[33]   Construction Debris:
USA 9: Detail (c)—Nantucket House Waste Stream Data—American Institute of Architects (AIA)
http://www.aia.org/aiaucmp/groups/secure/documents/pdf/aiap072739.pdf.

[34]   Gauley River History: USA 11: Detail (a):
https://www.nps.gov/gari/learn/historyculture/a-timeline-of-gauley-river-history.htm

[35]   Hydropower: USA 11: Detail (a):
http://www.hydro.org/tech-and-policy/faq/.

[36]   Oil for Transportation: USA Conclusion:
In the United States, we use 28 percent of our energy to move people and goods from one place to another. Source:
http://needtoknow.nas.edu/energy/energy-use/transportation/.

Chapter 8: Central America

[37]   Sacred Cenotes: Mexico 2: Detail (b):
National Geographic magazine: http://ngm.nationalgeographic.com/2013/08/sacred-cenotes/guillermoprieto-text.

Chapter 9: Big Cities

[38]   Street Cars: Big City 2: Los Angeles: General Motors Street Car Conspiracy: https://en.wikipedia.org/wiki/General_Motors_streetcar_conspiracy.

[39]   Sixteenth Street Mall in Denver: Big City 2: Los Angeles: https://en.wikipedia.org/wiki/16th_Street_Mall.

Chapter 10: Islands

[40]   Waterfowl: Islands 4: Spring Island, South Carolina: Detail (b): Clemson University: http://www.clemson.edu/cafls/departments/kennedycenter/.

Part 3: Commercial Impact

Chapter 11: Sustainable Smart House Design

[41]   Home Construction Costs: National Association of Home Builders: http://www.nahb.org/.

Chapter 12: Light It Up

[42]   War on Energy Waste Data: www.independenceled.com/war-on-energy-waste
Plus support data:
US Department of Defense http://www.defense.gov/About-DoD/dod101.

US Department of Veterans Affairs http://www.va.gov/health/findcare.asp.

General Services Administration http://www.gsa.gov/graphics/ogp/FY_2010_FRPP_Report_Final.pdf.

US Energy Information Administration http://www.eia.gov/consumption/commercial/data/2012/index. cfm?view=characteristics#b3.

Table B7. Building sizes

CO_2 Reduction Data Factored into This War on Energy Waste: http://www.eia.gov/tools/faqs/faq.cfm?id=97&t=3 and http://independenceled.com/led-tube-co2-reduction/.

Chapter 13: Key to US Economic Revival

[43]   Op-ed: The research for the article included the following sources:

Bureau of Business and Economic Research, UNM:

http://bber.unm.edu/econ/us-pci.htm.

US Green Building Council and Booze Allen's Green Jobs Study: http://www.usgbc.org/Docs/Archive/General/ Docs6435.pdf.

US Energy Information Administration:

http://www.eia.gov/tools/faqs/faq.cfm?id=86&t=1.

Center for Climate and Energy Solutions:

http://www.c2es.org/technology/overview/buildings.

US Department of Energy—Building Energy Data Book

http://buildingsdatabook.eren.doe.gov/.

US Department of Energy—March 2014 CALiPER Report 21: Linear (T8) LED Lamps

http://apps1.eere.energy.gov/buildings/publications/pdfs/ssl/caliper_21_t8.pdf.

Chapter 14: Perpetual Food Machine

[44]   Food travels hundreds of miles in America:

See CUESA (Center for Urban Education about Sustainable Agriculture) http://www.cuesa.org/learn/ how-far-does-your-food-travel-get-your-plate.

Average distances from farm to market: apples: 1,555 miles; tomatoes: 1,369 miles; grapes: 2,143 miles; beans: 766 miles; peaches: 1,674 miles; winter squash: 781 miles; greens: 889 miles; lettuce: 2,055 miles. Slate.com: http:// www.slate.com/articles/life/food/2008/09/whats_in_a_number.html. This article challenges the 1,500-mile statistic, based on various factors given the Chicago-based studies versus national distances. Organic Consumers Association: https://www.organicconsumers.org/old_articles/corp/foodtravel112202.php. "The distance that food travels has grown by as much as 25 percent," according to the report by the Worldwatch Institute, an environmental and social policy research institute based in Washington, DC.

The nation's reliance on a complex network of food shipments leaves the United States vulnerable to supply disruptions, the group argues. 'The farther we ship food, the more vulnerable our food system becomes," said Worldwatch research associate Brian Halweil, author of *Home Grown: The Case for Local Food in a Global Market* (World Watch Institute, 2002).

Figure 1: A system to feed the world cost-effective organic food. Source: Charlie Szoradi.

Part 5: Conclusions

Chapter 15: Local Future

45   SBN: http://www.sbnphiladelphia.org/.

46   BALLE: https://bealocalist.org/.

47   B Lab and B Corp: https://www.bcorporation.net/.

48   Judy Wicks, *Good Morning, Beautiful Business* (Chelsea Green Publishing, 2013).